AND THEY WONDER WHY WE DRINK

Newcastle United – The Quest for the Intertoto Cup

Billy Furious

Mag Publishing

D1336123

First published in Great Britain in 2007 by
Mag Publishing
56 St. Andrew's Street
Newcastle upon Tyne
NE1 5SF
mark.jensen@themag.co.uk

For further information or ordering, telephone 0191 261 5551

ISBN: 0-9544089-3-4
A catalogue record of this title is available from The British Library

Typesetting www.baselineshift.co.uk

Printed in Great Britain by Xpresslitho Limited.

Contents

Introduction

Rewriting History

August 2004: I was in The Tyne with my mate Bully. When I say we were "in The Tyne" I obviously mean the magnificently scruffy public house, not the river. We were not bobbing about like tatty old cormorants, pecking at a floating condom, it's not going to be that sort of book. Sorry.

Bully, from Great Yarmouth, an Arsenal fan visiting for my birthday, made the mistake of asking me if I was going to write another book.

Yes, I had already started it and was tremendously excited. This was going to be Bobby Robson's last season, Alan Shearer's last season and it was going to be great. The back story was going to be about me turning 40 and considering a life without football defining my every waking thought. The cherished manager, the iconic player and the battle weary foot soldier enjoying a last adventure together...

The next day Robson was sacked. The following March, Shearer announced he would stay on another year, "to the delight of every Newcastle fan" they said on the local news. "He's just ruined my fucking book."

What bounced the story on through two further seasons is: 1. A lot of what was going on during these supposedly dark times was really funny. 2. Sam Allardyce is probably football's Antichrist, sent by the Devil to destroy football and he needed to be exposed and stopped. 3. The simple question of why we keep going and why we drink so much had remained unanswered. 4. History was being rewritten by lazy or malicious hacks as it was actually happening and someone had to put over a different point of view. My next book, *Pissing In The Wind* will be available from June 2010. 5. Probably some pretentious nit-wittery about being in search of the soul of football in the 21st century. 6. I never did know when to shut the fuck up.

I write for Newcastle Independent Football Supporters' magazine *The Mag*. We don't call it a fanzine anymore because that would sound old fashioned and a bit common, when we are, in fact, glossy, vibrant and have interviews with important people.

I contribute because I like to swear in public, call people namesand to fight the idea that St James' Park (or The Theatre Of the Absurd as I have come to call it) is full of people crying and biting their fists over a lack of trophies. Yes we can do "livid" and "frustrated" but the sound coming out of the pubs afterwards is often laughter. Sometimes it's defiance, sometimes it's trench humour but mostly it's because we're daft. *Too Daft To Be Defeated* will be out for 2014, if I live that long.

Also, (and this will come as a shock to a lot of people) over the period of this story Newcastle United win more games than we lose and we win a trophy.

The story starts at The San Siro Stadium in Milan and should end at St James' Park in Newcastle at the Testimonial of Alan Shearer. But doesn't.

It's all stuff I wrote as or just after things happened; so some of it will make me look silly ("Boumsong had a blinder"). *The stuff in italics was added afterwards, either because things came to light subsequently or because it's funny or annoying or relevant.*

The dates on the chapters are when I wrote the chapter, not necessarily when the events therein took place. It is important for you to understand that this is not a reference book. There are inaccuracies and deliberate exaggerations and lies for comedy effect. All of it is opinion and not the views of anybody sensible. It's mostly about beautifully passionate, doomed drunk people going to the match.

Naturally within seconds of me adding what I thought was the final full stop and thinking "right, that's that fucker finished, let's get a beer", Mike Ashley bought a 42 per cent stake in the club and our world turned upside down again. This perfectly illustrates one of the reasons we Newcastle United fans drink so much – the bastards never let you relax for a second.

I would like to thank: Lynn for keeping me alive, Mark Jensen for his constant help and unwavering support, the gang of degenerates I drink with for their unwavering abuse, Bully, ADD and Lord Flynn of Jarrow. Biffa from nufc.com needs a special mention for tirelessly updating the best website in football and Tim Armstrong, who I have never met, gets a mention for writing songs that kept me going. In fact the unofficial soundtrack of this book is by one of his bands, Transplants; two songs: 'Diamonds and Guns' and 'DJ DJ', despite this book not being about any of those things. Watchmenow!

Chapter 1

11th March 2003

Have You Ever Seen A Mackem In Milan?

When Newcastle United returned to serious European competition for the first time in half a generation, the club's board of directors tried to "encourage" travelling fans to only travel on the club's own official trips. We were told that not travelling with the club would mean that you might not get a ticket and it was a policy they pursued with vigour, for some time. Presumably our club's administrators feared we would sack Antwerp like a crazed horde of drunken Visigoths if we were, at any point, left unattended. Fans who chose to abide by the club's wishes were treated to the best part of a day on a coach, were taken straight to the ground, without so much as a sniff of a drink and whisked off afterwards for another tortuous bus journey back to Newcastle. Fans who made their own way to Belgium offered moral support by waving frosty glasses of cool Stella Artois at the coaches as they passed by.

Partly because, in subsequent campaigns, those who chose to travel independently failed to besmirch the club's name by acting like barbarians, raping and burning their way across the Continent, and partly because it soon became clear that they couldn't actually stop us, the club changed its attitude. Free to make our own way to games we became resourceful, cultured travellers and are better people because of it.

Yet up to the game against Inter in the San Siro we still felt like uninvited guests at the swankiest party in town when it came to the Champions League. Keep our heads down, don't upset anybody and we will make a quiet and dignified exit before somebody recognises us as the scruffy-arsed interlopers we are and has us ungraciously hurled into the street. The national media certainly thought so and every defeat was greeted with a shaking of heads and a scratching of chins as we were 'found out' for being naive or not good enough.

Newcastle famously lost their first three games and won the next three, against Juventus, Kiev and (thrillingly) Feyenoord to scrape through to the second stage – partly thanks to Craig Bellamy's late goal in Holland and partly because Juve went to Kiev, played like men and won. Second stage and even some of our own fans were puffing out their cheeks, thinking we were punching above our weight.

Inter Milan beating us 4-1 at St James' Park felt like the start of our comeuppance.

We lost again in Barcelona before away and home victories against Bayer Leverkusen. To qualify we needed to win in Milan and then beat Barcelona at home. No one expected to do that but everyone wanted to see the San Siro and between 10 and 12 thousand Mags got to achieve that very ambition.

Wifey and I flew to Venice on the Saturday. Venice is brilliant, if you don't go when it's too hot (the canals stink) and it isn't rammed with bloody tourists. There are no cars and none of those irritating bastard scooters that blight the rest of Italy with their aggressive buzzing.

Important note: Don't go on a gondola! They're expensive and cheesy and you look like a twat. Look into the eyes of the people on them and you can see behind the forced smile as they rock perilously across the filthy water: "What the bloody hell am I doing this for? This man in the straw hat with the pole has got half my holiday money, he's staring at my wife's tits and what's that smell? This isn't romantic, it's fucking horrible!"

The vast majority of visitors only go for the day, so at night you pretty much get the place to yourself. Walking from bar to bar, through alleyways and sweeping over bridges you feel like you are haunting the place rather than sightseeing.

The trains in Italy are great, cheap, reliable and comfy. The journey from Bologna to Florence goes through Tuscany and is spectacular. Unfortunately the journey from Venice to Milan is bollocks. It's like travelling through bloody Lincolnshire for three hours: flat and featureless but without the cabbages. Milan itself is the least magical of Italian cities. It's a dirty, grey sprawling mass, it's functional and charmless and we couldn't find an Irish bar.

Hoity-toity travel writers and snobs moan about the rise of the 'fake Irish' bar but the most important things to have access to at home or abroad are a pint and a serviceable lavatory, 'fake Irish' bars provide both. Everything else you can live without and they are also meeting places for like-minded travellers.

Milan has a 'fake Scottish' bar. The Rob Roy is staffed by what appeared to be Mexicans, who speak neither English nor Italian and who don't seem to understand what you are trying to say even when you point at the pump and hold up two fingers. They look at you like you are trying to order a complicated piece of hi-fi equipment that you need to interact with a laptop computer, some magic beans and a hedgehog. But this was where we had arranged to meet friends so we were stuck with it. The last to arrive were Keith and Jackie who live in Newbiggin By The Sea and, like all people in a ten mile radius of Ashington, are known affectionately as Berb (Jackie Charlton calls his brother Berb, when he's not insulting him). Also called Berb is their charming daughter, both their dogs and everybody they know. People from Newcastle find this very amusing.

In a smaller, more traditional bar, where we were most welcome provided we stayed downstairs out of sight, we got talking to a big lad and a lass. Her English was quite good, he was learning, and the look on their faces when Keithy-Berb started explaining why Italy was different to Spain in a broad drunken Northumberland accent was worth the airfare by itself. Quite simply, they couldn't understand a single bloody word he was saying.

The big lad had a taxi and he explained to us that the bar was closing but that his friend had a bar if we were "still thirsty".

One of our crew, John, smiled a big daft smile and said, "We're from Newcastle, bonnie-lad, we're always thirsty."

The first texts arrived informing us that sunderland had sacked Howard Wilkinson and Wifey fuelled by beer could suddenly speak fluent Italian with the locals. Her confidence extended to local geography and undeterred by the fact that this was her first day in the city she marched off in search of our hotel, with me whimpering, "surely we should get a taxi?" God knows what happened after that but we woke up in the hotel the next day.

Sightseeing in Milan away from the spectacular cathedral (The Duomo) involves long walks, daredevil runs across busy roads and, ultimately, disappointment. After hours of tramping around trying to shake off our hangovers, peering into hideously overpriced shops and wondering what use is a canal with no water in it, we walked back towards the Rob Roy. We bumped into a lass who sits three rows behind us at SJP and two excitable young Mag sellers who told us that the whole city was beer-dry for the day.

"You've got no chance," they said. Instantly thirsty we scuttled up to the Rob Roy where all the draught beer was off except Tennants stout. There were, however, three bottles of Corona in the fridge.

"Three bottles of Corona please." The Mexican looked at me like I'd just tried to push live eels down his trousers. "Them," pointing, them there, sell them to me. Tres, trois three, per favore, Si?" He shook his head and waved his arms saying, "Is gone".

"Is not gone, you crazy Mexican, is there." He eventually gave me the bottles with a "what the hell are you going to do with these" expression as if I had just asked for the shit off his shoes and could he stick a bit of lime in it for me?

"I've been here since Sunday," said another lad at the bar, "and they've sold out of beer every bloody day. It's a pub as far as I can tell but getting a drink in here is a friggin' nightmare."

Our friends turned up and without so much as pausing dragged us off to the little bar round the corner. Once again the owners chased us down into our cellar and brought us cold beer and free food so we didn't have to come out. The taxi driver came and practised his English on us, he asked how many Newcastle fans would be at the game. "Ten thousand." He didn't understand "ten thousand".

Wifey says "diecimila" and his mouth dropped open. He'd only met 12 of us and now we were telling him that another ten thousand just like us would be swarming all over his city.

So much for the "dry-city", we were drinking until about an hour before the match. The latter couple of hours being in a little cafe up near the stadium where once again the owner brought food. The idea that people would just drink seemed alien to some of our hosts and giving us food seemed to give the process some point.

We walked to the ground buzzing with excitement and fear. Our team needed to play well. We didn't expect the win we needed to qualify and a draw seemed fanciful, as long as we did ourselves justice and didn't get humiliated we could go home with our heads held high.

The San Siro is a magnificent monster, it shone, enormous in the night sky, with a famous spiral staircase on each corner. Inside, what turned out to be twelve thousand screaming Geordies were almost swallowed up in its 80,000 capacity. We had the lower tier of two behind one of the goals and we looked brilliant and sounded magnificent, a sea of black and white, in full voice. The nerves jangled like a derby match but the thrill was awesome. The teams came out, Bobby Robson's proud beaming smile visible from what seemed like half a mile away and the noise all around us was unreal, a swirl of colours and lights, with flashing cameras. Our singing went up a notch, as if we were trying to bring an air of determination to our players through sheer force of will and noise. "Geordies in the San Siro", went the song as if we couldn't believe it. We were living a dream but the harsh football facts were shaking us awake.

Within seconds of the kick-off Inter had a really good chance, Emre blasting over after a defensive mix up. "Wake up Newcastle man, for fuck's sake!"

Newcastle did wake up. For the next twenty minutes we stood strong, passed, moved, tackled and went blow for blow with the team top of the Italian league. Solano rattled a shot off the bar that came down and hit Toldo, the Inter 'keeper, on the back and bounced just wide and there was a huge "Ooooohyabastard!" from the away fans. Laurent Robert was tackling back and getting forward down the left, Bellamy's movement was causing havoc and Speed and Jenas were cool as fuck in the middle. Solano nearly scored again when Shearer pulled off wide and drilled in an evil low cross that Nobby came onto at the back post and blasted off Toldo.

The Italians had won in Newcastle within minutes of the game being kicked off. Bellamy had petulantly poked Materazzi with his toe and the big Italian squealed and rolled and on the floor like a stuck pig until Craigy was sent off and our bemused and shocked troops unravelled before our eyes. The realisation that tonight was not going to be so easy slowly dawned on our hosts and the institutionalised cheating started. The diving, the moaning, the lying, the sneaky fouls, the crying and arm waving that drives British fans to an indignant fury. Conceicao the Portuguese right winger was the worst offender, marked brilliantly by Bernard, he never stopped diving or complaining all night. Bernard took the ball cleanly time and again and Conceicao eventually dived two-footed over the ball on Robert and got booked.

That was the exact point the ref went from playing a blinder to having a nightmare.

Bramble was booked for a handball he knew nothing about as he slid across the grass with the ball behind him. A foul was given against Bernard for an immaculate tackle on Vieri. One side was cheating and one side wasn't; and the ref couldn't get his head round the idea and kept trying to balance things up. It sounds like a cock-eyed and biased view but Robson simply wouldn't stand for gamesmanship and our players' behaviour was impeccable.

Our team and support were starting to swell with confidence, I distinctly remember thinking, "These blue and black bastards are terrified of us, that's why they're cheating so much." Off the pitch the Inter fans in the tier above us had kept a steady barrage of bottles, coins and spit dropping onto our heads, so our formidable collective hatred and fury was turned right up.

Bellamy raced into the channel on the right, skipped past two defenders and drove the ball low across the goal, where Shearer slid in to score.

Like many Italian grounds, the San Siro is all-seated, with the definition of the word 'seat' somewhat stretched. A bit of bottom shaped plastic bolted to the old terracing is not actually a seat now is it? Whatever, the point is we were all standing on our seats, all twelve thousand of us and the goal brought along with the traditional jubilation a spectacular communal disregard for our own safety. There was utter mayhem as we leapt, fell, embraced each other, screamed, punched the air, abused our tormenters and tried to get our minds round the idea that we were actually winning.

Suddenly we didn't want to "make it to half-time", the Italians were in disarray, Robert broke clear on the left and whipped in a cross that four Newcastle players were racing towards as Toldo desperately snatched it away.

The memorable thing about half-time was that people were laughing and smiling and shaking their heads in disbelief. On the steps up to the toilets I came across a policeman who was joining in, he was doing a little dance and shaking hands with passing fans. Turns out he was an A.C. Milan fan and was enjoying himself immensely at his enemies' expense. Unfortunately neither he, nor any of his colleagues, were prepared to do anything about the fact that loads of bastards were throwing stuff at us, but at 1-0 up we could tolerate it.

Almost straight from the kick-off everything appeared to have gone to shit. Bramble confidently brought the ball out from the back but went on to confidently fall over and confidently lose it. The ball was knocked wide and the cross came in and Vieri leapt up behind two defenders to head in the equaliser. The noise was unreal, like nothing we'd ever heard before. It was a deep booming roar like four planes taking off at once and it went on and on. We defiantly got behind our team but you couldn't hear us, just the roar of the home fans. I was standing right in the middle of twelve thousand Mags and I could see their mouths moving but I couldn't hear them. Now we were in trouble.

Our players didn't seem to think so and almost at once Gary Speed curled a beautiful ball out to Robert who hit a wicked swerving, dipping cross that Toldo fumbled and spilled out to the in-rushing Shearer.

To my dying day I will see Shearer, right in front of my very eyes putting the rebound in and running, with his arm up, straight towards me. As I remember it we shared a bonding through joyous shock. The feeling only lasted half a second before I got a tremendous bash from behind as the crowd exploded. I twisted in mid-air to see that Wifey was OK so I fell two rows and landed on my back, bent uncomfortably and upside down across a seat, a celebrating mass of bodies falling towards me. I just had time to think, "oh shit!" before the impact. I couldn't feel anything, "I've broken me fuckin' back in the San Siro."

"Cool."

Fans dragged each other to their feet and eventually I was uncovered, back unbroken but very sore. Missiles rained down from above, a flare that looked spectacular on the T.V. burning bright red smoke didn't start its life amongst the Newcastle supporters, it was thrown at us by some fucker in the upper tier.

Inter were given a great deal of help getting back into the game by Andy O'Brien's nose. He got clobbered in the face and it wouldn't stop bleeding and the fourth official wouldn't let him back onto the pitch. Our team fought on bravely with ten men when we could have been pressing home our superiority. O'Brien came on after what seemed like ages but was probably five minutes but had to be taken off soon after because the blood wouldn't stop flowing. Aaron Hughes came on and our defence was still getting to know each other when a debatable foul was given on the corner of our area and Cordoba got up outrageously high to head in a second equaliser.

Still our boys wouldn't give up, still they played with a confidence we have rarely witnessed. Bellamy raced through at an angle, Toldo came out and Craigy went down. The Italian defenders and keeper swarmed onto him accusing him of diving as our fiery tempered young dragon contained himself heroically (which wasn't always the case). He never asked for a penalty but the defenders' reaction ensured he was booked, which was a bit bloody rich coming from them.

Minutes later and a defender gave Shearer a vicious kick in the kidneys from behind. Our fury at the injustices our team were suffering was added to by bombardment from above, reminiscent of the Anzacs landing at Gallipoli.

Newcastle had other half-chances and they never gave up; Inter, team and fans, were petrified but time slipped away, culminating in Inter being awarded a free-kick on the corner of our area. Three minutes (seriously three minutes, I re-watched the match on video) later, after protracted pointing, shuffling and re-spotting they took the free-kick from the edge of the "D".

We clapped off our heroic team at the end with lumps of pride in our throat then turned our attentions to the bastards still throwing stuff and spitting at us from above. Our fury was massive, the indignant frustration unbearable. I saw a friend, Peter J, a nice family man who works in a bank, shouting in the face of a policeman. The police just watched, they could see the culprits but did nothing. A plastic bottle half full of piss crashed off the seat next to me and I looked into the eyes of the thrower, "If I see you outside, I'm going to rip your fucking lungs out!"

I've never been in a fight at a football match in my life but I can confidently say if they had let us out at that point I, like thousands of other half-decent, law abiding folk around me would have been right into it. Suffice to say for all their bravado within the ground, outside the Inter fans had all scurried away. Which was for the best.

We had a long period to cool off before we were let out, during which time we amused ourselves by singing (To the tune of *She'll Be Coming Round The Mountain*) "Have you ever seen a mackem in Milan? Have you ever seen a mackem in Milan? Have you ever seen a mackem, ever seen a mackem, ever seen a mackem in Milan? HAVE YA FUCK!!" We sang it with gusto and relish and we sang it constantly; while we were away our 'rivals' had sacked their second manager of the season on their way to becoming the worst team in Premiership history.

Highlights of the match were replayed to us on a giant screen and there was a twelve thousand person audible gasp as we saw that Toldo HAD made contact with Bellamy when Craigy got booked for diving and we should have had a penalty.

We trudged away from the stadium with a smouldering, disappointed pride.

What we learnt from the trip and why this game is so important is the fact that Newcastle United, team and fans, came of age as a European force. Under Bobby Robson we went to Inter Milan with a weakened team and gave the bastards a bloody nose in their own back yard. It didn't matter that we hadn't won, those fuckers knew they had been in a game against a damn good team with an away support beyond their comprehension. We took over twelve thousand fans, made a magnificent racket, caused no trouble and came away with a feeling that we had looked the world square in the eye and said, "We are Newcastle United. Are you impressed? Because you bloody well should be!" We confidently started talking about the chance of adventures in Madrid or Paris.

We thought we had arrived, we had the players, the fans, the stadium and the manager. Instead we fell into a horrible personality crisis, confusing the team we could be with the team we are. Things got messy.

Chapter 2

8th June 2004

The Lap of Honour

Since gaining promotion to the Premiership some 12 years ago the Newcastle crowd has demanded, and been rewarded with, a lap of honour after the final home game of the season. Since that promotion there has never been anything tangible to celebrate, apart from European qualification and the mutual respect between players and fans for at least 'having a go' together. Exhausted players with their socks and their excitable children round their ankles trudge round the pitch one last time, smiling and waving to the fans who clap their hands sore, choke back tears of pride and look forward to the next season when, with just a touch better luck and one or two new faces, we would really have something to 'honour'.

Ten minutes from the end of our last home game of the '03/04 season against Wolves it was announced that the players would be remaining on the pitch to say 'Thank you' to the fans and the booing from the crowd was deafening. It was an unplanned and spontaneous show of frustration, as was 95 per cent of those present turning their backs and walking out on the final whistle. The players were reportedly 'shocked', manager Bobby Robson was livid and, apparently unaware that the cameras were still rolling and transmitting to the bars within the ground, complained bitterly and compared our reaction with the massive show of support and defiance witnessed the day before at Elland Road as Leeds United were relegated. Some in the national press reported that the crowd's reaction was to the insipid performance on the day that ended with a 1-1 draw against a pitiful Wolves team. Some suggested that it was the frustration of being knocked out of the UEFA Cup by Marseille in the semi-final a few days beforehand, which had added to 35 years without a major trophy. There was certainly an element of both but what most of the press and definitely Robson misinterpreted was the fact that the crowd's reaction to the

Wolves game was the culmination of a rubbish season. Bobby and his apologists could point to the European semi-final and fifth in the league as being quite acceptable and certainly better than most seasons in living memory but the truth was that Newcastle never got going all season. They spluttered into life occasionally with a 3-0 win at Southampton in the FA Cup, a fine 2-1 over Chelsea and steady progress in Europe but most Newcastle fans aren't that daft. The '03/04 season was fuckin' awful, with spineless performances, long balls being lumped at Shearer, misplaced passing, players being picked week after week despite poor form or fitness, other players not being given a chance, hollow excuses and a steady stream of piss running down our backs while the manager told us we should be thankful for the refreshing spring rain he was providing.

Two years before, Newcastle had potentially the most vibrant and exciting young squad in the Premiership. Credit where it is due, that team was Robson's doing, he built a team which was thrilling to watch and frighteningly quick and fit. If we went behind in games, crowd and team didn't care because we kept bouncing back and a close game with ten to fifteen minutes left, generally meant we were going to win. Defeated managers would complain about having matched us for 80 minutes and we would laugh at them because we knew it was true and we also knew that the last ten were as unavoidable as a mile high tidal wave. Top at Christmas and flying, Newcastle got bogged down with injuries, most notably to Craig Bellamy and we finished fourth BUT this brilliant young squad, with Robson's wisdom and backed by the second biggest crowd in the League, could only get better.

Or so we all thought.

The following season, spectacular progress was made in the Champions League, culminating in a proud night in Milan but this masked the fact that Newcastle scored fewer goals and won fewer points in the Premiership than in the previous year. Chelsea and Liverpool imploded and gifted us third place which seemed like progress, as did the addition of Jonathan Woodgate, but something was wrong. In the run-in of that season Manchester Utd turned up at St James' Park and walloped us 6-2. We had been getting cocky and they smacked us silly. The lesson was not learnt in time for the start of the new season. A straightforward qualifier in the Champions League against Partizan Belgrade was going well with a hard fought 1-0 away win. At home however we were timid and wary and Robson's team and tactics didn't seem to make sense. He was beginning a vendetta that would eventually drive the popular Nobby Solano out of St James' Park and was frustratingly sticking with the Ameobi/Shearer forward line which had constantly failed to work. The lovable uncle persona had slipped, Robson appeared belligerent and stubborn and many of his favoured players looked to have grown spoilt. Belgrade deserved a 1-0 win on the night and dumped us out on penalties. The whole of the previous season's achievements, the effort, the worry, the relief and the glory, were shat away in one teeth-grindingly irritating night. The story of the season was set.

The aforementioned games against Southampton and Chelsea were the only domestic games Newcastle performed well in over the whole 90 minutes. We had some good results, especially at home, but that has to be set against this being the poorest Premiership season since its inception. Creditable draws against Man Utd and Arsenal showed we could just about match the big teams but we failed to win at home against Birmingham, Bolton, Aston Villa, West Brom (in the League Cup) and Wolves. Our home defeat by Blackburn Rovers over Christmas being one of the most dismal and shocking performances served up in years. Fans were coming back into the pub after that game literally screaming with frustration.

Away from home the story was even worse: two wins; a comeback after a terrible start at Fulham and a hilariously ill-deserved victory at Middlesbrough. There were the gutless surrenders at Bolton and Manchester City where we barely strayed into opposition territory after half-time and we also conceded late equalisers trying to hold onto what were fortunate leads at Birmingham, Portsmouth, and Blackburn. Newcastle didn't beat any of the bottom nine teams away from home who were all bollocks.

While there was still a chance of a Champions League place or a European final Newcastle's fans backed their team and hoped for the best – but the defeat in Marseille followed by the shambolic show against Wolverhampton were the final straws and we were in open revolt against the team and manager.

Hugo Viana, a player who cost £8.5 million, a player Robson insisted would replace Gary Speed despite being slow and unable to tackle or head a ball was booed onto the pitch. He had avoided a challenge in the build-up to Marseille's second goal and perceived cowardice is the worst crime you can commit on a football pitch in these parts.

Truth is, I was praying for a 'lap of honour' at that Wolves game for no other reason than I could show my disgust at an under-performing team and a stubborn manager who wouldn't admit when he was wrong and who insulted anybody who suggested otherwise. I knew from the pub conversations beforehand that I wasn't alone in taking all the lies about pitiful performances really fucking personally – I didn't expect over 40,000 other fans to agree with me. All season we had had to put up with players and manager saying no one was more disappointed than them and that they understood how we felt – now the fact that they were shocked and annoyed with us showed that they had no bloody idea just how pissed off we were with them and by turning our backs on them they could no longer ignore how we felt. The tiny minority of the misguided and the wrong who stayed behind to applaud the team called us fickle and spoilt but most of us would be back, so we weren't being fickle and what the bloody hell did we have to be spoilt about?

Ravaged by injuries, Newcastle still had two away games to play for reputations to be mended. A chaotic 3-3 draw at Southampton and a nail-biting 1-1 at Anfield while Man Utd were holding onto a 2-0 lead at Aston Villa despite only having nine men, saw us into the UEFA Cup by securing fifth place on goal difference.

Bobby Robson called us "ungrateful" because there was a time when we would celebrate into the night after finishing fifth. Chairman Freddie Shepherd, who seemed to be sharing the fans' frustrations throughout the season, inexplicably said, "You don't sack Bobby Robson", and we fans wandered off into the summer confused and utterly in the dark as to what the hell was happening at our football club.

At the end of the same season Gerard Houllier, whose Liverpool team beat us to fourth place and who had actually won trophies for his fans and board, got the sack.

The next campaign was going to be captain Alan Shearer's last, it was also looking likely to be Robson's and the way I was feeling it was also probably going to be mine.

Chapter 3

23rd June 2004

So What Happened In The Summer?

Venus passed between the Earth and the Sun for the first time since 1882.

Moving a little closer to home or zooming in from space if you like these things cinematic; in Iraq bombs went off on a daily basis and servicemen and civilians died with depressing regularity.

Norway became the second nation, after the Republic Of Ireland, to ban smoking in public places. Meanwhile U.K. Health Minister, John Reid, warned against anti-tobacco vigilantism, defending cigarettes as "one of the very few pleasures available to the poor".

Ronald Reagan died.

The village of Fucking in Austria voted to keep its name despite the cost of replacing stolen traffic signs.

The secretive Bilderberg Group, who many conspiracy theorists think run the world, met near Milan, specifically due to the lack of mackems, who are never welcome at that sort of thing.

In Newcastle the ruling Labour Council lost control of the city for the first time in 30 years – whether the good people of Tyneside were protesting about the war, immigration or the fact that smug bus lane fixated mad people had now brought the entire city to a standstill twice a day, nobody really knew. That Gosforth-bound traffic was now parked across the fast lane of the central motorway thanks to the latest ill-conceived bus-lane lunacy was as maddening as it was dangerous.

The Liberals stormed the Civic Centre despite the fact that they would, more than likely, be more rabid about fucking bus lanes than the smug ninnies they ousted.

And the football? There was no fucking football, bollocks to them, they can fuck off.

No local papers, no transfer speculation, no counting the days, nothing. We are not speaking to football in this house and we are not speaking to Newcastle United in particular. Sometimes you look at your life and what have you done with it – you never expected to cure cancer, join the Wu Tang Clan, get a part in Star Wars or turn out to be Spiderman but come on. You've been to literally thousands of football matches and spent an obscene amount of money and all you get is the right to experience more disappointment. Seriously, you would be better off financially if you took heroin. You would be healthier, happier and would bring less shame on yourself and your family if you took heroin for 20 fuckin' years. Bastards.

Football is a sickness, a dirty addiction that eats away at your mind. You flip straight to the back page of the morning paper, straight past the tragic early deaths, people losing their jobs, old people attacked in their own homes, disease, famine and proposed bus lanes. And for what? To find out if some jumped-up little prima donna thinks his team can win its next match. We feast hungrily on unsatisfying titbits of non-football to get us through to our next fix. Well I'm done with it, bollocks, I don't want to think about it, talk about it or have it soiling the gusset of my life for a moment longer.

In my mind I slammed a door behind me when I left St James' Park after the Wolves game. Now I went back, opened the door, checked everybody was still there, saw the entire staff gorging themselves on ill-deserved luxury: house slaves roasted a swan on a bed of panda tongues and unicorn horns; enormous cigars were lit with burning season ticket applications and they were all laughing at me. I stuck my fingers up at them and slammed the door behind me again.

That would teach them and for further effect I won't hand in my season ticket renewal until the very last possible moment. "I want two. Nearly a thousand pounds you say, here's your money and damn your eyes!"

Oh, doesn't the new away kit look nice. When's it out, I must get one straight away. And that season we just lived through? Yes the really frustrating, annoying and shit one. That's the one. Yes, I'll have the DVD of that as well please.

When are the fixtures out?

Oooo, England are playing.

I love football me.

In 2007 a new bus lane was put outside Newcastle Central Station, ignoring the fact that cars would have to cross it to get into the car park. In the first week over three hundred people, some puppies and (thankfully) Jade Goody were killed. Bus lanes have now caused more deaths than smallpox and still the madness continues - when I miss the local news I sometimes have to make it up myself – later we'll have all the region's sport but first a Gosforth man today discovered that he was Spiderman: "it's fuckin' brilliant, I can run up walls and everything, so if you see that Green Goblin tell him I'm gonna fuckin' knack the mackem twat".

Chapter 4

25th June 2004

En-ger-land. Club or Country?

I have been writing a regular column for *The Mag*, Newcastle United's premier independent supporters' magazine, for well over ten years. In this time I have learnt that the one thing guaranteed to get complaints is to write about the state of the England team.

You can insult people's opinions ("If you think Laurent Robert is a shit footballer you are a fucking idiot" being a regular favourite of mine), their religion, their musical taste. You can question their loyalty, their sexuality and their personal hygiene and mostly people just laugh it off or assume you are talking about somebody else.

I've written about subjects as varied as D.I.Y. (don't do it), the state of the British film industry and ferret racing BUT if you so much as mention the national team the letters pour in. "This is a Newcastle fanzine, I don't care or want to hear about England!" Rabid football fans rant for pages about how they hacked through the jungles of Borneo to see a Newcastle under-11s reserve team kickabout but how they would rather have their eyes gouged out and their arms chopped off than watch an England game or support the country they were born in.

Yet the streets are deserted during competitive England matches and during Euro 2004 if your car didn't have a flag of St George flapping off it you were obviously some kind of treacherous spy.

This isn't a problem, it's merely a reflection of how football fans are. 99 per cent of us would rather see our own team win the League Cup than see England win the World Cup and you should be very suspicious of the other one per cent. But the truth is you don't have to make that choice, it's not a decision you can make. People can turn their support for the national team on and off like a tap and that is fine.

During the season international matches are a nuisance, especially friendlies and everybody, except the England manager and the F.A. wringing the last shillings out of the parents of children blowing annoying little horns, would rather they didn't happen at all. Domestic teams see their best players pointlessly risking injury but competitions like the European Championships are a splendid sunny distraction during the summer and if they happen to trample all over Wimbledon and Big Brother, all the better.

Last night England were knocked out on penalties and we in our pub, like in tens of thousands of others across the English supporting world, were distraught. Why play with four attacking midfielders (Lampard, Scholes, Beckham and Gerrard) then try to defend a 1-0 lead for 85 minutes? Why does the nation's arse fall out when a game goes beyond extra-time?

Today I have a stiff neck from looking up at the telly in the pub and a sore head from the drink. The flags on the cars are starting to look tatty, many will no doubt snap off and cause major road accidents. I'm afraid to turn on the radio because they will be over-egging the fallout when the truth is, it wasn't Newcastle so I'm pretty much over it. There will be a pang of regret from time to time; Paul Gascoigne, sliding in at the far post and missing the ball by what professional tradesmen refer to as "a fanny's hair" against the Germans in 1996 still makes me howl like an abandoned puppy but set next to the pain my own team has provided – it's nothing.

Over coffee in The Back Page (sporting memorabilia shop run by Mag Editor Mark Jensen and DJ Mad Mick – opposite the Newcastle Arms) Mick had the club v country dilemma nailed; "When Newcastle lose you wake up and you're in a bad mood before you can even remember why. I was up an hour today before I even remembered England had played".

Chapter 5

12th July 2004

All Other Sports Stink

The papers have been desperate to talk about football and have been running round like headless chickens looking for a new angle on flavour of the moment, Mr Wayne Rooney. The lad hasn't kicked a ball since going off injured against the Portuguese and he has nothing else in the world of interest to offer BUT damned if that's going to stop a media feeding frenzy. *The Sun* sign him up for 'exclusive' stuff and residents of Liverpool get righteously indignant because of the paper's cock-eyed coverage of the Hillsborough disaster. Quite right, bear that grudge, but away from Merseyside who the fuck cares what Wayne Rooney has to say about anything. He is a good footballer – end of story. Exactly what kind of enlightenment do the people at *The Sun* expect young Wayne to impart on this troubled world? "I played football then ate me tea", fucking brilliant.

The Chronicle, entertaining as ever on a Saturday, have crudely hacked off the head of Newcastle's only summer signing so far and grotesquely affixed it, Frankenstein-like, to the body of another Newcastle player to show us stupid and unimaginative folk just what James Milner might look like when he turns out for Newcastle. Why thank you.

We are supposed to be deep into summer by now but still the country is bogged down in filthy grey drizzle, with intermittent downpours and gales strong enough to uproot soft southern trees. Weekends drift by with the answer to far too many questions being, "I don't really care".

"Euro 2004 final, Portugal v Greece?" – sigh
"What do you want for tea?" – fffer
"What time do we finish work?" – errrr
"Can Jenson Button win the British Grand Prix?" – who?
"Can Little Timmy Henman win Wimbledon??" – what? No, wait! No! No

he can't, ha ha-ha. The rest of Wimbledon is thrilling with the proper players scuttling around performing brilliantly at pace, culminating in a final between Federer and Hewitt who are so far out of Henman's league it's hilarious.

But….whatever.

"Other Sports" are all methadone. Distractions. Granted they have their moments; Stevie Harmison turning West Indian wickets into fucking splinters sets the pulse racing, Valentino Rossi tyre to tyre with Max Biaggi on bastard-fast motorbikes briefly holds my attention but compared to the all-consuming, sense-numbing brain fuck that is watching Newcastle United, they are nothing. And everything else is a stupid waste of time. Golf could be a good game – if they only played it in thunderstorms using copper clubs, I'd watch that.

Rugby is just silly and the whole sport should make up its mind if it's going to be properly violent or properly gay. Take weapons onto the pitch and beat each other to death or just get on with shagging each other, this tedious wobbling about in the middle ground seems tiresome and pointless.

Formula One? Multi-million dollar cars that would be buggered if they ever encountered a speed bump (or a bus lane), zipping past at a thousand miles an hour, trying to give you a migraine? No thank you – souped up milk floats with co-pilots armed with high powered paintball guns? Now that's more like it. And why don't they dress little monkeys up in jockey-style racing silks and attach them to the backs of greyhounds? You could make millions showing monkey-greyhound racing on Pay-per-view. Probably.

The trouble is that even if the season started today I would be no happier – the prospect of relying on Newcastle United to alleviate inner frustration is too hideous to contemplate – it would be like drinking Jack Daniels to get sober. A weaker man could turn to religion but God and I haven't been on speaking terms since he let Cantona score at the Gallowgate End in '96.

Chapter 6

27th July 2004

You Can't Buy That Kind Of Luck

I'm wandering up Northumberland Street minding my own business when I spotted her. A green-eyed gypsy girl and she's coming towards me. She must have set out to get me before I noticed her as she's already moving like a shark through the crowded street – eyes locked on mine. It happens a lot and it drives Wifey mad; firstly that anybody who is a bit strange, pissed or mental speaks to me in the street and worse still that I take the time to talk back to them. I always like to think that Romany folk can see that I have a magical aura and are drawn to me accordingly, when the truth is that I probably look like the kind of twat who might just give them a fiver for a coloured pebble.

"Would you buy a charm from a gypsy?"

"Well you tell me, would I?" I stare straight back, smiling, thinking, "That should unsettle her". But I'm so far out of my depth here someone should call the lifeboat. She doesn't even flicker, the green in her eyes is as hard and as cold as the stones in her hand. And she's off: "You are going to London, never let a woman break your heart, trust in me and in God, watch out for a man called Tony and remember me on the 29th of next month."

Years ago I bought a charm from a gypsy, a brass coloured boot, I was 18 and had just been paid. I wore it on an old bootlace round my neck until my skin went green. I kept it in a drawer from then on and soon after met a girl who was far too cute for the likes of me. The same girl now tells me off for talking to these people, which isn't my idea of gratitude. But what I really need now is something that will get Newcastle off to a good start in the Premiership. Something that I can move from one hand to the other in the last ten minutes of an away game at somewhere like Blackburn that will turn the whole season. Chelsea may have Roman Abramovich with his £200 million war chest but Newcastle United will have me and my little magic rock.

It's at that moment that I realise I'm actually looking forward to the new season. The signing of Patrick Kluivert tipped me back into thinking positively about football. At work Mick (a canny lad) and I have been jabbering about formations and other signings non-stop since the notoriously stroppy Dutchman turned up at Newcastle International Airport. I've got my tickets for the home Rangers friendly and the bus booked for Celtic away, Nicky Butt is on his way from America and Manchester United, I've subconsciously been looking in shops for 'away match clothes', my application is in for Boro tickets and I've started buying two newspapers a day again.

I'm shifting my judgement of Robson, his team and last season. We had bad luck with injuries, how can we be expected to play decent football on that shitty pitch. Now Robson has got rid of Speed; seven good years service but now nearly 35, Viana, Caldwell and Lua Lua shipped out and a magnificent new pitch for us to zip the ball about on. We might even have a decent year.

Final touches are what's required; Bobby Robson still needs a right-back and I need something in my pocket to fiddle with that isn't going to send me blind.

Hard green emotionless eyes draw me back: "You are outgoing and bright. To get on you need to study, there are plenty more fish in the sea." I think she might actually just be making shit up now, "you are careful with money and good with your hands". I'm afraid I laughed out loud at that bit and walked away.

"You shouldn't walk away from a gypsy."

"You'll see me again and I've only got a twenty."

"I can give you change," at which point I imagined an old style bus-conductor ticket belt and a gypsy ticket winding out that promised the bearer good fortune. Which kind of undermines the magic.

I will think of her on the 29th of next month? We play Villa away on the 28th.

"I'll see you again, take care of yourself," I say, for some reason worried for the safety of someone who can see into the future.

I might have gone back but that bit about being careful with money and good with my hands was so far wide of the mark she might as well have said, "You are a large bosomed dentist from Barbados and you can fly". I didn't think enlisting this woman into the cause was going to be any kind of help at all.

31

Chapter 7

17th August 2004

Rangers, Celtic, Rangers, Celtic, Rangers, Celtic

I adore Scotland for more reasons than I care to list and I have all the time in the world for Glasgow and the people who call it home. Barrowlands is the best live venue in Britain, there is a chip shop outside it that does the most scrumptious mushroom bhajis, Glaswegians (Or "soap-dodging Weedgie bastards" as my friend from Edinburgh insists they prefer being called) provide that buzz of energy that can make a whole city vibrate and, like New York or Newcastle, it's intoxicating if you have the courage to meet it head on, but Celtic and Rangers can both fuck off if they think they are ever getting into the Premiership. It's a ludicrous idea, would be to nobody's actual benefit and anyone suggesting otherwise is an idiot.

For a start, who would sanction it? The top English teams have full grounds already and don't need the only positive thing the Old Firm have to bring to the table, namely, a large away support. The next level down don't want another two teams squabbling over the League Cup, UEFA Cup qualification and everybody else would be two League places nearer relegation.

The problem for Celtic and Rangers is that they have maximised their own market and despite qualifying for the Champions League every year, don't appear to have a pot to piss in. The TV cash in the Premiership must look very inviting to them. And that is my problem because.............?

The Old Firm bitch on about their own League not being competitive enough, then every time a player or manager at another Scottish team so much as looks like making an impact they steal him clean away. They have bullied their way into the very position they complain about.

The baggage they would bring would be extraordinary. If Celtic fans want to pretend to be Irish and Rangers fans want to be English and if the pair of them want to refight ancient battles, let them do it in a field somewhere like those sad fuckers who dress up as Roundheads on a weekend, don't drag me into it.

Like comedian Denis Leary says, "I didn't make the world, it was like this when I got here", so I don't want to hear about why they are anti-English either, it's got nothing to do with me. And anyhow, historically the Scots have spent more time kicking each other in the bollocks than they have spent being oppressed by the English and it's rarely mentioned how they rushed south and sacked Hexham when the English army was off in an Anglo-French bundle in 1346.

The day after the *Evening Chronicle* pictured the windows of The Tyneside Irish Centre being boarded up, 15,000 Rangers fans descended on Newcastle for the Newcastle/Gateshead Cup. This auspicious object was in fact a rather attractive pasta bowl but for once was a trophy with our actual name on it. Of course we didn't win it, we never win anything. The other teams involved in the two day tournament were Real Sociadad and Feyenoord, managed by potty old Ruud Gullit. Tickets for the two days and the four games therein were a mere forty of your English pounds. Thankfully they were taking Scottish pounds as well, otherwise the attendance would have been embarrassing.

The day after I let my excitement run away with me and rushed to St James' Park to hand over my money, Sky announced that they would be showing all four games on the telly in my house (this was obviously not an exclusive deal, everybody else in the country could have it at their house as well). The crew of delinquents, drunks and deviants I drink with pre-match can number as many as 20. Only myself and Guy stood defiantly in an almost empty Trent House as Sociadad and Feyenoord did little more than kick chunks out of our beautiful new pitch.

We got to our seats in time for the penalties, decided that we had no interest whatsoever and went back downstairs to get another pint.

Newcastle beat Rangers convincingly 4-2, with a thumping low penalty from Shearer, a snap-shot from Bellamy, a scorcher from Ollie Bernard and a back post poke-in from Dyer. The crowd gave a massive and warm welcome to Nicky Butt, only to realise that the substitute was actually another diminutive gingerish fellow, the presumably rather chuffed Martin Brittain. "How kind," he must have thought. "Who's he again?" I asked.

"He's actually very good," said Guy who, to his lasting credit, takes an interest in the reserves and youth teams. Young Brittain spent the rest of the game giving the ball away, crossing into the crowd and falling on his arse. Guy shook his head, I chuckled and the Rangers fans sang *Rule Britannia* and *God Save The Queen* (unfortunately not the Sex Pistols version) before taking a dislike to Alan Shearer for appearing to kick Jean Alain Boumsong up the arse. Robson took him off, as he later explained, to save him from "filthy chants out of filthy mouths."

Day two and even less people turned up to see Newcastle lose a tedious game 1-0 to Sociadad. The highlight, the reason many were there, was to welcome Patrick Kluivert onto the field for the first time in a black and white shirt. He came on for Shearer, looked rusty but had our best chance of the match, which was cleared off the line.

Despite the expectancy of widespread drunken pillaging the Rangers fans were no trouble at all. 15,000 people drinking, singing and making arses of themselves in Newcastle on a Saturday night is obviously just a drop in the ocean.

Celtic Park on a warm Wednesday night three days later and again the atmosphere is rowdy but friendly. The pubs around the ground are shabby as hell, the draught beer is rancid, the floors are tiled, presumably so the blood and broken glass can be swept off at the end of an evening and you can't understand a bloody word anybody is saying.

"Wevonli goat heavyencans hen," shouts a ferocious looking woman over the jolly pro-IRA songs on the jukebox.

I blink at her. I don't know any of those words. "Goat? What goat?"

She shakes her head like she has been wasting her time talking to a deaf Chinese person and dumps a can of beer next to my watery Guinness and the two pints of lager that were presumably pumped out of the hold of a partially submerged Clydeside dredger. I give her money smiling and nodding like a deaf Chinese person. "The nice lady says she has only got heavy," Alan holds up the beer, "in cans."

Oh.

A call comes in on somebody's mobile: "They've had to shut the training ground because of the conjunctivitis."

The four of us change pubs, subconsciously moving away from the stadium until we end up in a place where there is a carpet on the floor and the bottled cider that Peter J has been looking for. Alan has to drive when he gets back to Newcastle so only three pint bottles of Magners are ordered with three pint glasses half filled with ice. "It's lovely," says Peter. Tony, the fourth of our happy band, steward of our coach, massive Clash fan and all round good egg looks at Peter like he has put a rotten old fish in his hand and told him to have a bite. I am equally sceptical: "Cider Peter, are you sure this isn't going to end up with us pissing ourselves on a park bench and swearing at pigeons?"

The pub is small, hot, smoky, clammy and crowded. Yet a single gulp of icy cider cools, cleans and calms the soul. "Bloody hell!" I gasp. Drink it greedily and order some more.

In the ground, I am wedged in with my hands on my knees like I'm six years old in a crowded church, between Peter J, who is no stranger to a meat pie, and an enormous bloke with a shaved head and heroic moustache who immediately gets into a slanging match with two really pissed kids who insist on singing 'No Surrender To The IRA' and *Rule Britannia*.

"That shit has got fuck all to do with Newcastle," he growls.

"We're just winding them daft fuckers up man."

"That's not the fucking point," and this extract from The Royal Debating Society goes on for the entire first half. Boring as it gets, it's better than the match. "This argument has got nothing to do with me but for the record I agree with you," I tell the big lad as I squeeze out and over the back of my seat into an empty one behind. If they were going to start swinging at each other I wanted out. Peter J, who for some reason was watching the match whilst wearing sunglasses, was oblivious.

I have little room to criticise oblivion here, Celtic changed virtually their entire team at half-time and I didn't even notice. Bellamy, who was busy all night, scored to put us one up after about an hour and once again Shearer was taken off, replaced by Kluivert.

Celtic scored with an unmarked header at a corner and a deflected shot in the last minute to win 2-1. No points were lost and we weren't out of any sort of cup but the manner of our defeat and the identity of our opponents made it hard to stomach.

Back on the coach we watched five episodes of *The Royle Family* back to back, which, good as it is, is a bit much. But there was a time when all there was to do on a coach trip returning from an away match was to breathe in other people's farts and we were back in the Toon for 1 am, so you can't knock it

35

Chapter 8

17th August 2004

Away To Jolly Old Boro

Pre-match.

Last season at Boro we had a great time, not so much the game, which was truly awful, but the atmosphere. "Pogo if you love the Toon", "Shoes off if you love the Toon" and best of all the mass dancing and singing of Boro's own *Pigbag* theme every time one of their hapless goons blazed a shot over the bar. We all had a laugh and no one died, what could possibly be wrong? Everything it seems, our reckless behaviour was endangering innocent lives and our ticket allocation had been cut from 3,000 to just over 2,000 as some sort of punishment.

(Middlesbrough have done the same thing to Manchester United supporters in recent years: were we the only two groups of fans to stand up, or were these the only games the home team were likely to sell out of tickets?)

You have to wonder about the person or persons who work at Middlesbrough as safety officers? I have thought about little else this week (apart from conjunctivitis) and it's quite a picture I have painted for myself: shifty weaselly little men; snidey, dickless peckerheads puffed up on their own self-importance. Rubbing their sweaty palms on their cheap nylon trousers in a darkened office, twitching with an almost sexual excitement, confirming their self-importance as those nasty Newcastle fans are taught that they must learn to play by the rules or suffer the consequences. This may be an unfair and inaccurate picture but it's one I will personally enjoy perpetuating.

Let it not be forgotten that these people used the 9/11 attack in New York to stop Newcastle and sunderland fans wearing comedy gas masks and radiation suits when visiting the Riverside. They take themselves soooo seriously that they are prepared to use other people's horrific deaths to stop what amounts to nothing more than a bit of light ribbing. So should we be surprised that the explanation as to why Newcastle's ticket allocation was cut by around 800 for this game included references to the Hillsborough disaster? Is there no level to which these greasy little Jobsworths won't stoop? Apparently not.

How dare they? How fucking well dare they. To the best of my knowledge no one ever died at a football match because they took a shoe off and waved it in the air.

And our version of the Boro lot, the (deep breath) "Newcastle United Safety Advisory Group Under The Chair Of The Newcastle City Council" rather than telling the Boro creeps to "give us our bloody tickets, then fuck off and grow the fuck up, you dismal little bastards", actually start to lecture us on how to support our team. They announce: "The objective of a supporter should be to come along and enjoy a match, shout and cheer in support of your team and stand at times of excitement – but please think of the consequences if you persistently stand." Which means that you are allowed to stand but only when you are "excited". Personally at last season's game I was excited from lunchtime until about one o'clock the following morning – I couldn't believe we had won a game when we were so shit.

AND it was the Boro safety people who called off our game at the Riverside the year before that (after an injury-hit Boro had been battered by five, midweek by Aston Villa) because of a bit of snow on the Friday. Snow that had all melted by three o'clock Saturday. "It was dangerous," explained my friend Brian (a Boro fan), "there was the very real danger that you were going to give us a right twatting." So it was a bit rich of Steve McClaren to turn up looking smug on TV referring to our request for the game to be postponed (because our squad is afflicted by a hideous eye infection) that, "these things happen in football, injuries and illness. The game should be played." If we got the points and they got the conjunctivitis we wouldn't be able to stand up for laughing.

Post Match

Most fans seemed to travel by coach and what a pleasant surprise to find ourselves in the ground over an hour before the game was due to start. It is traditional and expected for the Cleveland cops to leave us rotting on the side of the A19 until five minutes to kick off, but despite turning up suited, booted and ganghanded, then dragging us all off our buses for a full search, they allowed us to go almost straight away. Problem being, there was no beer for sale in our little corner, granted the stuff they usually sell us is pissy weak slops that they have no doubt washed their feet in but it acts as a placebo. During the game the police and stewards tried all game to get people to sit down and some very stubborn lads who refused were hoyed out. Most of us sat for a second or two before jumping straight up again because we were "excited" which, as we know, is allowed.

Newcastle supposedly had nine players unable to travel, with those remaining training in parks, on their own and changing in their cars. This turned out to be a smokescreen and Given, Robert and Dyer turned up with what looked a pretty handy squad. We were without four centre-halves but Elliott and Hughes coped manfully and Boro rarely got at them anyway, such was the brilliance of Nicky Butt. Even the notoriously hard to please fans among us were raving about him afterwards, his tackling, his composure, his positioning and the small matter that he always passed the ball to a black and white shirt.

Just over a quarter of an hour in and Riggott fucked up, Bellamy whizzed away from the Boro defence, round the keeper and 1-0 to the good guys.

We dominated the first half but we defended deeper in the second half and a Boro goal was always coming. Given made one brilliant save then Downing scored with just under 20 minutes left. Dyer came on for the exhausted Milner and Ameobi came on for Robert in what seemed a bizarre substitution until Shola turned out to be a quite splendid left winger. Strong and skilful, he was a constant help at the back and a menace up front, until he burst into the box and was up-ended by Zenden. Shearer smashed in the penalty then went off and Kluivert came on.

Boro had gone at this point, their neat passing got very sloppy and heads were dropping, the crowd were muted and we were bouncing. Dyer skipped free down the right and crossed low, Kluivert missed it altogether but Jenas was flying in behind him with the goal gaping. Somehow, from what seemed like six inches out, he missed. That was about 89 minutes and you couldn't help but worry. Then with 90 minutes gone Dyer slipped and fell and Zenden crossed. Mendieta, in front of Given, was offside and Hasselbaink ("Fat

Eddie Murphy, you're just a fat Eddie Murphy" – song of the day) punched it in with his fist.

We would probably have taken the draw beforehand but it was a sickening way to drop two points in the end. Cheating like that should get a five match ban, and the guilty party should be forced to play in bright yellow marigold gloves for the rest of the season so we can all see where his sneaky hands are.

Chapter 9

27th August 2004

Another Quiet Week In Newcastle

"Everybody is in the same boat and we are all rowing in the same direction" - Bobby Robson.

While we're doing nautical metaphors: two weeks into the season and the 'boat' was spinning around, shipping water in a maddening chaotic whirlpool. Crew members were thrashing about in incompetent panic, one had, reportedly, been refusing to row at all, one was last seen swimming for shore and the rest appeared either on the brink of mutiny or ready to man the lifeboats.

Cap'n Bobby described reports that Kieron Dyer had refused to play on the wing at Boro as "utter rubbish" and made a joke of the idea that Dyer had a 'camp' saying, "I don't know about a camp, he's got a nice house." (*)

At Boro Dyer came on as a sub, appeared to refuse the captain's armband, pouted about and fell over to allow Boro to score and by the end of the week his 'camp' had put out a statement apologising for his not wanting to play on the wing. But not before he came on as a sub for England against Ukraine in a friendly international at St James' Park, where he was played on the wing and was booed by the crowd. Even ignoring the fact that England fans from Boro and sunderland would have been gleefully booing until they went purple or passed out – it was a savaging the boy would have to work hard to get over. Remarkably things got worse as Jonathan Woodgate was sold to Real Madrid for £15 million. Opinion was split, even inside single heads, between "£15 million is a lot of money for a player who doesn't play", Woodgate having only played thirty-odd games out of a possible 120 since arriving from Leeds and "we have just lost the best defender I have ever seen playing for Newcastle." It helped that he wasn't going to be playing against us for a little while but £15 million isn't "too good to turn down" (B. Robson) and the whole transfer was dealt with in a haste that seemed indecent. Chairman Freddie said we had a plan to replace Woody, Capt'n Bobby said he had no idea who we would be getting.

No one blamed the player for going: never mind the fact that Real Madrid have brilliant players and a damn sight better chance of winning stuff than Newcastle United, he would be playing in the sunshine and the Newcastle summer had been utterly fucking dismal. The crap grey weather that usually departs with the Hoppings annual fair and Wimbledon had stuck around all summer and on the night of the England friendly against Ukraine a violent and spectacular thunderstorm rattled the windows of the restaurant I was celebrating my birthday in.

England manager Sven Goran Eriksson single-handedly ruined the international friendly in this country and although the rules had been changed to stop his usual dozen substitutions the game still seemed a pointless exercise. An expensive exercise in irrelevance for everybody, except for those keen to boo their teeth loose and for Shaun Wright-Phillips who bolted half the length of the pitch to score England's third goal. A goal that was enjoyed just as much in the pub as it would have been from a £40 seat. Possibly more so; England games are so detestably blighted by unruly children, incessantly blowing annoying plastic horns, that digesting a scrumptious dinner with a cool pint in front of a large screen, seemed much the better option.

By the time Newcastle's first Premiership game came around it was entirely possible to have seen five games at St James' Park so the giddy excitement of seeing the pitch for the first time was a little diluted. Familiar faces roll in, quieter, a little greyer round the temples maybe. But the buzz is still there in your stomach, your heart still races at kick-off and Newcastle are playing Spurs whom we like to thrash handsomely. There have been a couple of frustrating exceptions but generally Tim, our Spurs mate, will spend the evening claiming that at least four of Newcastle's goals were offside. It has come to the point where he can be applauded into the pub with the firm belief that he has brought our three points with him in his overnight bag.

After a sparkling first half in which Craig Bellamy was magnificent and only Paul Robinson in the Spurs goal stopped us being 3 –0 up, Newcastle faded alarmingly.

Timmy the Tuba (actually Atouba but the P.A. announcement wasn't that clear) scored after 51 minutes and although other chances came and went Newcastle United descended into a farcical mess. The highlight of the silliness came on 77 minutes when Robson made a triple substitution that had nothing to do with football and everything to do with political expediency. Shearer had looked tired, slow and ineffective but, presumably so as not to upset him, he was left on. Keen for Ameobi not to feel like the fourth choice striker he was brought on first, Dyer was rushed on before Kluivert so people were applauding players onto or off the pitch and would be too confused to boo as well, and both the wide players were taken off. Newcastle now had four strikers on the pitch and nobody to supply the crosses; the first corner we won everybody stood around waiting for somebody else to take it. Craig Bellamy eventually wandered over and hoofed the ball high into the Gallowgate End.

We lost 1-0 and the team was booed off.

Amidst all the gnawing frustration, hangovers and latent fury of the next day we were supposed to take Newcastle United's reported interest in Wayne Rooney seriously.

(*) In an exclusive interview with The Mag in March 2007, Kieron Dyer denied that he refused to play on the wing at Middlesbrough and pointed out that he had played all across the midfield, as well as up front, when asked to do so. He had spoken to Robson about his not playing wide but there was no refusal.

The amount of abuse Dyer took seems particularly unfair in light of the fact that, as The Journal claimed in September 2004, two other players had flat out refused to play wide but that Dyer didn't want to name them and drag them into the firing line with him.

It is also our understanding that one of these players, when asked to play wide in the pre-season friendly against Rangers, told Bobby Robson and John Carver to "Fuck off" but was never punished.

Chapter 10

3rd September 2004

Being 40

I didn't mention that my birthday was my 40th. I was reluctant to do so because being 40 is like being on mild drugs. You wander around slightly bewildered by the world wondering if it's the drugs/being 40 or because the world is essentially confusing. Your best friends know you are on drugs/40 and will use this rare moment of emotional vulnerability for their own amusement, otherwise you are fine as long as nobody knows. Providing you don't start jabbering gobbledegook, befriending lamp-posts or trying to stare into a different dimension, people around you will carry on as normal. If you let the cat out of the bag those people's perception of you changes, they take a mental step back, pop you into a completely different box and wait for you to start acting weird. Women find you less attractive, they raise their eyebrows and say "Really, never?" in a way so sweet that they think you haven't noticed how disgusting they now find you, like hair is sprouting out of your nose and ears before their very eyes. An inner voice is screaming at them, "Even standing near this man is desiccating your ovaries, quick, run".

This is the best argument against ingesting even the softest drug there has ever been. The government should start paying me.

To add to my general state of befuddlement, this self same calendar year I have moved into a house *(previously I lived up a tree, near some bins and before that, Benwell)*. Three bedroomed, semi-detached, gardens to front and rear, life was suddenly different. For example, when the sun comes out now I don't think, "Oh good the sun has come out!" I think, "I must mow the lawn and get a load of washing in." When did I turn into that fucking person? I hate that person and consequently the urge to rush out and get drunk, have a fight and a huge tattoo is overwhelming. In fact I need to get lots of stuff pierced and become a roadie for Californian punk rock band Rancid. This sort of thing troubles me; at the frozen veg in Asda I regard myself as a class traitor when I choose petit pois over peas and now I'm in a bloody garden centre?

Garden centres bring my advancing years into sharp focus. My fear and subsequent fascination with them dominates my thinking at present. It is an utterly baffling and alien universe full of brightly coloured things that I don't understand at all. Compost, hardy perennials, tropical fish; Wifey and I didn't know the first thing about any of them but she has been devouring information, using her growing displeasure with Newcastle United to fuel her plant-related fires. I push the trolley, pay half and try not to speak or break anything. All the other customers know how to go on, they are tranquil, know why they are there, know exactly what they are looking for and they terrify me. Any second one of them will point at me and shriek "Imposter!" and I will be pursued off the premises by an angry, casually dressed, mob wielding garden implements that I don't know the names of.

Perhaps I thought all this domesticity would turn out to be some sort of buffer against the ongoing pain caused by following Newcastle United, like supporting football could be turned into some sort of hobby, an idle distraction if you will. I try; the morning after the Norwich match I get out of bed and announce cheerily, "A week and a half and we'll be on holiday, we can get some plants for the beds you dug, get the patio laid maybe. And Bully is coming up at the weekend and there's the party on Saturday."

Wifey scowls at me and says, "and that wasn't the first thing you thought of when you woke up" and I'm caught bang to rights. My coat, Toon top and boots are still on the floor by my chair (I have "a chair" now – for snoozing in) where I sat shouting "Bastards!" at the *Match Of The Day* highlights of the game we'd just got back from. A game where Newcastle had worked themselves into a 2-0 lead and then let Norwich deservedly claw it back to a final score of 2-2, with Norwich having had a couple of decent chances at the end to actually win it. My life is confusing enough without those incompetent fuckers trying to get us all relegated. Dyer somehow got 85 minutes in the centre of midfield despite the fact that he was rubbish from minute one. What the hell was Robson looking at?

Bully is my man, we lived together in abject poverty, in the draughtiest flat in the world before I moved in with Wifey and he was best man when we got married. He lives at the other end of the country and we see each other once or twice a year. He is my punk rock conscience and laughs at the idea of me struggling round the garden with a lawn mower. He supports Arsenal, drinks too much, smokes way too much, doesn't always eat properly and sabotages his own relationships with women. On a purely health front, I will live twenty years longer than him which he genuinely couldn't give a fuck about, which is one of the many reasons I love him so much.

His arrival and my birthday drinkie on the Saturday night means I don't go to Aston Villa. Instead I take him, and the poor woman he is presently inflicting himself on, to the Baltic so we can walk across the brilliant footbridge and afterwards we have a couple of pints in The Tyne.

Back home we sit down in front of Sky Sports, the pangs of desperate guilt and regret are brought to a head because Patrick Kluivert is finally making his full debut in place of Alan Shearer and I'm going to miss it. The Sky panel makes a big deal out of Shearer being out, unaware presumably that Shearer had a stinker against Norwich and was well overdue a dropping. Comparisons are made with Ruud Gullit dropping Shearer five years earlier and finding himself out of a job soon after, the difference nobody seems to pick up on is that Gullit replaced Shearer with Paul Robinson who is now at York City whereas Robson replaced a different Shearer (the 33 year old version) with Holland's all-time top scorer. We are a goal down within minutes.

John Gregory is watching the game on our behalf and relaying his thoughts back to the studio, which is an entirely unsatisfactory state of affairs but putting the radio on instead would involve moving from my chair.

I wake up.

We are 2-1 up. Kluivert has scored! And Andy O'Brien. My mood has changed completely. I am bolt upright and excited. This doesn't help, Villa make it 2-2 then the Villa keeper, Sorensen, deliberately handles the ball outside the area to stop Bellamy scoring, even Gregory, former Villa manager, says he should be sent off. Sorensen, who in the past has been a damn nuisance, twice saving vital penalties against Newcastle, only gets a yellow card and then makes a good save to thwart Robert's free-kick. It proves to be the turning point because our players are weak in the head. Arsenal or Manchester United would use the injustice to spur them on, we use it as an excuse to lose 4-2. I desperately try to get back to sleep during the last ten minutes but the game is over by then, we've given up.

Sunday morning after a night out in Newcastle with 25 or so of my friends and I'm fine. The hangover is testimony to a good time but my main problem is that I still haven't seen Kluivert's goal, or so I think. My car has been broken into and so has Bully's. We both lost nothing but some CDs each but the dashboard of my car is mangled where the clueless fucker tried and failed to rive the radio out. The police come and later a nice lady who dusts for prints. On T.V. Kluivert receives the ball with his back to goal, turns and scores. Bully doesn't really care about his car and I give him a pile of CDs to listen to on his way home. I on the other hand am horrified, not just at the hassle this is going to take to sort out but what it is going to turn me into. No sooner have I got my head round the idea of being 40 and going to garden centres at the weekend than I am now going to be the sort of person who jumps up and looks out the window whenever they hear a noise in the street. I'm now totally fucked off and hungover, Bully is leaving, my car is going to be in the garage forever and my football team is bollocks. Depressingly, the latter is the most important problem and the one I can do least about – I really think I wouldn't be having these outrageously violent revenge fantasies - about catching the cunt robbing someone else's car and sticking a claw-hammer through his fucking skull and seeing his ugly useless whore of a mother crying on the news about what a good boy he really was - if Newcastle had won their first three games and were playing well.

We decide to go to the garden centre anyway. Before we get half a mile up the road I realise that the indicators are knackered and we have to turn round and go home. In that time my phone has vibrated three times, three messages. I don't care who they are from or what they are about. I just get through to the insurance company when Wifey rushes in and says, "Robson's been sacked".

Fuck!

Chapter 11

10th September 2004

Sir Bobby Robson and I

There is a phrase in television called 'Jumping The Shark' – it is of American origin and comes from an episode of *Happy Days* when The Fonz, on water-skis, had to jump over a pool with a great white shark in it. Basically it is the precise moment in time when something previously well thought of suddenly becomes embarrassing, unwatchable garbage. At this point it's over, it doesn't matter how good it used to be, you have to scrap it and move on, for everybody's sake.

Football managers can 'Jump The Shark' – you can only work out when retrospectively but if you think about it it's obvious. Dalglish was doing OK until he sold Sir Les Ferdinand and Gullit was actually doing a fine job until he walked on the pitch to take the acclaim of 30,000 of us singing his name at Old Trafford after the FA Cup semi-final against Spurs in 1999. A magnificent tactical display after which he appeared to go stark-raving mental, his eyes spinning in their sockets like a crazed weasel, he seemed to think, "See. I know everything. I'm great I am!" From that exact moment he was doomed and we crashed and burned along with him.

So, did Bobby Robson 'Jump The Shark' when he signed Lee Bowyer? Certainly it felt like an uncomfortable compromise to our principles having such a notorious fellow in our colours. *(Bowyer doesn't appear to have bat wings or have the number of the beast burnt into his forehead but bad Ju-Ju follows him around like a curse. Look at the downfalls of Leeds Utd, Newcastle United and West Ham and consider the common element).* You've got to admire the self-confidence in Robson's own man-management; turning Newcastle United into Bobby Fagin's Home For The Rehabilitation Of Naughty Boys, where there would no doubt be close harmony singing from ruddy-faced scamps who would "put the show on here" and save the orphanage. It didn't work out like that, I bumped into Mick Martin of Toon fanzine *True Faith* at an away game last season and asked him what he thought was the matter with our underachieving heroes. "The problem is, we have got a team full of bastards," was his concise reply.

You would have thought Bobby Robson had died and that Freddie Shepherd had pulled the trigger over the next week or so. People queued up to say how marvellous he was and the papers lamented his passing. "He was a great man and the game will be poorer without him," was the overriding sentiment.

Over the years I have fallen out with and fallen in love with Sir Bobby Robson more times than I care to think about (he is no doubt unaware and unconcerned by any of this.) This waxing and waning of emotion is not, in my opinion, because I am flighty or fickle, it is because the man is an enigma: wise and perceptive at one time, stubborn and inflexible at another. Charming one day, obstinate and infuriating the next.

As manager of Ipswich Town, winning the 1978 Cup Final against Arsenal was like him winning a war for football's living soul. Ipswich were vibrant, exciting and dashing, while Arsenal were a meticulously tedious team who deliberately spoiled football matches that they generally went on to win. Ipswich fizzed around in hot, sunny, perfect Cup Final weather and missed chance after chance while the cynical Gunners waited for the one lucky, ugly twist of fate that would seal their inevitable victory. Roger Osborne scored for Ipswich and like many a neutral I leapt across the living room, in my case from the midst of Spangles, bubble gum football cards and clumsily customised Subbuteo players.

As England manager he dropped Kevin Keegan yet persisted with Paul bloody Mariner and Phil bloody Neal. He further snubbed me over the years by often choosing Mark Hateley over Peter Beardsley, John Barnes over Chrissy Waddle, and by not taking Paul Gascoigne to the European Championships in 1988 where his stale old England team lost all three games. I would like to think he would admit that the teams that served him so well in the '86 and '90 World Cups were nowhere near the teams he intended when he set off. This is both a criticism of his stubborn loyalty to the wrong players and a compliment to his genius in pulling together a great team during a crisis. The 1990 team, re-forged mid-tournament amidst evil and malicious media coverage, was a tactical masterpiece of flair, passion and power. Robson's

England (who deserved to meet the most swashbuckling Italian side in living memory in a final that the football Gods deemed instead to be fought out between ghastly Germans and cynical Argentines) exploded football into the 1990s and the shock waves of that blast can be felt today. All his players from that period adore him as do all England fans over a certain age and there is no need to start poking his achievements with a stick at Barcelona, Porto, PSV Eindhoven and Sporting Lisbon.

The story goes that on taking over at Newcastle United Robson saved the club from relegation and made us into a top four team which, again, you could consider true enough not to quibble with, except Thora Hird could have taken over Newcastle at that point and saved us from relegation merely on the basis of "not being Ruud Gullit". It is unlikely that Dame Thora would have got us to the semi-final of the FA Cup however, where we suffered a cruel 2-1 defeat to Chelsea that still hurts more than any of our lost finals because Robson's team played so well.

Sir Bobby boasted that before he turned up the club "could only dream of playing in Europe" when we had already tasted the Champions League under Kenny Dalglish and were actually in the UEFA Cup the day he walked in the door. His first full season in charge was actually the worst season Newcastle endured since arriving in the Premiership, admittedly we had finished lower in the table in the two previous years but both those had brought Cup Finals. In retrospect the 2000/01 season can be seen as transitional, at the time it was simply "shit". The fans blamed dour coach Mick Wadsworth; the *Evening Chronicle* printed the results of *The Mag's* readers' poll just after Southampton came in to offer Wadsworth a coaching job.

Question: " Do you want Bobby Robson to stay?" Answer: Yes - 94%, No 6%. Question: "Do you want Mick Wadsworth to stay?" Answer: Yes 23%, No 77%. According to Robson himself, this tipped the balance in Wadsworth's decision to leave. Not for the last time Robson was livid with his own public, in this case he should have been grateful because in blaming Wadsworth the fans were letting Sir Bobby off. Wadsworth recommended, and Newcastle acquired, some awful bloody players during that time; Fumaca, a Brazilian who could fail to control a ball and fall over it in one fluid movement, Bassedas who cost £4.5 million pounds but didn't appear to be good at anything and Daniel Cordone who looked canny at first and had earrings that were "welded" into his ears but who turned out to be a major league loon with no understanding of the offside rule whatsoever.

After Wadsworth left, the quality of the players coming into the club took a noticeable upturn. Bobby bought and stuck by Laurent Robert when many people thought him a lazy player and a luxury. Robson recognised him as a luxury we could afford, saw how the Frenchman stretched the game and for three seasons Robert scored or set up more goals than any midfielder in the Premiership who wasn't called Giggs or Pires.

Like most fans, I thought the purchase of Craig Bellamy was a mad and expensive mistake and like most fans I was delighted to be proved spectacularly wrong. The following season Newcastle were reborn as the fittest, fastest and most exciting team in the country. The spirit was such that with ten minutes of a game left and a goal down you didn't think, "I hope we can equalise," you genuinely thought, "We ARE going to win!" Bellamy's injury and three consecutive games against Arsenal meant we slipped out of the FA Cup and the title race but Robson takes sole credit for building a belting, young team that could only get better. Or so we thought. The following year, be it because of injuries or the fact that the club were overstretched in the Champions League, Newcastle weren't as thrilling, scored less goals and (crucially) on meeting Manchester United at St James' Park with an outside chance of the title were horrifically battered 6-2. But that season we left the San Siro the better team against Inter Milan and Bobby Robson had taken Newcastle United further than we had ever been in our lives. We could look anybody in the eye and fancy our chances, that was entirely Robson's doing and our love for him was immeasurable.

Criticising Bobby Robson in public is seen in many quarters as being on a par with being caught in a darkened room with your trousers round your ankles, the bleeding corpse of the Easter Bunny in your hands and a Bowie knife between your teeth.

It would be a horrible person indeed who could actually bring themselves to dislike Mr Robson, yet during the 2003/04 season he seemed hell-bent on forcing just that.

"He was a great man and the game will be poorer without him" – which is undoubtedly true yet the interests of the game are not necessarily the same as the interests of Newcastle United, loved though he remained. How many other fans would have wanted Robson to take over at their club? Throughout the season Robson stuck by players who were playing badly and lost his temper with anyone who suggested so. He insulted his own fans openly calling them "muppets" and "budgerigars". He told those of us who had never played the game that we didn't know what we were talking about. This attitude is prevalent throughout football and it drives fans mad because it is so insulting; we have never worked in the circus but we know a clown when we see one. Bobby tried to convince us that Hugo Viana, who couldn't head the ball or tackle, was the natural successor to Gary Speed, one of the greatest headers of a ball the Premiership has ever seen. Then in a game against Everton, with Speed off the pitch getting stitches and the crowd getting restless for six minutes, Robson made a show of walking out from his dug-out putting his fingers in his ears and turning round in a circle so everyone could see what he thought of their opinions. He spent £8.5 million pounds on Viana but plainly thought having ten men on the field was a better idea than actually playing him.

He spent £7 million on Carl Cort who played a dismal number of games in three years and was eventually off-loaded to Wolves for £1.5 million. All top managers make big mistakes, Arsene Wenger spent a fortune on Wiltord and Alex Ferguson bought Diego Forlan but when the Cort signing was described as a failure he publicly hit the roof and said he hoped Cort would come back to kick us in the pants. His vanity being such that he would rather his team lost points than for his judgement to be proved wrong.

In what seemed an act of spite he sold Nobby Solano (a player once linked with a £10 million move to Real Madrid) to Aston Villa for a measly £1.5 million after consistently leaving him out of vital games and criticising the player's change of heart about playing for his country. Robson claimed Solano got a new contract because he said he was retiring from playing for Peru. This might be a genuine gripe but would Robson have stood in the way had he been manager of Stuart Pearce when he came out of international retirement? During his time at United, Nobby was a decent man and a brilliant footballer who brought the best out of other players, most notably Kieron Dyer, with whom he shared a rare and special understanding on the pitch. Solano had fallen out with his national coach and when that coach left there was no reason for such a popular player not to answer the call-up. The fact that Lima is on the other side of the planet is geography's fault, surely not Solano's.

It was said that Newcastle fans were split over Robson's sacking and in my view that was true. All the fans I spoke to who actually went to matches could no longer put up with the team lumping the ball in the general direction of Alan Shearer and playing rubbish football. Then there were the sentimental fans, many of whom didn't actually go to (or more precisely, have to endure) matches, who viewed the game through news coverage. The second group are entitled to an opinion, my grandfather didn't drive a tank across the African desert for nothing, but they have to accept that it is an opinion that carries no weight.

The team were playing badly all season with flashes of luck or individual brilliance winning us matches against a backdrop of ugly football and that means: a) Robson was telling them to play like that, or b) the players weren't doing what Robson told them. Those are the only two options available and they are both the manager's fault. It sticks in the throat to be called "ungrateful" by Robson as well; "ungrateful" for what exactly, all those trophies we won? We paid his wages for five years and because we can be trusted to keep turning up every week, he was given tens of millions of pounds to spend on players and he thinks we should be grateful? Sir Bobby Robson was given more time and more money than most managers and it didn't work out so he got sacked, that's how football works.

"With hindsight he should have gone in the summer," wrote one journalist. No, with eyes he should have gone in the summer, Robson had assembled a bloody good team but they just weren't doing it for him. "People have short memories," he snapped at the time but he was wrong because we all remembered that his team had been brilliant and now they were a pale imitation of themselves. St James' Park was silent for most of 2003/04 with 50,000 fans frustrated and disappointed. We had all seen worse teams than this but that was not the point, the players had no fire in their bellies anymore and that was a worse crime than simply being "not good enough". The players Bobby defended so loyally consistently let him down.

Certainly the situation could have been handled with much more dignity than the way things actually worked out. Robson was hung out to dry with the chairman saying this was his manager's last season and players being bought and sold reportedly without his say so. "You don't sack Bobby Robson," Shepherd said (presumably hoping Robson would walk out after being publicly undermined) then when it came to it, "I didn't want to be known as the man who shot Bambi" when he eventually had no choice. Shepherd was thus the bad guy when he was actually only guilty of being too sentimental; giving Robson more time and believing in the fairytale that would end with Newcastle winning something and Uncle Bobby and Alan Shearer skipping off together into the sunset.

As it was, the end was handled shabbily and far from being pleased or relieved when it came I, like most of the country, felt genuinely upset for Robson. "I'm going to go away and think about what I'm going to do with the rest of my life," he said with tears in his eyes.

"Oh my God," I thought, "we've killed that nice old man."

Forgetting as everybody always does; that Bobby Robson is much tougher than he looks and this is a crucial point. With each report of his failing health I have considered ditching this entire chapter for fear of being accused of any disrespect to Mr Robson. But I think it's patronising and ageist to talk of him merely being a dear old gentleman because it is only half the story. He is also a gnarly, battle-scarred and bloody-minded old warrior which earns him a whole different level of respect that must not be overlooked. Besides, Newcastle fans are allowed to criticise Bobby cos he's family, if you are not in the family and you criticise him we'll likely swing for ya.

Chapter 12

12th September 2004

The Media Circus

Sky Television has been accused of many things over the years: top of the list is providing the financial environment where bog-standard footballers get to flounce about like movie stars. You can forgive Sky that because the same money has meant we have seen many of our generation's finest players perform on the same pitch that once provided the likes of Frank Pingel or Malcolm Brown for entertainment.

It also appears to be the case that Sky want a hand in the running of the game from top to bottom, to the extent that an ideal situation for presenter Richard Keys would be himself, dressed as Nero, passing final judgement over the outcome of games. The ref gives a goal and we all look to the Sky-box to see if Emperor Keys concurs. He checks with Andy Gray and they observe the replay. We wait, then a hairy hand is raised and the goal is "good" and we may commence to celebrate. But as we leave the ground it turns out that the opposition shot that came down off the bar in the last minute actually crossed the line, so before we can get to the pub for a celebratory drinkie, Sky have given the equaliser and altered the score and the league tables accordingly.

This may yet be a year or two away but we have their worst crime with us every minute of the day. Sky Sports News, a 'dedicated' 24 hour, rolling monster. What's wrong with it?

Well, it's hideously addictive for a start, more so than crack-cocaine apparently. If you subscribe you are at once horribly and hopelessly hooked. It's the first thing you think about when you wake up and the first channel you flick to whenever you enter your home. This despite the fact that most weeks nothing of any real importance happens at all – what shock developments are going to take place at 3.30 a.m. on a Thursday? Yet here I am perched on the edge of the sofa, full of apprehension, like I'm about to lay an oversized egg.

Our freshly scrubbed and eager presenters are poised and ready to unleash excitement on us at the drop of a hat. "Will the hat drop and if so which way and in whose favour, we'll ask Tony Gayle and Alan Mullery if this is the most historic hat-dropping in the history of football, right after the break." Meanwhile the world is in flames, murderers stalk the streets, children are eating themselves to death and here I still sit. Waiting. Waiting to hear what Clive Allen thinks about the chances of Crystal Palace winning at Everton.

Harmless you think? Really? Well you're wrong because the worst side-effect of this 24 hour saturation, never once blinking news, is that ill-educated, slack-jawed, unemployable halfwits know that if anything happens at Newcastle United at all, they can pull on their best sports casual wear and drag their knuckles up to the ground secure in the knowledge that they can embarrass the entire city by standing gawping behind the man with the microphone. This must gain them some sort of credibility with other cap wearing, sunken-eyed ninnies or loose-knickered girls with cheap jewellery because they flock like starlings and worse still, some of them are asked to speak to the nation on my behalf. This despite the fact that they have never been to a game in their lives and can't actually manage a coherent sentence.

Somebody needs to get along and talk some sense so the whole country doesn't think we're all subhuman fuckwits BUT woe betide anybody who tries to set themselves up as a fans' spokesman: "Many are called but few are chosen" (Hunter S Thompson).

And many have found themselves getting an earful of abuse or a smack in the head for assuming they speak for the Geordie nation.

Writing for *The Mag* you get many invitations to turn up in front of a microphone and make a tit of yourself and the novelty quickly wears off. The night before Newcastle played Manchester United in the FA Cup Final a man rang up and asked me to pop my replica shirt on and get myself down to the Central Station for a live interview for the six o'clock news.

"We're interviewing fans travelling down to London."

"But I'm not going tonight and I'm not going on the train."

"Oh that doesn't matter no one will know."

"No, I don't think so."

"But it's live national TV news."

Who gives a fuck? Until you see that in your place they've got some excitable, gurning loony in a daft jester hat with jingly bells hanging off it saying, "Aye man canny, we're gonna win 5-0 nee botha. Toon Army Toon Army!" And the nation shakes its head.

Fortunately *The Mag* has Alan Harrison as unofficially delegated Minister Of Information, so the rest of us don't have to bother any more. Alan is calm and composed in front of a microphone and won't, like me, turn instantly into Porky The Pig (" I aaah b b b b er der er"). He enjoys the hob-knobbing and particularly likes to turn up at the BBC in Newcastle where he can make goo goo eyes at Carol Malia.

Unfortunately Alan is also a good friend and so the fact that today he has given the nice man from Radio 5 Live my number means I feel obliged to tell the nation what Newcastle fans think of Graeme Souness. I still try to wriggle out of it, "I haven't got any legs," I lie.

"We'll send a taxi," they promise.

Oh alright. After all, I've got a book coming out some time in the future and I might make enough contacts to get invited onto the splendid Simon Mayo show to talk about it. Then Radio Newcastle ring as well and before I know it I'm jabbering into any old pink-shirted newshound's microphone about our new manager.

I told the taxi driver that my mate Spuggs had this really great idea about our new manager being gangster Paulie Walnuts from T.V. show *The Sopranos* because he already has black and white hair and he can whack the useless bastards in the team round the back of the head with a shovel if they didn't do as they were told. But I bottled out and ended up repeating, "His main qualification is that he isn't Steve Bruce, David O'Leary, Glenn Hoddle or Terry Venables," for an hour.

Strawberry Place was buzzing with media vans, cameras and eager well-dressed young men scurrying about. A Range Rover approached, similar to the one Souness left Blackburn in and the poor bloke in it got a hell of a shock as the collective media sprang briefly in his direction.

Nothing happened.

Nothing at all. Souness didn't show up, nobody from the club came out and I didn't get to argue with curmudgeonly Peter Allen on Radio 5 Live because at the last minute he got Craig Bellamy instead. "How dare you," I thundered at the researcher, "you'll be telling me there aren't fresh cut flowers in my dressing room next". The traffic roared and rattled past like it does every day and slack-jawed, unemployable half-wits in ill-fitting sportswear stood about 'in shot'.

Would I like to come back at six for a piece for BBC News 24?

"Thank you, but no."

Because what our club needed right there and then was for all these people to bugger off and let us get on with being a football team again. Not a media circus, not a chaotic soap opera, not a laughing stock, just a football team.

Some chance.

Chapter 13

16th September 2004

A Chairman's Lot

Football supporters' relationships with the chairmen of their clubs can appear complex but essentially they are very simple. The fan wants a chairman who keeps his head down, writes fat cheques for international star players, doesn't charge them too much money to get into the ground, tells them how marvellous they all are and never takes a penny out of the club. The complexity in the relationship begins with how the chairman copes with these unreasonable demands. Unless he can work out a way to let everybody into the ground for nothing AND buy all the world's best players he will be criticised in some quarters. So Freddie Shepherd naturally got some flak for, in his own words, "Shooting Bambi" when he eased Sir Bobby Robson and his favourite golf club out into the street. The sentimental types wanted Freddie stoned out of the parish for this crime while the quieter majority said he should have pulled the trigger in May, so how could he win?

What people have to bear in mind is that Mr Shepherd is no fool, he knows full well that as long as the team is winning Newcastle fans don't really care how much the people running the club pay themselves or that another member of Sir John Hall's family has attached itself to the communal teat. We may all think Sir Bobby came to a shabby end but were we ever going to walk away in disgust?

We were all supposed to be up in arms after Freddie and Douglas Hall were all caught up in the *News of The World* 'scandal' wherein the pair were accused, amongst other things, of calling all the women in Newcastle "dogs", Alan Shearer "Mary Poppins" and boasting about how much money the club made off replica shirts, but that year we also got to an FA Cup Final, so we ignored the lot of it and eventually turned our contempt on Kenny Dalglish instead for being over-cautious against superior opposition.

There was a representation of our chairman in *Viz* after "Dog-gate", playing the drums and grinning like a simpleton at some strippers whilst saying, "I like big jugs, me" which was very funny. However, if you see the original manuscript of what he and Dougie really said to the Fake Sheik at the time, the pair were stitched up like post bags in a prison. Alan Shearer was called "Mary Poppins" because off the field he didn't get into any bother, hardly an insult, and everybody knows that replica shirts are overpriced. Newcastle United reportedly sell the second most club shirts on the planet, which is one of the reasons we can afford decent footballers to wear the real ones – it's simple maths.

As to the "dogs" thing, they were specifically talking about prostitutes in Newcastle, which isn't a nice way to talk about working girls living life as best they can admittedly. But to this day you get old boys blustering away in the press and even sometimes in *The Mag* about how the pair of them had "insulted our wives, mothers, friends and daughters" which is obviously not the case. Unless of course your wives, mothers, friends and daughters offer sexual gratification to strangers for coin of the realm, in which case you've probably got a bit more to worry about than a couple of blokes shooting their gobs off.

There have been real crimes committed that got less headlines, like people being turfed out of the seats they had sat in for years because of expanding corporate seating. This specifically split up the people in The Milburn Stand who used to start a lot of our singing and the atmosphere in the ground is poorer because of it.

It is around this point that some ill-informed journalist will knowingly state "but when it comes to money for players no Newcastle manager for over ten years can complain about lack of funds." This does rather paint the Hall and Shepherd families as jolly Geordie philanthropists when it's the fans' money that is spent. Spent rarely from a considered position of squad strengthening but all too often idiotically thrown at players and agents in panic only a few months before the manager is removed. But we are expected to give our chairman credit for what is his job?

To this day I want to grab people by the throat who trot out this line and violently explain "We give him money, he spends some of it on players" – as comedian Chris Rock says (albeit on a different issue) - "It's what you're supposed to do, you dumb motherfucker!"

But we do compete in the transfer market, the ground is now magnificent and the training ground is awesome yet still there is an air of distrust from fans and media towards the chairman.

Unsubstantiated rumours of shady dealings are devoured with appalled relish, despite a lack of any evidence: "Did you know Shepherd sold the club the shovel out of his garden for half a million quid?"

"That's nowt man, he sold all our names and addresses to the Triads and the next time we play the mackems all our houses are gonna get robbed."

Neither of these things happened.

Mr Shepherd was quoted as saying that the next Newcastle manager after Bobby Robson would be a Geordie. A sceptical media had this down as a straight choice between Alan Shearer and Steve Bruce and were winding themselves up nicely to throw the quote back in Freddie's face when Robson's coach, Geordie boy John Carver, took charge of the team against Blackburn. The chairman, on this subject at least, was a man of his word. Graeme Souness watched his old club take on his new from the stand.

Newcastle won 3-0. Flitcroft nudged a Robert corner into his own net, Shearer scored with a great header and Andy O'Brien turned and finished like he was Thierry Henry for the third. Happy times indeed until someone in the pub said, "Mind, Blackburn were fuckin' shockin'!" and somebody else pointed out that Souness had built that team and we all stared into our beer for a second or two.

Anyway, if Souness turned out to be a mistake we could always blame the chairman.

Chapter 14

20th September 2004

Hapoel Bnei Saknin

What rude and unpleasant house guests we had at SJP yesterday. We have extended them every courtesy right down, apparently, to giving them a lift up from London in our team bus. After this display we should have pointed them in the direction of the National Express depot for their lift home and told them they had ten minutes to get off our property before we released our flying monkeys.

I checked this back on the video when I eventually stumbled through the door last night and they really should have had two players booked inside the first 33 seconds. But this ref was taken in like so many before him. It used to be African players and more recently Koreans; they kick the hell out of you then look all innocent and the refs seem to think, "bless them, they don't know how to play properly yet," and give them a patronising little ticking off. Hapoel Bnei Saknin, from Israel, are a heart-warming mix of Arabs, Jews and Africans and for all we know Gypsies, homosexuals and crippled circus freaks and are thus a beacon of hope in a cruel and bigoted world. Unfortunately by the time the Portuguese dimwit in the yellow caught on to the fact that they were also ruthlessly violent, the game was already lost from his control. For an hour they had been blatantly hacking Newcastle players late and/or from behind and when they finally got a reaction it was from Nicky Butt, who had only been on the pitch two minutes and really should know better. Perhaps given that he was once lifted up by the neck by David Batty during Newcastle's 5-0 win over Manchester United, he thought you are allowed to do that up here. And let's face it, we fans all think you are, the ref however thought otherwise, the Saknin player made a meal of it and both sides, after an unseemly scuffle, were down to ten men for the last half hour when we decided 2-0 was enough and left Patrick Kluivert up front on his own.

This brawl at least livened the crowd up a bit, a rubbish game and a big fight. Welcome to Newcastle Mr Souness.

Chapter 15

21st September 2004

Lies, Damn Lies, Statistics and Bastards

Hypothetical situation: Alan Shearer doesn't score for five games. Media scream "Goal drought!" Shearer scores in the next two games but they are both penalties.

Going into the next game; "Shearer hasn't scored from open play for eight games," it is helpfully pointed out, like a penalty is some kind of bastard back-stair sort of goal that we don't talk about in polite society. They exist but they are common and vulgar.

Shearer scores with his arse in the next game and thus having scored in three consecutive matches is "in a rich vein of goalscoring."

And so Newcastle went to Southampton where they "hadn't won since 1974" and weighed down by the fact that they "hadn't won away from home since October 21st 2003".

Ominous signs indeed that overlooked three small but somewhat relevant points:

Newcastle massacred Southampton 3-0 in Southampton within this same calendar year (FA Cup).

Newcastle actually last won away from home on March 26th 2004 (3-0 at Real Mallorca in the UEFA Cup).

Southampton are fucking shit.

Newcastle beat Southampton 2-1. They made heavy weather of it and needed a belting second goal from Stephen Carr but Given didn't have to make many saves. The Saints put more and taller forwards on to lean on our 'shaky' defence but hardly a chance was made.

Shearer tried to claim the first goal despite the fact that his shot was going into the sea before Prutton deflected it into his own net but his major contribution was beefing away corners at the nearpost with his heroic and increasingly scarred head.

However, the major talking point was the fact that Souness played Shearer and Kluivert up front with Bellamy on the wing, which was a bloody mess truth be told, but when your team wins away from home ("in the League" – as they kept quickly and quietly post-scripting every minute or so on Sky) for the first time in 11 months, who's complaining? Not, fucking well, us.

Chapter 16

25th September 2004

Brian Clough R.I.P.

Match Of The Day opens. Gary Lineker, crisp peddlar and sometime TV presenter has his sombre face on. Brian Clough is dead and the cameras show that all round the country players have their heads bowed in thoughtful deference to a great man.

Thank God they didn't show St James' Park where the players were warming up and the idiot DJ was playing Republica's *Ready To Go* over the tannoy. What the fuck is wrong with this sodding Football Club? I know it was expecting a bit much to hope for a minute's silence for Johnny Cash or my cat (both of whose recent departures have left the world a much poorer and darker place) but this is Brian Clough here people. We have had minute's silences for Princess Margaret and The Queen Mother, who had as much relevance to football as squirrels do to powerboat racing but we choose to ignore the passing of Brian Clough?

Our old matchday DJ, Rob, played The Clash, The Fun Lovin' Criminals, Led Zep, The Transplants (oh yes) and every week The mighty Ramones. "Hey Ho Let's Go, Hey Ho Lets Go", yes let's, dammit! We had credibility, hey new DJ, give us our Ramones back, the fuckin' mackems play Republica ya arsehead! The daft bint singer wore a red and white shirt and performed the stupid song ("Standing on the rooftops avvin' it" - what the fuck is that all about?) when they opened the new ground. Do you know nothing?

The fixtures have been kind to Souness; lining up muppets more rubbish than the new Robbie Williams single for us to knock over while he gets his feet under the table. West Brom are already woefully bad but they also played 120 minutes in the week and have all, apparently, been punching each other in the head and pulling each other's hair for the last fortnight because they all hate one another so much. Consequently Newcastle could afford to be a bit unsettled and off-balance without any real fear of not winning. Kluivert played in the hole behind Shearer and Bellamy, a hole so deep in fact that we could barely see him for an hour.

Bellamy had been a handful but a crude Darren Purse challenge effectively put him out the game. Purse claimed to have made no contact, which makes him a fool or a liar cos Craigy's ankle took a wallop that threatened his inclusion in a game five days later. As Purse also brutally elbowed one of his own players in the face we can give him the benefit of the doubt as far as lying is concerned and be content with him simply being an imbecile. His clumsy bundle into the back of Kluivert after Patrick had skinned him may have looked soft but it was a deliberate infringement and the ref had no real choice. Obviously Gary Megson thought otherwise but Gary Megson is a self-deluded ginger gas-bag who thinks speaking softly to the press makes him seem wise and screaming and waving his arms about on the touch-line makes him a good coach. He is wrong on both counts.

The real turning point was the introduction of Robert and anyone in attendance thinking otherwise should have Laurent's name and date of birth tattooed onto the inside of their eyelids. He instantly gave us the width to pull West Brom apart, he crossed for Kluivert (who, having climbed out of his hole, was sublime) to score the opener, then nearly uprooted the Gallowgate End goal with a shot that thumped against the underside of its crossbar.

Jenas sprang to life on the other wing about the same time and his energy and ability stamped the last vestige of chance out of Megson's shower of shite. Skipping past a defender and clipping the ball back for Milner to bundle, then thrash, home the second and doing the same for Shearer five minutes from time.

The ease with which Horsfield scored West Brom's last minute consolation gave us cause not to get too carried away in a 3-1 win but we should have won and we did, so you can't knock it. However, you'd doubt that a curmudgeonly old genius like Mr Clough would have enjoyed it.

Chapter 17

21st October 2004

Not Going

I love going to away matches; the travelling, the excitement, the beer, the crack and that pure adrenaline rush you get when you go into a strange ground. Surrounded by hundreds of friends, soulmates and fellow drunken degenerates, yet with a strange view and strange people shouting abuse at you in a peculiar dialect. I feel alive, I feel a physical surge of pride and energy; born to this noble purpose of supporting my team and representing those who couldn't be here.

Yet I missed four games in the last month, my reasons for doing so sound like wet excuses and I hate myself.

Perhaps I'm being a bit harsh for not going to Saknin. A trip to Nazareth to play a team of Arabs, Jews and Africans was obviously an adventure but no one is going to begrudge me my next Cup Final ticket because I missed this one.

Newcastle wore yellow shirts and got the crap kicked out of them. Again. But ended up winning a messy game 5-1 with two goals from Kluivert and a hat-trick from the boy Shearer.

If you want to bollock me for not being at Birmingham, then feel free but I am not giving those fuckers 38 bastard quid. No chance, they are taking the fucking piss.

Strangely enough this very month the Football Supporter's Association brought up the subject of price-capping and somebody from the Premiership said, "Ask Arsenal fans if they would mind paying an extra £200 a season to see the likes of Henry and Pires and I don't think many of them would complain." OK, fair point but using the same argument - ask me if I want to pay £38 to get into a scabby ground with Robbie fucking Savage and Emile bloody Heskey on the pitch. Not that Birmingham always charge this much, like many teams they indulge in the loathsome practice of bouncing their prices around to punish the teams who have a decent away support. Imagine if Asda employed a man to walk in front of your trolley putting up the prices of the stuff you needed: "Sorry that tin of beans is now a pound."

"But everyone else only paid 36p," you would rightly complain.

"I know but a lot of people like you buy beans and we thought it would be OK to charge you more. We can make more money that way you see?"

"What about this toilet roll?"

"Normally it's £2.27 but I reckon you can afford at least £3, if we think you might need a poo soon we'll charge you £4."

Of course we can always shop elsewhere for beans and poo-roll, you can't go elsewhere for Birmingham v Newcastle, this is the very definition of extortion. That sound you can hear is the ghost of Al Capone clapping.

As it turned out it was, apparently, a good game, JJ scoring early for us, Brum going 2-1 up and Nicky Butt equalising with a scissor kick in the 67th minute. Robert hit the post, with the keeper static, from a 40 yard free-kick in the last minute.

Is that the sort of thing Darren Ambrose is capable of doing? I only ask because he was in the team instead of Robert for the game at Charlton two weeks later, when the first serious grumblings about Souness began.

I had every intention of going to Charlton, Wifey's best mate from uni is married to a Charlton fan and we were going to go and see them, take in the game and come home on the Sunday. Then Sky got hold of the damn thing and moved it to the Sunday which ruined everything. Yes, yes, I could still have gone but the effort and expense required to go in direct proportion to the distance my fridge is from my favourite armchair made it less than appealing. Getting home at midnight with work a five o'clock start the next day, meant going felt like little more than an expensive point of principle and for all the excitement an away game brings, the joy of opening a beer and already being home should Newcastle lose, well…….

Anyhow, ask yourself, who lost out from my absence at the Valley? Did Newcastle lack vocal support, was there an empty seat? No, some younger, drunker travelling desperado got to go to the game because I didn't, either that or some London based Geordie who doesn't get to see her/his team as often as I do.

Not going makes me a good person and somebody out there owes me a pint.

As to the game; Newcastle dominated possession in the first half without really making any clear-cut chances. In the second half Bernard slung in a cross and Bellamy threw himself at the ball with a heroic disregard for his own personal safety and his header smashed into the Charlton net and we were 1-0 up. Newcastle then set about strangling the life out of Charlton with tidy passing until yet another defensive aberration breathed life back into our victim. O'Brien sold himself and Lisbie nipped past him where Stephen Carr was waiting to poke the ball into his own net. Lovely.

Shearer had a shot cleared off the line, then cleared a shot off his own as both teams went for the win, Given made a great save and the ball bounced in a frighteningly erratic way around our penalty area and in a frustratingly erratic way around theirs. Both sides could have won and a draw was about right but there was a sting in the tail.

Craig Bellamy was taken off, presumably because he had just played back to back games for Wales and because we had an away trip in Europe looming. *The Sun* reported that Craig said in the direction of his manager, "Are you joking, you fucking prick."

This was what the press had been waiting for; many players appear to chunter under their breath, but the interest on which 'errant star' Souness would fall out with first was growing by the day. Like a class full of snotty-nosed sneaks the papers squealed for all they were worth. Patrick Kluivert had been photographed coming out of a London nightspot some weeks earlier and they all started eagerly banging their desk lids. Souness shrugged that one off, "It was his day off but I might have to speak to him about that shirt he was wearing," was our manager's response, which pulled the rug out from under them. But now it was "sir, sir, Craig Bellamy swore!"

Things threatened to get ugly, Bellamy and manager were reported to have had some sort of physical altercation in the week and neither looked happy. Then we whisked off to Athens and got on with the football.

Too short of cash, no holidays available, too short notice. I'm getting used to this and, oh look, it's on the telly. Splendid, feet up, crisps, nuts and a four pack. "Play up the Toon". What am I turning into?

The thing is, only about 300 fans went to Athens.

European campaigns are tests of brinkmanship. Most people can only afford a limited number of trips, the majority can only manage one in my experience.

Bearing in mind that Newcastle took over 12,000 to Milan two years before, that means that the vast majority were, like me, keeping their powder dry. I hate to admit it in public but the small band of heroes in the away enclosure vs Panionios actually made me feel better about myself.

Apparently the grass was too long. Souness claimed the ball wouldn't roll properly or something and Newcastle won a scruffy-arsed game 1-0 after Shola Ameobi came on and fell over in the box twice. The cumulative effect gave Shearer the chance to score from the spot.

Panionios never looked like scoring and with three of the five teams getting through from the group, a couple of home wins should see us through.

Then, after over a month of being exactly the sort of ignorant, lazy, know-all, armchair expert that I have always hated we finally got a home game and I could turn into a proper fan again.

Chapter 18

29th October 2004

Walking In A Keegan Wonderland

No one in the footballing world needs to be told how important Kevin Keegan has been to Newcastle United, how he pulled the club from nowhere by signing as a player, then how he transformed our lives as manager. It's too easy to get misty-eyed and romantic about it all but when strangers broach the subject I long ago took to shrugging it off and changing the subject. Keegan taught us to think big but he also taught us that the next game was the biggest game, not the one last week or last year or five years ago, the next one. So it's best not to think about how we nearly won the title, best not to think about the 4-3 defeat at Liverpool that some people bang on about being the best game ever and best not to think about all the other what might have beens. You would drive yourself mad.

We remain grateful and that's enough.

The home crowd went berserk when Kevin Keegan first came back as the enemy and the media lapped it up. We played Manchester City in an FA Cup tie in February 2002 and the 1-0 Newcastle win was lost beneath the local fan frenzy, the media hysteria and a thousand flashing cameras. You could barely see Keegan come out the tunnel and take his seat in the away dug-out, such was the mob of photographers waiting for him.

Two and a half years later and the national media barely noticed that Keegan was coming home again. Manchester United were playing Arsenal on the same day and nothing else existed. Keegan took his seat and the crowd barely flickered with recognition. Fair enough really, Keegan had been back twice and been beaten twice since the Cup game and this barely seemed like the same man.

The infectious enthusiasm, the barely containable energy, the aura of pure confidence were presumably still there in some measure but to all intents and purposes this seemed like a broken messiah to us. "And we should know, we've followed a few."

The game was a classic, a belter. 0-0 at half-time there were seven goals in the second half with Newcastle netting the winner in the last minute. "Classic Keegan" thought the world, like he invented 4-3 as his signature dish. But this new Keegan was having none of it and a lot of the shine was taken off the afternoon because of his moaning about the ref and his uncharacteristic bad grace. Yes the ref made mistakes but few in favour of Newcastle United and the fact that the man in black was cheered ironically by the home crowd, when awarding a free-kick in the 80th minute, tells you all you need to know about the differing perspectives.

Keegan complained that our first goal came from a free-kick that shouldn't have been given, when Bosvelt clearly caught Butt, and Robert curled the ball delightfully past a static David James. Keegan complained our second goal, a penalty, was a mistake by the ref, Carr was clean through and James brought him down and could easily have been sent off (Shearer BOOM 2-0). Mr Keegan, it seems, didn't notice that Nicky Butt played the ball when City were given the penalty that made it 2-2 or that it shouldn't have been a City throw that led to Wright-Phillips making it 3-3 (Robbie Elliott had flicked in our third in the meantime). Overall he also seemed to miss the fact that Newcastle were the better team and had more chances than City. He didn't even appear to notice the attempted streaker, who was clumsily wrestled to the ground in an undignified flurry of naked limbs and luminous jackets before he got past the advertising hoardings, let alone onto the pitch.

Perhaps Kevin had been at City too long by this point. The whole club lives its life in the shadow of its obvious superiors and this affects it to the core. Manchester City are Manchester United's bitch and they know it and they don't like it. This can make City's fans either hilarious or bitter and resentful and too many of them fall into the latter category. They behave like fucking mackems for the most part; self-deluded, puffed-up gobshites with a shitty fucking attitude and no bastard manners.

"Where were you when you were shit?" they constantly ask us. Getting more fucking fans at our games than you scabby fuckers and that's a fact. When Ollie Bernard wriggled past Willow Flood to pull the ball back for Craig Bellamy to score in the 90th minute we weren't even thinking about

Kevin Keegan, nearly 50,000 people were too busy jumping up and down and gleefully sticking their fingers up at the away section.

The following Wednesday Manchester City lost at home to Arsenal's youth team and Keegan looked even grumpier.

We are grateful enough for what he did for us to not enjoy seeing him look like that.

Chapter 19

30th October 2004

Taking Children To The Match

Half-term and £5 for kids, 42,153 in SJP. The decision makers got it right and we shouldn't be shy to say so, credit where credit's due and all that.

After the mad bear-pit of the Man City game where the crowd rocked harder than Motorhead and the mutual dislike between us and the Manc-mackems had the place crackling, this was a considerably more sedate affair.

It was terribly fashionable to take a child to this game and, darlings, you simply weren't dressed without an excitable cherub clutching the hand you usually use to hold beer with. Wifey and I borrowed a couple from Wifey's sister so as not to feel left out, which is a much better idea than actually making your own in our opinion.

Why waste your life feeding, clothing, cleaning and putting up with a person who will no doubt bung you in an old folks' home and steal all your money just because you've started shitting in your pants during *Songs Of Praise*? No, it's much better to borrow one that is already house-trained that you can give back the moment it threatens to become difficult.

So we had a male, Stefan, who is 12 and already a veteran fan, and a female, Kirstin, who is 9 and was going for the first time. I feared she only wanted to go because she thought she was missing out and would get bored and want to go home before half-time but I know nowt about kids me.

One swift pint outside Luckies and no swearing? So how exactly young Kirstin got to be shouting "Referee that was bollocks!" in the 90th minute I don't know but it was nothing to do with me.

We scored after 78 seconds with Robert firing in a savage corner that Jenas got the last touch on before the ball bobbled into the Norwich net.

The rest of the half was magnificent entertainment. Souness tells us that Kluivert isn't anywhere near match fit yet, so how good is he going to be like when he eventually is? Better than this? Bloody hell!

(Sadly we will never ever know. In 2007 after a short spell at Valencia he was released by PSV Eindhoven, 4 goals in 26 matches in two years since leaving Newcastle, a large part of his potential intact.)

Kluivert's touch, his movement, his intelligence and his composure are already so far above everybody else's that you can't help feeling a bit embarrassed for them. He's behaving like a diamond as well and never stopped talking to Shola, right down to encouraging him to take and score the penalty.

Later, Ameobi got his legs tangled up with a Norwich player and Huckerby scored from the spot. This was one of the few acts young Darren performed in the second half that he managed to complete without ending it sitting on his arse looking at the ref. "Now he's just cheating," Kirstin informed me at one point, stamping her little foot. Bless.

Half the crowd had enough confidence that our defence would see the game out to leave early, secure in the knowledge that they weren't going to miss any extra time or penalties. I don't know whether to be impressed or annoyed.

Chelsea at home in the next round, the game's on the telly and the prices have gone up. Credit where credit is due; the decision makers are idiots.

Chapter 20

4th November 2004

The New Wimbledon

"At every level of this game, be it Premiership, Champions League or World Cup, 90 per cent of games are decided by set pieces and so we work very hard to make sure the players here are effective in that area." Sam Allardyce

If the press reports are to be believed, Newcastle United approached 'Big Sam' for the manager's job before they rang Graeme Souness. Unsubstantiated rumours even went as far as claiming that he had been up on Tyneside for a look around before turning the chance down. If true, then we dodged a fucking bullet because this man's team is one ugly piece of work and we would not stand for this sort of shite. The steady decline in Bolton's gate, despite the rise in their League form and the presence of all the irritating family-friendly bollocks (mascots, people running around with flags, incidental music when they score, fireworks etc) suggests the locals are getting a little bored with watching this non-football. And who can blame them when a player of Okocha's ability is used for nothing more than launching the ball into the area at throw-ins. Wimbledon were harder to get rid of than genital warts (apparently) and now we're stuck with these horrible bastards, crashing about like boorish vandals.

We were bullied out of the game, which is annoying because we should be tougher than this but how Diouf stayed on the pitch was as much of a talking point. He was booked for taking his shirt off after scoring in the 52nd minute, which was one of his minor crimes. Obvious dives, late and dangerous tackles, throwing the ball away, being a twisty-faced fucking baby.

Darren Ambrose hammered in a great goal, the best of the season so far, beating two players and rasping a shot into the top corner but we never got to grips with Bolton's strong-arm tactics and Kevin Davies bundled in a winner for the home side on 70 minutes. Our manager wasn't happy: "We knew what to expect when we came here and we got it. They try and intimidate you with set plays and it has worked for them because they've got the win. Okocha must have sore arms after the number of throws he launched into the area. It is not pretty, they launch balls into the area from every set piece, but they are fourth in table so it's working for them. I'd love to be able to say that style of football has died out, but they are high up in the league so they will be pleased with how they play because it has proven to be effective."

Allardyce replied: "Poor old Graeme, he is knackered because little old Bolton have beaten his big Newcastle United, but he should just comment on his own team and not mine." *(It is important that you remember this quote).* And the press roundly condemned Souness for sour grapes despite his being, essentially, right.

We always played badly away to Wimbledon, at home we played our own game and generally battered them, away we tried to play like them and weren't any good at it. One of the frustrations of getting older following this football team is the same mistakes being repeated again and again as you hurtle towards a premature, never seen us win fuck all, grave. Newcastle had gone ten games unbeaten before this game and Souness had been saying for weeks he would learn more about his players when they lost.

(It is May 15th 2007 as I do the final read through of this chapter. It is quarter to twelve in the morning. In an hour and a half from now Sam Allardyce will be unveiled as the new manager of Newcastle United – a revolting fucking development in my opinion but more of that later.)

We appeared to get the Bolton game out of our system with a 2-0 win over Dinamo Tbilisi.

Those of us who bothered turning up left the ground feeling as though a chance was missed here. We will never have a better chance to score ten goals in a game than this for the rest of the season. We finished the game having had 20 shots, we carved them apart with some great football, Kluivert was magnificent and Robert and Bellamy will never have so much space on a football field in their lives but it didn't quite click.

One of the million reasons I love Laurent Robert so much is that I don't understand him at all, he looks so fucked off when he is subbed but after the third change was made and he was still on the pitch, he lost all interest. Up until then he had been fantastic; his crossing, his shooting, the moment where he jumped up and caught the ball on his foot and brought it down in one movement. He had a hand in both goals and the half-pitch sprint to cover for Bernard that had the astonished crowd on their feet and shut up his detractors for ten seconds was worth the entrance money alone. But he suddenly started wandering around with his hands on his hips and giving the ball away. Graeme Souness was clearly fuming and I worry that the fools who don't like our genius will get their way sooner rather than later. Our lives and our team will be poorer whenever he leaves and anyone who thinks otherwise is a bastard. Complaining that he can't tackle is like pointing out that he's not a very good goalkeeper and can't juggle moonbeams but saying he hasn't got 90 minutes in him is harder to argue with. Then, to make things even more confusing, in the last minute he rips off from the halfway line, knocks the ball past the last defender, scorches round the other side and blasts a shot that the keeper does well to beat away.

This game wasn't about Robert though, for an hour Patrick Kluivert had the crowd purring. He was involved in all the best stuff and the ball he put in for Shearer for the first goal was a work of art. Even though he tired again, he was man of the match by a mile and there was a chance near the end when, with no backlift and little room, he curled a shot just past the post and everybody in the ground was willing it in.

Unfortunately, everybody in the ground only numbered 27, 218.

Chapter 21

14th November 2004

Being A Good Loser

At Newcastle United, being gracious in defeat is a character flaw. Those who are may give the impression that they are serene and mature but really they are being weak-willed and pathetic. They are admitting that failure is an option, that being incompetent and lazy is acceptable, that injustice should be tolerated and that some bunch of bastards coming to St James' Park and beating the home team is OK by them. It's not and that is why God in his infinite wisdom invented pubs so we could drink beer and complain. Bitterly and for ages.

No one had got too carried away with Souness as manager, simply because he had been getting away with poor tactics against poor teams. We were winning games despite the fact that he was cramming three strikers into the team and playing other people out of position. If he persisted it was only a matter of time before we came a cropper. Nobody expected it to be bloody Fulham.

The old adage that "if you are 2-0 down you may as well have a go and lose by four" was disproved once and for sodding all as well. By the end of this game Newcastle had two defenders on the pitch and four strikers. We had 25 shots at goal, of which 20 were on target and had 19 corners to Fulham's nil. Our manager pointed out, quite correctly, that Fulham keeper Mark Crossley had the game of his life and that Fulham's first goal came after an outrageous foul on Alan Shearer. Souness was also sent from the dugout for kicking a water bottle after a blatant penalty wasn't awarded but that doesn't begin to tell the story of why we lost this game. You could claim bad luck that we didn't score more goals than Bellamy's heroic header; Kluivert hitting Crossley on the forehead with one of his many shots but even acccepting that and all the other excuses how the hell did Fulham, bloody Fulham, score four goals at our ground? Rank bad defending, possibly the worst I can remember in a very long time, rotten even by our own rotten standards and with Chelsea and Man Utd to come in the next week, we were not only livid, we were worried.

(Carling Cup v Chelsea)

It's a constant struggle not to become mean-minded and jealous when thinking about Chelsea. It's like those rare occasions when somebody nice wins the lottery, you worry that other people's shitty attitudes will spoil their good fortune. If you ignore the money and simply look at the football team and the performance from this game you might have to hold your hands up. Terry and Gallas are magnificent defenders and the former's two hour war with Alan Shearer was worth getting to the ground for on its own. The midfield works as a unit when it hasn't got the ball and attacks with pace and imagination when it has. In the pub afterwards, you could say, "We lost to a good team in a good game so fuck it, let's have another beer" and be as pleased as it's possible to be after your team has lost a football match - except that we are all such bad fucking losers.

So bollocks, Chelsea are not nice people, they were despicable before the Russian turned up with his billions and I think they may have ruined football for a lot of people. Players like Cudicini, Parker and Johnson should be playing every week for somebody, not being well-paid reserves, and the power imbalance their money gives them is disheartening. The bar has been raised impossibly and artificially high for too many teams to aspire to. Without a seemingly inexhaustible pile of cash behind to back it up you can have the most loyal fans, the best youth academy and a genius for a coach and it will never be enough. This seems an unpleasant and harsh crystal ball to be looking into, especially for Newcastle United because essentially Chelsea have muscled ahead of us. I may be wrong here but if Chelsea hadn't struck it rich then all the best elements of this team would have been scattered through the League, making it more interesting for more teams. Perhaps I'm a communist but I would always prefer 20 people to win £1 million than one person to win £20 million and a part of me can't shake the thought of William Gallas in a black and white shirt.

Bobby Robson liked him, Chelsea were about to financially implode (with the joyous side effect of chairman Ken Bates living in a skip, having to tie up his pissy old trousers with electrical wire) and our present defensive problems wouldn't even be an issue. How can we hope to compete with a team that can afford to pay a player (Crespo, reportedly) over £100,000 a week while he is on loan at another club. Mourinho is a good manager as well, who buys good players so we can forget about selling them any of our misfits at an inflated fee.

"I have never seen Titus Bramble play as well as that," said Mourinho. We have and know better than to get carried away but with Johnsen assured and composed next to him, our defence played its best game of the season against some good players. None of whom were Joe Cole, the irritating little show pony. A monkey dressed as Hitler, riding a little bicycle and blowing a trumpet would be as entertaining and about as much use. He also seemed determined to get sent off; diving, whining and kicking people. As we know, Mourinho is no mug and after an hour he was dragged off and replaced by Lampard. Chelsea's other subs were Robben and Gudjohnsen and therein lay our downfall.

Both scored and our extra time subs, Hughes and Ameobi, were unlikely to do the same.

0-0 in the 90th minute. A free-kick on the edge of the area to us. I've got £10 on Robert to score first and if it goes in, I'm in the pub inside ten minutes with £120 in my fist and Newcastle are in the next round. Cudicini again goes full stretch and it's the fat end of an hour before I get back to the pub, never mind the money or being out of the cup that we all secretly thought we were going to win this season.

Bollocks.

The simmering resentment and begrudging respect we eased out of our systems with cold beer on the Wednesday was nothing to the blazing fury after the Manchester United game. Long before the match ended most of the ground had turned into Tourettes-monsters, screaming and swearing at everybody and everything. Souness still trying to play Kluivert, Shearer and Bellamy in the same team, Rooney left utterly unmarked after seven minutes, Rio Ferdinand and Gabriel Heinze apparently being un-bookable, Ronaldo being more of a diving, insufferable little show-off than Joe Cole, the referee for missing Rooney shoving O'Brien in the back then giving a penalty to Manchester United seconds later, two decent Newcastle goals disallowed and an ill-deserved last minute third goal from the worst Manchester United team seen on Tyneside in living memory.

Even our goal was irritating. Shearer tackled Wes Brown in a Peter

Beardsley styl-ee then skipped past two defenders to score yet another brilliant but essentially pointless goal against the team he famously turned down twice. Oh how he loves scoring against them and oh how they hate him doing so and oh how much we Newcastle fans enjoy both those facts. But as with the thumping free-kick he hammered in down there a couple of years ago and with his goal in the famous 5-0 win, they had the last laugh. And for all the reasons they have given us to despise them over the years, that is the hardest to deal with and being a good fucking loser doesn't help one little fucking bastard bit.

Chapter 22

10th December 2004

What We Think We Know

A friend of mine once said that he hated European football because "it turns football supporters into accountants. It's nothing to do with football and everything to do with working out how much money the club is making." This seemed like a semi-interesting point but the true football obsessive becomes a self-appointed expert on everything. Never mind 4-4-2, sweeper systems, diamond formations and our opinion of fancy-pants, twinkle-toed Brazilian soft-shites who insist on playing in a 'hole' that doesn't exist in this country. No, we also think we understand revenue streams, costing, TV money and cashflow. This financial whiz-kiddery absolutely always results in us thinking that our club should have "about twenty million pounds to spend on new players come the opening of the transfer window", which rarely turns out to be the case.

But that is barely the start of our layman's expertise, oh no. We are all unqualified physios demanding to know what incompetent buffoon is responsible for all the ham-string strains our squad is afflicted with. The nutritionist we never trained to be wants to know what the players are eating that leaves them lacking in energy for the last 15 minutes of any game and the psychologist we're not knows exactly which players need encouragement, a kick up the arse or the threat of having their testicles set on fire.

Given the time to think, the world becomes an avalanche of worry sweeping us all to an early, frozen grave. And the bastard A1 gives you all the time you need to think and so to worry. By the time you hit that painful, dragging period of ghost time 50 miles south of Scotch Corner, where miles per hour in the car bear no relation to the actual distance you are travelling, all semblance of enjoyment has evaporated. The day after we won 2-0 at Palace should have been no trouble, Kluivert's sublime flick and Bellamy's lashed second should have been enough to see us through to Monday at least. But Palace were garbage, really fucking bad – so where does that leave us? God knows. All you want to do is get home, but now you are an amateur biochemist working out if last night's drink has worked its way through your system far enough to risk being stopped for speeding. Nasty, evil, selfish fuckers your drink-drivers, and you would hate yourself forever if you caused a serious accident by turning out to be one. So, when did you have your last drink, how much did you have, how quickly does it wash out your system and is it worth the risk of clamping your right foot to the floor in an attempt to get home half an hour earlier?

The same bloody road two weeks later and this time it's worse because Newcastle United have been butchered at Chelsea again. We could never win there when we were brilliant and they were crap, so it should come as no surprise but 0-4 always stings like a bastard and no amount of "we played well for the first hour" is going to help us here.

In between these two capital visits our team did its best to confuse us, winning 4-0 in Sochaux in a game that we should have been losing at half-time but should have won by six or seven by the end (Bowyer, Ameobi, Bellamy and a 90th minute belting free-kick from Robert). Then we drew at home to shoddy bloody Everton who despite being third in the league, were decidedly unimpressive. Bellamy is fast but the Everton defence made him look like he had been fired out of a cannon as he blasted away from them to put us 1-0 up after five minutes. We wasted chances to claim the second goal that would have led to the ritual annihilation the Scouse-mackems always so richly deserve and they equalised and nearly won it at the death.

Post Chelsea, I mentioned to Wifey that I thought we had stood a chance of getting something at Stamford Bridge and she looked at me like I was mental. "Don't be so stupid!" she said with her eyes and then with her mouth. And that's my problem at the minute, I keep getting confused with the team I know Newcastle United can be and the team that they actually are. Some fucking expert. The more you try to learn the less you realise you know. I resolve to ignore the football media for the next week secure in the knowledge that my lack of participation will be of no consequence to anybody. I shall remain blissful in my ignorance until the Portsmouth game.

But the day has a sting in the tail.

Newcastle United are drawn away to non-league Yeading in the 3rd round of the FA Cup. And one thing we at Newcastle are experts on, one thing that every man and woman knows to be a bastard fact is that we are now in for a fucking media pantomime with us as the villains. Booooooooooooooooooo!

Chapter 23

20th December 2004

What Not To Wear

Wearing a replica shirt, or any colours for the match, is starting to feel increasingly daft and away from home it's just ludicrous. Why mark yourself out as any sort of target and, more importantly, why deny yourself access to any chance of getting a drink on enemy soil? Obviously, if you happen to stumble across a pub that has been swamped with jolly drunken Mags the day is all the better but being turned away from a cool refreshing pint and throat lubricant just because of the colour of your shirt is a silly risk to take. I'm aware that inside the ground we, as Newcastle fans, have a duty to perform and what we wear is part of that duty, so for my own part I'm happy to provide the black in the sea of black and white.

I used to be one of those people who thoughtlessly pulled on a football shirt to watch Newcastle games on the telly but then I saw that John Burridge interview where his wife said he put on his boots and gloves to watch TV games and I thought, "what a loony," before realising what I did was only one step away. I also like wildlife programmes but I don't dress up as a wombat to watch them and the less said about my viewing of *The World At War* the better.

My problem the morning of the Liverpool game is that it is perishing outside and the thick, cosy black sweatshirt that I wear away from home is frozen solid to the washing line. It should be dry and toasty warm on a radiator but that would have involved me not going out and getting drunk and forgetting all about the twat. The only other top thick enough to stop my ageing and thinning blood freezing in my veins has a small red and white dice motif on the breast and I can't be going to Anfield to support Newcastle with anything red and white on ……..or can I?

December 18th 2001, a couple of days off exactly three years ago, I bought that top. In an act of rank cowardice James, Lucy, Wifey and I, all Newcastle fans, forsook all contact with Newcastle's mid-week game at Highbury. New York City's finest, The Fun Lovin' Criminals were playing live in Doncaster and what they had to offer compared to our team's traditional collapse in the face of Arsenal's brilliance did bear thinking about. The Crims rock live, they're funny, entertaining and cool as fuck – whereas the previous season Newcastle lost 5-0 at Arsenal. So off to Donnie we drive.

The gig was on at a sports arena on a retail park in the middle of nowhere. There was a bar with a TV but it wasn't showing Sky so we were utterly ignorant of what was going on until Wifey demanded I ring Bront to find out what had happened.

In the toilets with the racket from the stage booming and echoey, phone clamped to the side of my head it was ages before Bront screamed, "WHAT!?"

"What happened?"

"We're winning 2-1 but it hasn't finished so FUCK OFF!" and with that he slammed the phone down, no doubt convinced that I had ruined whatever spell was holding our lead. I stood for a second in utter shock before rushing back to tell the others, except what could I tell them? I'd jinx it for sure so decided to wait and call back for the final score. On stage Huey (singer/guitarist/main man) slides straight out of *Big Night Out* into the opening riff of *Scooby Snacks* and the place goes crazy. At the back a pair of bouncers feel the need to keep an eye on the man hopping from one foot to the other singing along to the song but adding the words "c'mon c'mon C'MON" to the end of every line. On the last note I run back into the toilet and hit redial.

Bront answers the phone in a somewhat untraditional fashion. "YEEEEAAAAHHHHHHAAAAARRRRHHHHHHH!!!!!!!!!!!!!!!!!!!!!!!!"

"What, what, what, what?"

"We won 3-1, Robert broke at the end and got another one, Henry's gone off it, Shearer's pulling him away from the ref, fuckin' brilliant. Get in you fucking bastard! We've gone top of the league!" A swift match report ensued, before I scooped up a round of drinks and found the others. In the drunken ecstatic mayhem that followed I bought an overpriced hoody with the Crims logo on it. A pair of red and white dice.

All this has raced through the fuzzy, hungover head over which I pulled the top with the offending red and white on it. No one batted an eyelid when Alan Harrison and I squeezed into a bar opposite the famous Kop and bought our pre-match drinks. We further amused ourselves by dodging the piles of dog shit in the beer garden and counting the accents of those decked out in serious red and white, none of which were Scouse.

In the ground the unseasonably bright December sun shone harshly into the eyes of the away support who sang "Feed the Scousers" and "You Nicked My Stereo" at our hosts whilst trying to work out our team from their silhouettes.

Shay Given in goal: at least he isn't being asked to fill in on the right wing.

Andy O'Brien at right back: a lifelong centre half asked to fill in because Carr is injured. Andy has taken to his new role less like a duck does to water and more like a duck does to being asked to play lead violin with the Moscow Symphony Orchestra.

Robbie Elliott and Titus Bramble at centre half: Robbie is a diamond of a lad, unflappable and strong. He is also a left back playing in a strange position and is vulnerable to pace. The kind of pace maybe one would associate with Milan Baros. Five rows in front of us somebody has a stuffed donkey in a Newcastle shirt and our fans are singing "One Titus Bramble" at it. He is our best defender.

Ollie Bernard at left back: was our best defender until his bitter contract row with the club that seemed to distract the hell out of him.

The midfield has Lee Bowyer out of position on the right wing, the (still) unpopular Kieron Dyer, the out of sorts Jermaine Jenas and James Milner on the left wing. Souness has dropped Laurent Robert again because "he doesn't work hard enough on the pitch or in training".

Up front Bellamy has pulled out just before the kick off with a bad back and Patrick Kluivert, lacking any kind of fitness (match or otherwise), has been drafted in because we have no one else to partner the increasingly erratic and bizarre Shola Ameobi. Two rows behind me the lad who spends 90 minutes shouting "YOU'RE FUCKING USELESS!" at his own team becomes my personal favourite for the job as our next manager.

The last vestiges of our hope are clung to, only because for the first half an hour Liverpool are as bad as we are.

Then out of nowhere Newcastle score a beautiful goal. Dyer tearing into the heart of the Liverpool defence before putting in Bowyer on the right who pulls the ball back for Kluivert to score. Bloody hell.

Now all we have to do is hang on for ten minutes......

Ten minutes later and we are losing 2-1. By the end we are let off 3-1. Lee Bowyer appeared to spend the entire second half trying to get sent off. He was rewarded with not only a dismissal but a suspension that gave him Christmas off, after kicking people violently under Graham Poll's nose until the poor bloke had no choice but to wave his red card. Our awful defence got no help from our neglectful midfield, our brittle confidence and pitiful mental strength led to utter capitulation and I skulked back to Alan's car, thankful that the Liverpool fans laughing at despondent folk in black and white chose to ignore me.

Point of interest 1 *- The Fun Lovin' Criminals were asked if they had any interest in "English soccer" on Radio 5 Live a year or so later and Fast (keyboards, trumpet) said "we are down with the Geordies" before they were removed from the show because Huey kept saying "Muthafucka".*

Point of Interest 2 *- Following the resignation of Tony Blair in May 2007 Gordon Brown re-emphasised his commitment to compulsory ID cards. One of the many civil liberties this will infringe on is my right to grab a sneaky pint behind enemy lines. If the man on the door of a pub can read "address Newcastle" I'm not getting in now am I? Never mind the fact that they had ID cards in Nazi Germany and look where that got us.*

Chapter 24

3rd January 2005

Perspective?

We may have all skulked away from Anfield with our tails between our legs but Newcastle fans are all too daft, pig-headed and proud to go away quietly for long. On Boxing Day news of the tsunami that hit South East Asia hadn't sunk in properly as a sea of black and white washed up on Blackburn's metaphoric shores. The back-up support, dressed for the match but watching the game on legal and illegal pub TVs across Newcastle were still mostly in a post-Christmas haze and the enormity of the tragedy just wouldn't compute. "Some unlucky people have died but everybody else just got a bit wet, sounds like a laugh. Let's get drunk and watch the football."

You feel guilty enough for having used words like 'catastrophic' and 'disastrous' to describe your team's defending when those words belong on the other side of the planet. Having completely underestimated the tsunami devastation you feel even worse. Well I did. But such is football, nothing else matters when the game is on and the extremities of your feelings are never in any perspective. The beauty of Robert's ball through to Dyer's perfectly timed run brings nothing but joy. The sloppy equaliser brings nothing but fury. Robert twatting in a free-kick from 30 yards = euphoria and elation and the worst player on the pitch (Andy Todd) bundling in a second for the home side leaves you with nothing but despair and frustration.

Two teams who were never either going to win the league or get relegated got a point each from a 2-2 draw.

In South East Asia it is estimated that around 230,000 people died.

The minute's silence for the tsunami dead before the Arsenal match was immaculate.

No one could remember the last time we went into a home game so lacking in hope. That magical fourth, fifth or tenth drink that suddenly inspires belief, bravado and confidence only brought a, "well, we'll give it a go" attitude. And we did give it a go, crowd and players.

This match proved a lot, you came away thinking, "we have got good players, they have got spirit and fight in their bellies and we do love them and believe that we can break out of this downward spiral. Get the injured players fit, the new players in, take a breath and let's fuckin' go!"

Of course a daft fuckwit of a ref always stokes the flames of our seemingly dimmed passion. When the cross-eyed fool finally got round to booking Ashley Cole he made a show of pointing to the three other previous places on the pitch where the odious little twit should have had his name taken. Arsenal's 'gamesmanship' is ingrained, systematic and they expect to (and mostly do) get away with it. Perhaps when we are Champions we will be afforded the same treatment – I guess none of us at this game will ever know. For the record *The Journal* stats quoted our 7 fouls committed to their 23 and in my view they committed more that went unpunished.

One of the key players in this tremendous performance was Shola (sigh); whenever you get to the point where selling him is not enough, when you actually start looking on the internet for quotes from hitmen, he has a game that makes you love him again. He has been pants all season, then he gives Sol Campbell the kind of game he will not want again in a hurry. Playing up front, on his own in front of a five man midfield, Ameobi worked his nuts off. He tackled and battled for every ball, he won stuff in the air and he had our best chance, which Almunia in the Arsenal goal did brilliantly to claw round the post.

Kieron Dyer was full of mischief and Steven Taylor did a remarkable job of marking Thierry Henry and then there was Craig Bellamy: his dislike for playing wide right seemed to be offset by his obvious greater dislike of Ashley Cole whose overreaction to a stray finger got Bellamy sent off three years ago. By overreaction I am obviously avoiding saying that a waft of a pinky finger sent a grown man crashing to the floor clutching his face was a deliberate attempt to cheat. In the same game that Alan Shearer had beseeched the ref not to send off Ray Parlour, despite the fact that he had just committed his fifth bookable offence – ho-hum, thems the breaks.

Bellamy gave the England left back a chasing. Every time Cole tried to get forward, Craigy got in behind him, and Cole resorted to desperate hacking and at one point jumping up in the penalty area and punching the ball away. It was the crucial point of the match. Half the ground exploded, the other half believed them and we were still wondering just who would take the obvious penalty as the daft ref waved play on. This cranked the indignation up a notch and we were still roaring our boys on when Vieira, with virtually the last kick of the half, tried a shot that took a deflection off Jenas and looped over Given. In the last minute of the second half Jenas tried the same thing from the same position and the ball bounced harmlessly through to Almunia. And that was all that was in it, this is the best you get to feel when you've lost a football match and there is no shame in taking heart from it. It's a question of perspective.

Chapter 25

5th January 2005

The Transfer Window
(players throwing themselves through it)

Getting through to January felt like a trip aboard a three-wheeled wagon. Cherokees, in the form of the worst teams in the Premiership, were gaining on us fast and more of our wheels were threatening to come off. More wheels were needed but our options seemed limited and none of the players we had been linked with seemed available. The size of the club's 'war chest' (as the papers like to call it) or 'wheel budget' (as I shall call it to overburden an already creaking metaphor) was an unknown quantity, as was trust in our new manager's judgement. In the pub before the Arsenal game, I posed the question to the gang of degenerates I drink with as to who they would like Souness to buy and was surprised that they had more opinions about who they didn't want than who they did.

I was at once besieged by opinion, the best of which follows. Be warned, some of them had been on the drink for a while and the opinions quoted are not necessarily in agreement with my own.

John Hartson: "He's clumsy and shit and has got fat ginger man-tits."

Robbie Savage: "He's not really a footballer at all, he nods his head like a knock-kneed mule when he tries to run fast, it's pathetic."

Anyone from Blackburn: "I know managers have players they go back to their old clubs for but Souness should forget he was ever at Blackburn and treat everybody there like Robbie Williams would treat anybody else from Take That - 'They're all shit and I never want to see any of them again, ever.'"

Sweep: "He's way cooler than Sooty, the whispering little fucking sneak, and he likes Motorhead but Graeme shouldn't overlook the fact that he is essentially a glove puppet with no legs. He wouldn't be much help at all. He's better than John Hartson mind."

El-Hadji Diouf: "The twisty-faced bastard. Never mind the spitting, anyone who ever saw The Damned at the Mayfair in the 80s has seen real spitting, so that's nowt, it's the diving and the ground-banging and most of all his face. Once you started punching him, you wouldn't be able to stop."

Robert Huth: "He's still got bits of Alan Shearer's scrotum stuck between his studs from that tackle last season, the twat. If we bought him Shearer would have to smash his face in. What's the point of buying a player who is going to be hospitalised the second he gets out of his car?"

Velma from Scooby Doo: "She would lose her glasses at corners."

Phil Neville: "Why can't he shut his mouth? Why, why, what's wrong with him?"

Anyone Scottish: "As a nation they have completely lost the ability to play football. Maybe Thatcher poisoned them, I don't know, but whatever it was that gave the world Gemmill, Souness, Dalglish, Strachan and Hansen has been utterly eradicated. It's reached the point where it's cruel to encourage them anymore. They should concentrate on being managers or pundits or sitting on park benches swearing at pigeons. Play to your strengths."

Robbie Keane: "It's that rubbish celebration basically. Even if he scored for us, in the last second of the Cup Final, against sunderland, you would still want to tell him to fuck off. A forward roll and pretending to fire a little bow and arrow, what's that all about? Honestly, it's rubbish. If you saw him in a bar afterwards you'd say 'thanks but fuck off!'"

Private Godfrey: "Not even if he brought some of the cakes his sister Dolly had made. Which quite frankly is unlikely what with him being so very very dead."

Francesco Totti: "No use to us because our lass would shag him 'til he was blind, at the airport, as soon as he got off the plane."

Mungo: "From *Mary, Mungo and Midge*. Or Midge. Or come to think of it Mary, they all seem two-dimensional."

Ming The Merciless: "He might be an evil genius but having a bald bloke in a dress in the team would make us a laughing stock. Not as much as having Hartson in the team though, obviously."

For my own part I have been giving the same answer for ten years when asked who I think we should buy. The entire Dynamo Kiev back four, they are always huge, fast, well organised and brutally violent. I couldn't name one of them but they seem to relish the cold and are always awesome. Always.

The distinctly un-Russian Jean Alain Boumsong and Celestine Babayaro were both ready to crash through the transfer window like Batman and Robin on 1st January but the F.A. gave themselves the nice long Christmas break that the players and managers wanted but couldn't have. The window was shuttered, barred and bolted until after our game at West Bromwich Albion on the 3rd. At £8.5 million Boumsong was obviously going to be the answer to all our defensive problems and we couldn't wait to get him into the team.

For now the team had to manage, to press on and to cope. Which at this time of year is all any of us can hope to do. Wifey and I stumbled home from a friend's house party at 4.30am, numbed against the cold by flaming sambucas, tepid champagne and enough lager to float a small boat. We woke up (still pissed) five hours later, enjoyed a hearty breakfast and then, drinkwise, went our separate ways. Wifey determined to detox and I determined not to sober up until I had to go back to work.

The wagon's wheels were still spinning with the hope that the Arsenal game had given us and Birmingham were seen off before half-time with Shola finally making heading look an easy thing to do, nodding in the first, and Bowyer accepting one of the four chances he was presented with. Terror briefly reverberated through the ground after Heskey got one back but Jermaine Jenas grabbed hold of the midfield and we finished the stronger, Bowyer missing narrowly and Dyer rattling the bar.

By the time of the televised game at West Brom days later we only appeared to have the one wheel left. The wagon was dragging along the road and those pulling it looked flogged half to death.

Fortunately, because West Brom were awful, it finished 0-0.

Chapter 26

10th January 2005

Nothing Happened
(except our paranoia increased)

Newcastle United, only ever described as 'Mighty' when drawn against the lowest available opposition, played Yeading in the FA Cup third round at Loftus Road. We won 2-0. That's the end of that.

There was no story, no scandal, no bully-boy tactics from nasty Freddie Shepherd. The pitch was shabby and Newcastle didn't seem to know how polite it was to actually try in the first half. Yeading had one decent chance, Newcastle played better in the second half and scored twice. They should have scored more but that whole cow's arse/banjo equation where one is brought into contact with the other was still proving to be a bit of a problem. In hindsight we were never in any danger, not that you would think so if you read the papers the next day where even the quality press, who should employ people with a little more sense, snapped and snarled spitefully. We suffered descriptions of new signing Alain Boumsong being turned inside out by a plucky young upstart called DJ Campbell who actually didn't get a shot off in the whole game. Credit to Yeading for not behaving like greedy, crazy-eyed howler monkeys like bastard Stevenage did a few years back and good luck to them because of it but the whole televised exercise just made the BBC look silly. Gary Lineker jiffled about like he had involuntarily weed a little and John Motson, who is now single-handedly responsible for keeping the memory of Newcastle's defeat at Hereford in 1972 alive, seemed frustrated that he didn't get to re-live his first and finest hour. Bowyer tapped in a Bellamy cross and Ameobi headed in the second, very good, can we go now?

Likewise a week later Newcastle beat Southampton. Newcastle United replayed their Groundhog Match, going 2-0 up against a shit team, letting them get a scruffy one back and hanging on for grim death at the end. Shearer came back from a series of niggling injuries and that seemed to put a spring in everyone's step. He blasted in a penalty despite the presence on the pitch of ref Uriah Rennie who hates him.

Titus Bramble clipped in a second. Lanky circus freak Peter Crouch bundled in one for The Saints and Steven Taylor performed a heroic block in the last couple of seconds for us to hold on.

For an hour we were brilliant then, once again, the whole lot just fell apart in front of us. The frustration and panic in the crowd is mirrored by those on the pitch and the last minutes of games, against even the poorest opposition, have become almost unbearable.

Chapter 27

23rd January 2005

"A Man Should Be Treated Generously Or Destroyed"
(Niccolo Machiavelli, 1513)

Arsenal played a game of football against Newcastle United live on Sky. Arsenal won 1-0 and Newcastle hung on to that score thanks to the acrobatic brilliance of Shay Given. Then right at the end Bowyer had a chance to sneak an equaliser and failed. It would have been an undeserved point but no less undeserved than any number of points that rotten teams have snatched from us this season. An unremarkable afternoon except Bellamy was dropped because he was injured. Or so Souness said. Sky unforgivably got access to Bellamy (who couldn't keep his mouth shut if you stuck his head in a Glastonbury Festival toilet) and clapped their hands with glee as Newcastle United turned into a stupid fucking soap opera for them. Again.

Within a week the phrase, "Once again the good name of Newcastle United has been dragged through the mud" became a cliché. So what good name would that be exactly?

The whole truth eventually came out with no one with any credibility arguing with Graeme Souness' final account: "After Friday's press conference at St James' Park I arrived at the training ground to find Craig Bellamy in the dressing room and with his boots off. He told me he felt his hamstring was a bit tight. But my first-team coach Dean Saunders informed me that Bellamy had told other players in the dressing room he was going to feign an injury *(at last we found out what Saunders did for a living – club snitch)*. I took him to see the chairman on Friday afternoon at St James' Park and he admitted to both of us that this was true. I asked him in front of the chairman if he had feigned an injury and he said `yes'. I told Bellamy that he had to apologise to the rest of the players, but I then found out later that he had not done so. That was on Friday tea-time and that's when I decided he wasn't going to be in my team at Arsenal. If he had apologised he would have been in the team."

Worse stuff came out with reports alleging that Bellamy had told new signings Boumsong and Faye that Newcastle United was "a shit club with a shit manager".

Filled with the self-important egomania that a fat wage and Sky Television encourage, Bellamy, instead of apologising, invited Sky Sports News into his home for another exclusive: "He went behind my back and lied to my face," whined Craigy (dressed in a rather nasty shirt) which apart from summoning up a picture of our manager slithering round our best striker like a big eel is just silly. Is that what you're upset about son? Ah bless......

This is football Craig, everybody lies, you know that, what are you, four? Remember that big Italian who rolled on the floor when you poked him with your foot – he was lying. Remember when you scream and swear at the linesman for flagging you offside when you are (what's the word I'm looking for here? – oh yes, that's it) "offside", you were lying. The game is riddled with lies, from the chairman of Real Madrid saying he has no interest in buying David Beckham to me saying I will only have the one pint before going straight home after the match on Saturday. Badge kissers, journalists, fans screaming for penalties at every 'ball to hand', when you told the chairman you would apologise to your team mates for walking out of training – lies lies lies. Grow the fuck up.

Bobby Robson was quick to offer an opinion but in doing so inadvertently confirmed our deepest fears. That he gave up trying to control Bellamy months ago. He figured it a trade-off because of what Bellamy did on the pitch but the effect that seems to have had on the attitude of the rest of our overpaid under-achieving squad is the very root of the club's problems. Under the last months of Robson's reign no player was improving football-wise and many fans dreaded meeting their heroes away from the ground for fear of having to punch one of the spoiled, snotty-faced, over-indulged little twats in the mouth.

In the end those self-same Newcastle United fans lost out because of the failings of others. Craig Bellamy had been Player Of the Season so far and he, like us, knew that he had been the single major factor between Newcastle United being OK and Newcastle United being good. Unfortunately he also seems to be a self-absorbed, mildly paranoid schizophrenic with Tourettes. He, like many other modern players, thinks the whole world does and should revolve around him and that's the main reason so many people are fed up with footballers and their shitty fucking attitudes.

To make matters worse a large proportion of our fans were already sick to the back teeth of the whole sorry lot up at Gallowgate. The last of our goodwill evaporated some time ago and we were living in a constant state of gnawing frustration.

Unless he had been hatching some Machiavellian plot to rid us of Bellamy, Graeme Souness was at fault here too. If he hadn't persisted with a formation that everybody in the ground could see was wasting our best player we wouldn't have been in this situation in the first place. And he got mugged like a sucker by Sky after the Arsenal game when he should have refused to comment BUT he is the manager and whether you like it or not our Chairman had to back him. Even if Craig Bellamy was the best player we ever had (which he's not) and Graeme Souness was the worst manager we ever had (which hopefully he's not) the player couldn't be allowed to win in this situation. Because what is important isn't all the shit that has gone, it's what we are going to do about it and what the consequences are of what we do. Sacking Souness might make some people happy but where would that leave us? The players would be walking out of training within a fortnight because the milk on their Coco Pops was too brown.

I like and admire Craig Bellamy the footballer, I will miss the hilarious, televised lip-reading and hate the idea of him playing for someone else, sold at a knockdown fee. I haven't made my mind up about Graeme Souness but Souness had to win this fight and he had to win it hard. Bellamy had to be crushed or shipped out and forgotten.

The fundamental problem that a lot of us fans have to get over is our own lack of self-esteem. Too many of us are too grateful to have a player as good as Bellamy and are prepared to overlook his many mistakes and faults when in truth Bellamy should be grateful for being allowed to play for us, with all the riches and comforts that privilege affords him.

Quite simply we have to replace Bellamy with somebody better and then we'll find out how good a manager we've got. Keegan replaced Andy Cole with Les Ferdinand but Dalglish replaced Ferdinand with dismal fop Andreas Andersson. Robson would have been forgiven selling Solano within a week if he had replaced him adequately. If Souness buys Hartson or Crouch or

Montella or Owen *(yes I did write this at the time, honest guv'nor)* we will have our answer.

Kieron Dyer, The Mag 214; "There was a lot made of the Craig Bellamy situation but I don't think the gaffer had any choice but to get rid of Craig after he'd gone on TV and called him a liar. I had a call from Craig saying he was going on TV to have his say. I pleaded with him not to do it. I then rang Steve Harper and asked him to try and talk some sense into him but it was too late, his head was gone. He's now moved on to Liverpool who are a massive club, but I don't think we are the only ones to miss out because I don't think Craig will be as happy with family life as he was here and the way he played and how he was loved by the fans. I still think he'll regret that day for some time."

Terry McDermott, in trying to gauge opinion around the club about Bellamy's possible return to Newcastle from loan at Celtic, said, "I've never come across so much hatred and unrest over one person. What I've learnt about him has astonished me."

Chapter 28

12th February 2005

Man City & Charlton v Rammstein & Green Day

The day of Newcastle's Wednesday night game at Man City didn't start well for Graeme Souness. He may not have realised it at the time but he had just made a massive mistake. In the frantic scramble between my getting in from work and getting sorted for the trip to Manchester he tried (via Sky Sports News) to explain to me that Craig Bellamy wasn't actually a very good footballer. For the sake of a steady ship we may have been prepared to believe that young Craig was the uncrowned King Of The Bastards, a malignant influence on team morale and we were best shot of him but trying to tell us that the player we all saw as being our best forward "didn't score enough goals" was basically telling us that all our opinions were wrong and that he had the real insight. Bobby Robson tried this 'you are all wrong, I alone am right' trick and it's about as good for manager/fan relations as sticking your hand up a tiger's arse just as it's about to start its dinner is for keeping your body scratch free.

Things got worse as far as the Souness P.R. machine was concerned when after the dismal home draw with Charlton on the following Saturday he tried to tell us that we should be more patient. "We need to learn to defend 1-0 leads" and "Modern football is more like a game of chess". Sorry, but I don't get up at five o'clock in the morning to cram my working day in before lunchtime, race around in a panic for an hour, then drive to the other side of the fucking country to pay thirty bastard quid for a game of chess.

Some serious lifestyle choices popped up between these two games: a drive to Manchester for football = expensive frustrating bollocks, a drive to Manchester to see Rammstein four days later (which cost less money) = mental German techno metallists rocking like fuck and shooting fire out of their faces. Rammstein live make you think every other band you've ever seen simply weren't trying, their music is enormous and they have fireworks, explosions and gouts of flame shooting 30 foot into the air. I went with my uber-Goth mates Paul and Denise who are always a safe haven from the stupid self-involved world of football and the trip home was spent mostly with our gobs hanging open in astonishment. The trip back from Manchester City was a depressing haul listening to the dismal opinions of idiots on crap radio phone-ins.

By the weekend the manager seemed quite happy with his team after a humdrum affair against Charlton that ended with the team being booed off. Three days later Green Day were in town playing a punk rock show at the Arena that had everyone who went grinning like a loony for three days, such was the joyous, life-affirming pleasure of it all.

Shouldn't our football team at least aspire to making us feel this good? "Hold onto a 1-0 lead" is a shitty, cowardly approach to football if you ask me.

Wifey asked if I wish I hadn't gone to Manchester for the football and I was about to bark, "Of course I wish I hadn't fucking gone, stupid fucking footballers, can't even pass a fucking ball to each other and I paid thirty quid to watch the stupid bastards not being able to do even the simplest part of what is, in the end, their bloody bastard job. Never mind wish I hadn't gone, I'm going to pay to have them all killed and I never want football, Newcastle United or Graeme sodding Souness mentioned in this house again".... when I thought about it for a minute.

The crack in the car with my mate Guy, who is different to me in every possible way (staunch Tory sensible to my anarcho-socialist, make it up as you go along, rant-a-lot, Rick Astley to my Rammstein) was fun on its own. Hooking up with Alan outside the magnificent City Of Manchester Stadium for a pint in a pub so rough I thought Guy was actually going to run away screaming, was an unexpected pleasure and Shearer rifling in a cracking shot to put us 1-0 up was all great.

Telling the tale in the pub before the Charlton game of how some daft old sod behind us said, "I have been watching football for 35 years and Patrick Kluivert is the worst player we have ever had," and of the ensuing argument, had our whole crew in bits (me shouting, "Are you blind, daft or both" while Guy quietly listed 20 former players who were worse than Patrick Moore, never mind Patrick Kluivert). Despite the stupid, pointless crap that we endured for 90 minutes and a 1-1 draw I loved it.

And the home game against Charlton, where the crowd fought a war of attrition with the manager over the introduction of some width and our players laboured for an hour to score a goal (Dyer, deflection) only to fuck up and concede the equaliser 48 seconds later? Well, what else were we going to do on a Saturday? And despite threatening to leave 20 minutes before the end out of sheer frustration we stayed and we would be back for the next game because the hope won't die. It's the hope that kills you and the hope that keeps killing you but it's the hope that keeps you alive.

Stupid hope.

Strangely after spending so much time together Guy and I find our opinions being affected by the other. For example I now think that Maggie Thatcher did the country a favour by stopping people having to work down mines for a living and Guy has got a Green Day album. Only joking. Guy hasn't got a Green Day album.

Chapter 29

20th February 2005

Fear & Loathing In The Snow

With any number of muppets left in the FA Cup it would have been easy to bemoan our misfortune at being drawn against the best team in the country so early. But where on the entire planet would we have the best chance of beating Chelsea, if not at St James' Park in the snow, three days before they play Barcelona away. Bring it on and give us Man Utd at home in the next round. Naturally Mourinho didn't like it and said that in Portugal the game would have been played on the previous Friday. Which would have been a bit tough on Newcastle who played away from home in Europe on the Thursday. Why not go the whole hog, Jose, and have Chelsea trot onto the pitch to play us in Heerenveen straight after the home side trudges off?

Chelsea had other problems and other fish they'd sooner fry; John Terry suspended, Drogba and Robben injured and Jose was pouting and twisting his face about the FA Cup not respecting Chelsea so Chelsea not respecting the FA Cup. Meaning? Lampard, Makelele, Duff, Gudjohnsen, Cech and Ferreira all didn't start.

This game HAD to be played and it HAD to be played right now. So the thick blanket of white stuff was not a welcome sight to bleary Sunday morning eyes. This led to frantic and pointless flapping around the Furious estate. Feverishly shovelling and sweeping snow off the path outside my house was never going to decide whether or not the game was played but deep down I felt I was helping. Pathetic isn't it? The sky was entirely blue, then half an hour later it was dark and grey and another blizzard mocked my feeble efforts. Then it was sunny again and Wifey was out giving a local cherub a carrot for the nose of the snowman that the little girl and her loving father had spent the last two hours toiling over. He, heaving a massive boulder of compacted snow around whilst she shoved what would turn out to be its wonky head. With stick arms, goggly lop-sided eyes and a simple grin, the addition of the massive orange nose gave the impression that a fat Phil Thompson was looking into my living room as the nice man from Sky Sports confirmed that ref Mark Halsey had given the pitch the green light. Then followed a strange three-way conversation.

Reporter: "Obviously the surrounding areas may still be a problem, the council gritter is just going past for the first time."

Me: "It's eleven o'clock! Stupid, penny-pinching Liberal council, shut some schools, sack some lollipop ladies, sweep the damn streets! And 'council gritter'? That better not be some filthy euphemism."

Presenter in studio: "So what can Newcastle do to make sure this sort of thing doesn't happen again?"

Reporter: "…"

Me: "Move us all to Jamaica, build an enormous dome over the entire North East of England, sue God. Silly woman!"

And what the fuck does 'surrounding areas' mean? Presumably we will still be expected to turn up for work in the morning? Clear the pitch and leave getting to the game, to us, we'll manage, OK?

This nervous tension would get worse for all of us as the day went on. But stamping through the day's fifth snow storm in the direction of the pub you couldn't shake the feeling that today was going to be special. Everybody in the pub thought we were going to win, the only thing that could mess it up would be silly tinkering from our manager. Having finally done as he was told in Holland (4-4-2, Robert playing) it would be an act of Bobby Robson size stubbornness to revert to a formation and team selection that was never going to work in the first place. The team news came on the telly, momentarily halting the hundred mile per hour shouting that passes for conversation in these parts, as well as the sloshing down of cold lager. We digested the information and there was much thoughtful nodding. Delighted as we were to see it, how dare Mourinho turn up here with an understrength team and expect to win.

Spirits lifted and suitably enthusiastic, the devoted masses loom large and impressive through the swirling snow towards their spiritual home. The extra hour in the pub, our collective yearning and that accursed hope have the ground vibrating.

We start well, crowd and team, passion and purpose and within four minutes we score a sublime goal. A great goal that is perfect for more reasons than it puts us 1-0 nil up. Robert and Kluivert have their critics and their disappointing games but it is they and what they *can* do that set us apart from Everton and Bolton and Blackburn and the dozen or so other humdrum teams in our dreary League.

Newcastle switch the ball from right to left, from Carr to Butt to Robert. Laurent takes off and whips in the cross, Kluivert (like Shearer, starved of this sort of thing) soars beyond the reach of Gallas and thunders the header into the top left hand corner of the net. What follows is not the wide-eyed delirious bedlam of old from the crowd. This team doesn't do 1-0 and we have got a lot of game left and we all know it. So we roar and we cheer and we clap, then like our team we get back to the job in hand. Nicky Butt holds the midfield together, wins the ball, cool and calm and vigilant. Unfortunately JJ keeps giving it away again and Laurent's delivery (or lack of it) is all over the place. Dyer is a constant handful, darting about, skipping past players, busy.

Chelsea, however are supremely confident. They keep the ball effortlessly and attack in great numbers. They leave three players up when defending a corner whilst Newcastle have everybody back. What the hell are Dyer and Robert going to give you when defending a corner? Leave them on the halfway line with the three or four players the opposition would need to mark them.

Seemingly out of nowhere Chelsea hit the bar. A cross is deflected, Kezman has nipped in and flicked the ball over Given. We scramble it clear and seconds later Dyer is bursting into the Chelsea area and it's their turn to scramble.

This half goes on forever and is gripping stuff to the extent that it takes all of half-time to get in and out of the crowded netties and many of us miss the chance to clap guest of honour Mr Tony Green – which is a shame.

There seems to be not much that Chelsea can't afford but what they can ill afford is a replay. Mourinho brings on Lampard, Gudjohnsen and Duff and Newcastle fans worldwide collectively gulp, all those players have hurt us before. It also thinks, "now if we did that, it would take about three minutes for some silly sod to break his ankle and leave us playing the rest of the game with ten men."

Three minutes later Wayne Bridge is stretchered off with a broken ankle after falling under a legitimate Shearer tackle. But much like the knight in

Monty Python's Holy Grail who has his arms and legs cut off and who still insists on fighting, Chelsea are too proud to fold. Too full of themselves to keep it tight and try to grab a goal that would give them a replay and a pretty obvious victory on a day less bizarre and stacked against them than this one. They pour forward, they still leave people up at corners and they still hammer straight at a door they think to be rotten and weak. A door that, despite its tatty reputation and appearance, is today lined with steel. And that steel is Titus fuckin' Bramble. Oh yes.

He has power, composure and speed of thought, foot and head, but it is his tackling that has the crowd on its feet. He hammers into them with frightening precision and timing. "He's going to get one of them wrong," you think, but he doesn't. Not one.

Laurent Robert declares himself 'extra man' and abandons most of his defensive duties, which is fine on one level because it keeps Chelsea stretched across the back but his final ball is generally awful.

Duff shows Robert how a winger should tackle back in denying a Carr chance but Laurent would point out that Duff injured himself in the process and limped about for the rest of the match leaving Chelsea, effectively, down to nine.

Still Chelsea attack and confused and frazzled of nerve, Newcastle wobble. The linesman doesn't help when a ball rolls out by his foot for an obvious throw-in and he gives a corner. If Chelsea were going to score this would surely be it and the crowd's blood boils with the injustice of it all. The heat is definitely turned up and the home crowd is awesome in its relentless racket.

As it happens, for all our fear Given has little to do except tidy up, largely thanks to a Babayaro tackle on Lampard with the outside of his foot that saves a clear chance.

Robert is getting a lot of the ball but by now our entire midfield is refusing to advance and he rarely has a clear target to cross to.

Five minutes of injury time comes up on the board and with Gallas limping Chelsea are down to eight fit players. Eight becomes seven when Cudicini races out of his area to flatten Shola and is sent off. Glenn Johnson, the right back, takes up the gloves and Robert who has tormented him all afternoon, inside and out, lines up the free-kick. Still Chelsea leave players forward so after Laurent has thundered his shot against the stand-in keeper's knees, we still have to rush around in near panic to stop the break.

Playing against seven with a midget in goal, you think you would wish the game would go on for another hour but the final whistle brings relief and you have got to hand Mourinho and his team credit for that.

It was one of those special nights afterwards, fuck the snow, fuck Chelsea and fuck work in the morning, get the bastard drinks in.

Stumbling home it was a shame to discover that Phil Thompson The Snowman had been savagely decapitated. It was more of a shame to wake to the news that another Thompson, Dr Hunter S, (author of *Fear & Loathing In Las Vegas* and inspiration to any writer worth a fuck) had shot himself aged 67. Thank you Doctor and Goodbye.

Chapter 30

27th February 2005

Songs About Murder

Three days before the Chelsea game, Newcastle played in Holland against Heerenveen and Graeme Souness appeared to be at a crossroads. Even the travelling fans mentally mashed up by Amsterdam's finest bakers could see the line-up made no sense; Shearer and Ameobi up front with Kluivert at the top end of a narrow midfield diamond, which obviously was going to leave us with three big blokes up front and no imaginable way of crossing the ball for them. Titus Bramble made the latest in a long line of defensive balls-ups and within 25 minutes we were 1-0 down, lumping the ball vaguely in the direction of the front three. Tyneside hummed to the tune of grinding teeth as the masses back home glowered at their television sets. Our voice in Holland, five hundred deep, gave vent to our frustration demanding the introduction of Laurent Robert, abusing the manager and even dusting off the old "Sack The Board" song sheet from way back.

It later became apparent that Souness had been planning the whole thing from the start, running the Dutch into the ground, softening them up for the introduction of Robert (Spurs manager Martin Jol was in the TV studio and he seemed so convinced this was the case that it was hard not to believe him). At the time it seemed like our manager was bowing to our collective will when after an hour Robert came on and the whole game changed. Laurent had put the killer ball through for Shearer to smash us level and the game was changed and obviously changed for the better when Carr crossed from wide on the right to Lee Bowyer who cutely flicked the ball (right foot behind left leg) into the Heerenveen net. The enigmatic Lee Bowyer (meaning capable of acts of surprising genius interspersed with moments of gross crassness) then got needlessly sent off for handling the ball deliberately.

The ten men hung on when they could have been putting the tie to sleep like a diseased dog but no matter, we could concentrate on Chelsea knowing the hard European work was done. The return leg, in front of 26,000 freezing diehards was over after 25 minutes, again thanks to Laurent Robert and the width he provided. An evil cross was desperately bundled into his own net by Breuer, then Shearer wellied in a second. Game over and nothing to do but avoid injury on the pitch and avoid hypothermia off it because it was bastard perishing.

Sunday morning 27th of February; third home game in eight days, against bloody Bolton with Nick Cave due at The Sage on the night time, singing songs about murder, rain and doomed relationships. It's gonna be a long haul this one. Longer than needs be as well because some knacker has decided we should kick off at 1 pm. Why, for fucksake, so we can see the League Cup Final? Who bloody cares, I can't see how anybody at Bolton wants to be reminded of their pathetic capitulation in last year's final against Middlesbrough and we sure as dammit don't want to watch them go about their anti-football without a half dozen or so strong drinks on board. There was an unseemly scrum around every bar in town as desperate Newcastle fans worried about watching the new Wimbledon sober.

Of course Sam Allardyce got very tetchy about Souness doing an Emperor's New Clothes on his team last October. Up to that point it was all "plucky Bolton" and "fighting spirit on a shoestring". Souness got accused of sour grapes but suddenly everybody started pointing, laughing and winning against Bolton and they plopped down the League like a lonely turd.

They pulled it round and were unbeaten in ten going into this game but their low self-worth was brought into sharp focus when about 14 people turned up to see their last FA Cup game at the Reebok.

Big Sam was asked recently about goal-line technology and he was most enthusiastic, "get everything on every decision", he stated, no doubt dreaming of a time when football could be 90 minutes of set-pieces, with him scientifically working out exactly where everybody should stand via his Satellite Lap-top And Dietary Coordinator, before yelling his instructions down his mouthpiece whilst chewing with his mouth open. How the away trips must have flown over at Bolton in the old days with Sam and Peter Reid seeing who could stuff the most Juicy Fruits in their faces before chewing like chimps at a termite mound.

First half: mostly rubbish, with Newcastle looking a bit leggy from

Thursday, failing to make any headway against Bolton's nine man wall of powder blue. Titus actually put in the two best crosses in the first half hour, Shearer shot wide and Dyer headed tamely straight at Juicyfruit Jasskelainen.

But what an enigma Lee Bowyer is, the same player who played like an utter fool at Man City, scored a goal so good that we should all meet up somewhere exactly a year from now to drink to its brilliance. Executing a Zidane style twist he left two Bolton players for dead before spraying the ball out wide to Carr who crossed into the area, where Kieron was waiting nicely for another nod towards Juicy. Bowyer, having witnessed the earlier effort, ploughed through the back of his team-mate and smashed his own header into the Leazes End net. Excellent, now let's play some football.

No, because Gianapopalopapop scored for them after some poor marking and then nearly did the same thing five minutes later.

The second half was all about Kieron Dyer. Yes, Shearer scuffed a couple wide and Boumsong had a header cleared off the line but it was Kieron who won us the game. His running with the ball was especially magnificent, the highlight being a run from deep inside his own half that ended with a crude Hierro trip on the edge of the Bolton area. Robert missed by a foot from the free kick, with Juicy stranded, but the damage was done. The fact that the daft, fat ref didn't send Hierro off galvanised team and fans and Newcastle laid siege to the Bolton goal. Dyer was at the epicentre of all that was most promising, culminating in a vicious volley into the roof of the net that won us that game. He was still sprinting past people in the last minute. Awesome.

Also awesome was The Sage by the way. Like a big glass hand grenade it stands magnificent and proud by the Tyne Bridge. Inside is just as impressive, most of all the sound in the auditorium, which was perfect for the intensity that is Nick Cave, from bombastic piano bashing to the tiniest ting of a cymbal. From some way in, people started shouting requests and rather than ignore them Nick said he was open to suggestions. There was much drunken Geordie hollering to which Mr Cave in his strong Aussie accent said, "I'm sorry I don't understand a single fucking word of what you guys are saying." I mention the gig, partly out of civic pride for the Sage but mostly because in *The Mag*, for his rendition of *Red Right Hand*, I awarded Nick Cave Man Of The Match.

Chapter 31

14th March 2005

Intimer-fucking-dation

So what makes a good home crowd and what effect does it have on the players? Sometimes you wonder, like when you see Aston Villa or Blackburn Rovers plying their trade in front of apparently disinterested and immobile spectators, staring blankly from amidst the spreading bald patches of empty seats. What's the point of them being there, what do they think they're doing because they sure as hell aren't helping? The home team can't be lifted and the away team can't be intimidated or fearful. At what point does a crowd start to affect either team? I've never even dreamed of being on the pitch at St James' (I have boring football dreams wherein I only have one boot, can't find my way to the pitch and Newcastle didn't need me anyway) but I have been going long enough to tell when and why the crowd help. Contrary to popular myth, size is only partly important; when 70, 000 Italians cheer a goal in the San Siro there is a terrifying sonic boom and your first instinct is to duck. Secondly this is wisdom because the bastards above you are about to afford you a wave of bottles and loose change but firstly it's because of the noise. On the other hand there were less than 15,000 in the Old Den when Newcastle last played Millwall there and it was as noisy and intimidating as hell.

The problem for clubs is that a lot of what makes a crowd effective is terribly politically incorrect and they can't be seen to be encouraging it. It's all about bullying, harassment and what an acquaintance of mine calls "the importance of intimer-fucking-dation". The problem for Newcastle United at this point in history was that the crowd wasn't doing its job. A hearty "C'mon!" at the start then we settle straight down into our seats for 80 minutes of moaning followed by 12 to 14 minutes of undignified panic interspersed with pin-pricks of pure pleasure and smouldering hatred.

What we really need to get the crowd going at the Theatre Of The Absurd is any two of: an extra hour in the pub, opposition worth getting on your feet for, or a daft ref who doesn't understand that officiating at Newcastle involves giving all the decisions, from penalties to throw-ins, to the home team. Pissed and indignant, we can make the world shake.

Sky loved our 4-3s with Liverpool last century and eagerly swooped on the chance to show our every encounter with them for years. Fortunately we served up enough turkeys for them in recent matches for the live cameras to leave us to get on with it in peace for once. Hence a three o'clock kick-off on a Saturday.

For an hour the crowd followed the familiar, depressing pattern; communal jeers and groans, sporadic applause and a few brave souls failing to get the lumpen lazy masses to join in with a bit of supporting. But something was growing, perhaps it was the memory of a time when Liverpool were worth beating. Perhaps it was the ref ticking off their violent players instead of booking them and indulging their frightful little ponces, who threw themselves to the ground squealing like piggies, with endless free-kicks but something was growing. Growing. Feeding off the tiresome abuse of Liverpool fans who have never seen St James' Park anything other than full but who still sing, "where were you when you were shit?" Feeding off the fact that our players were actually looking like they gave a fuck and devouring the fact that this was the worst Liverpool team in living memory and NOT beating them would be WRONG!!

It had been an unpleasant, grinding fascinating encounter with no shots on target but the crowd noise continued to grow. People were getting out of their seats, clenching their fists, clapping, singing, willing, roaring. Alan Shearer, (playing his 400th Premiership game) came to the East Stand corner of the penalty area, back to goal to control the ball. For the umpteenth time Pellerino was jostling and man-handling from behind, Shearer let gravity do its job and Laurent Robert lined up the free-kick. Liverpool had 19 year old Scott Carson in goal who had remained untroubled until this point and to his lasting credit he did get a finger tip to Robert's shot as it ripped and curled into the top left hand corner of the net.

(This free-kick was used as the climax of the film 'Goal' where the two central characters, Santiago Munez and Gavin Harris played up front alongside Shearer, Ameobi, and Kluivert. Given, Carr, Boumsong, Bramble

Robert and Dyer were the other players in a revolutionary 3-2-5 formation that must be worth a go. Meanwhile back in the real world...)

Through a frenzy of raised arms and leaping bodies you could see Laurent doing the gayest little dance before his team-mates descended on him. The next twenty minutes brought a ferocious determination from team and crowd. Patrick Kluivert came on, skinned Carragher but dragged his shot wide. That would have won it and it could have haunted us because in injury time Liverpool finally had a clear-cut chance and of all people it fell to Gerrard who, with 52,323 holding the same breath, fired wide.

The crowd had done its job and the players had responded but five days later the boot was on the other foot. A notoriously passionate and dangerous home crowd awaited us in Athens. Olympiacos had won all their home games in the Champions League without conceding a goal and were only dumped into the UEFA Cup by Gerrard not missing a last minute chance at Anfield. They had seen off Sochaux in the previous round, boasted World Cup winner Rivaldo in their starting line up and played in red and white stripes which are displeasing to us.

A large part of a home atmosphere is daring the ref. Do you dare give a penalty against Manchester United at the Stretford End, do you dare send off two players from the home team in the first half? Generally the answer is no but this ref fucked up. He had little choice with the first sending off; Kieron Dyer was about to nod the ball into the empty net after his shot had spun up from the falling goalkeeper and was shoved in the back as he jumped to do so. Alan Shearer hammered home his 25th European goal from the spot and the home fans and team got on with being hysterical. A legitimate but soft penalty conceded by O'Brien and despatched by Djordjevic failed to calm them down at all and the Olympiacos players, encouraged by fevered local noise, screamed in the ref's face and demanded sendings off for Newcastle for even the tiniest of infringements. The ref in turn was erratic and bizarre, overruling his assistant, waving play on after obvious fouls and blowing his whistle and waving his arms for no discernable reason. Shearer was upended on the edge of the area and we were somewhat surprised to be awarded a free-kick. Robert belted it into the net and did his gay little dance again.

Olympiacos, indignant, attacked. On the break from a corner Nicky Butt had his legs kicked from under him. The ref waved a yellow card at a player as a matter of little concern. But the linesman pointed out that the ref had got the wrong player, the trouble being that the right player had already been booked. Having already produced a card he could hardly take it back altogether and thus gave himself no choice but to award a second card to Kostoulas. This took time and looked confusing and farcical from within the stadium at the time but in the cold light of day it was correct. Would the ref have produced a yellow card for the foul if he had realised the player would have to be sent off, leaving these Greek maniacs with nine men for the entire second half? He was clearly madder than a badger sandwich but he wasn't that mad.

The second half consisted of Newcastle worrying more about the mad ref evening-up the sides than they did about passing the ball to each other. The same players who managed 71% of the possession of the ball against Liverpool couldn't string two passes together until Milner, on as a sub, was sent clear down the left. He twisted inside the defender and teed up Kluivert who bashed in the third.

Four or five goals would have seen us through to the next round comfortably but as Souness said afterwards, "Our great concern was we felt, with the pressure from the crowd, there was a chance we might get a red," and that, like it or not, is a home crowd doing its job.

Chapter 32

16th March 2005

And That's For Chas & Dave

21st of February 1987, White Hart Lane, fifth round of the FA Cup, Newcastle's inevitable march to the final, we were living the dream. It was the era of Beardsley, Goddard, Peter Jackson and the free-scoring Andy Thomas, we would soon have Paul Gascoigne back from injury and we had already put the mighty Northampton Town and Preston North End to the sword. We were the most underrated team in the country in my not very humble opinion and we were about to blow our cover by winning the FA Cup.

The terrace was heaving behind the goal, the official crowd was just over 38,000 and Newcastle had 10,000. Officially. Unofficially? God knows, there were no tickets, we paid on the gate. We were intoxicated with belief and strong lager. The Seven Sisters Road was awash with crazy fuckers who thought this a stop on the way to glory. We met some drunken bastard who gave Wifey a bunch of flowers and for some reason I had thought a bowler hat, with a black and white tartan band around it, acceptable attire. During the second half Wifey's feet barely touched the terrace as the heaving ocean of bodies, moved by some invisible moon, dragged the tide back and forth and up and down. She heroically clutched her increasingly bedraggled bouquet, while my hat went from an angle that could be considered 'jaunty' to one that was clearly 'distressed'. Breathing and seeing were both acts that took extreme effort, but this was pre-Hillsborough and we were veterans of stage-front gig survival, so we never imagined we were in any danger and at least we weren't going to get blind-sided by some stagediver's boot. Exhausted, drunk and sweaty you just forced your elbows into the back of the poor sod in front of you, gulped in the filthy, fetid, fart-ridden air and kept singing. "New-cass-erl, New-cass-erl New-cass-erl!"

Tottenham were awarded the most dodgy of penalties, the ref gave us nowt all day and then the swines played Chas and Dave at us on the final whistle. Out 1-0 and aggrieved to this day.

We have given them some hoofings since; the semi-final in '99, the 6-1 the season after but this was the first time we really paid them back for that shitty day 18 years ago. We paid them back because they had fought so bravely and in the end they were so hard done by. Never mind earned a replay, they could and should have won this game.

It all started so well, Dyer sprinting past Atouba down the right in the second minute seemed to have set the tone. The second time he did so, it was with the help of a lucky deflection but the ball span to Shearer who crossed to Kluivert who had lost his marker and who effortlessly slid the ball beyond Robinson.

A minute later Dyer skinned his man again, was brought down and Atouba was booked. A minute after that Kluivert had the ball in the net again. He timed his run perfectly, with Newcastle and Spurs players going away from goal he slipped through the gap, onside, and finished with an assassin's cool. The daft linesman raised his daft flag, something he seemed largely incapable of doing throughout the second half.

Dyer put a peach of a ball through for Shearer to run onto down the left, his cross was blocked but it seemed a matter of time before we got the second. However, from the moment Boumsong was erroneously booked for diving, the game began to swing the other way.

Tottenham were first to everything after that. They closed us down quickly all over the pitch, our midfield was forced into errors, with Amdy Faye having a dreadful afternoon.

Tottenham, so often the very embodiment of poncey, gutless cockney bastards battled even harder in the second half, whilst our players looked weary from Thursday night's game in Greece. They swarmed all over us, they looked bigger, fitter, quicker and it was exhausting to watch. Robbie Keane came on for the wretchedly poor Atouba and within five minutes had hit a shot Given did well to even see, never mind beat out. Yet before normal folk had a chance to rise and bring hand to applauding hand, Given had made an even better save from Defoe. Man of the Match in two seconds flat.

Kluivert had pulled up lame and Shola came on to help the over-manned pumps. Things were desperate from this point on, if we booted it clear they came straight back at us, if we tried to pass our way out they swarmed all over us and took it back far too close to our goal. Credit at this point to Stephen Carr who battled for everything, who never lost composure or ball and who did the job for us at the back that Shearer was doing for us up top. Leadership by example; blood, sweat and indomitable will.

The last ten minutes took an hour during which Spurs had two decent penalty shouts turned down and a goal disallowed. The roar of relief after four agonising minutes of stoppage time was a clear indication of how the afternoon went.

Too shattered and emotionally drained to leave the pub afterwards, the night went on far too long. Compared to how long it's going to take to get back from Cardiff it was nothing – but we wouldn't have it any other way.

Chapter 33

17th March 2005

Who You Calling Unsuccessful?

Our 100th game in Europe. We're all for hunger, drive and the next game being the most important one and the most tedious Newcastle fans are the ones who insist on living in the past but this is one hell of a landmark. Occasionally in life you need to pour yourself a large glass of something luxurious, sit back a minute and just smile.

"(slurp) A hundred games in Europe, you say? (sigh) A ten year old single malt scotch is it? Who'd have thought it. Num num num, ooh that's tasty. Oh it's all gone, never mind, I'll have another."

Apart from all the fun we've had, a hundred games in Europe is a sharp slap in the face for some of the dismal little fuckers who consider themselves our equals (yes sunderland, we are looking at you). Those who snipe and bitch will continue to do so, it's in their pathetic nature but we who have played a hundred games in Europe will look on them, as they deserve, like the shit beneath our feet, that we shall step around and ignore. You know we need to enjoy these moments because we are Newcastle United and any second the fucking roof is likely to come crashing in.

Think about this, European qualification represents a successful season and you can't play a hundred European games in a couple of years. Also, over 70% of those games have come within the last ten seasons which means over ten years we have had to have been consistently successful to clock up this century. Yes, yes we would all crawl under three hundred miles of razor wire to see our team win a trophy but cups are essentially flashes in the pan. Middlesbrough will no doubt continue to bang on about their League Cup win, but Leicester won the same cup a few years ago – does that put them on equal footing with a team who has played a hundred games in Europe?

In the meantime, well, it's been great and we have all learnt a lot. Our

European geography has come on a treat for a start but we have learnt many more subtle lessons; like European teams are generally only considered any good by the media when they have beaten us. If we beat them they are invariably 'disappointing'. So it was tonight, Olympiacos racked up ten points in their Champions League group and Liverpool only snagged them in injury time – they are no mugs, they have good players and we kicked their ass.

The very hardest part was done in Greece of course, where they have been formidable, while anything requiring a passport has been a bit of trouble for them but some credit where credit was due for us would be nice please.

It was the attitude of the home team that was striking from the off, with the intensity and effort levels astonishing given the amount of games we have played lately. Bowyer and Butt had the midfield by the scruff of the neck from first to last, the latter hammering a shot off the bar on the quarter hour but it was the form of Jenas and Dyer that had the post-match pubs purring. J.J. has been out of sorts recently but he was in fine fettle during this game, his running was superb, his passing intelligent and his composure assured but it was Dyer who shone brightest.

Playing off Shearer, with four other midfield options around him, Dyer sparkled and fizzed and scored a wonderfully cheeky goal. Back-heeling the ball into the net amidst the confusion caused by a Robert free-kick, "Cheeky bastard!" said everybody with a fat smile.

Shearer had three chances in ten minutes. Put clean through by Jenas he launched a left foot shot at the Toon-ultras in level seven (who were in fine voice by the way) then, from successive Robert crosses, he first missed the ball (by a distance that is technically referred to as "a gnat's chuff") than glanced a brilliant header just wide. Eventually Dyer, shiny new boots a blur, had to run the ball right up to the keeper from the right hand side before putting it on a silver platter for his captain. Bang 2-0!

In the second half Newcastle kept the tempo up and the ball pretty much to themselves. Our Greek guests got fed up, Bowyer squeezed a third under their international goalie and Kieron and Robert were allowed to knock off on the hour. Taylor swapped in from left back to have a go at senior centre-halfing, young Ramage finally got his boots mucky and Shearer went round the keeper and smashed a fourth into the roof of the net. There were still twenty minutes left.

Souness had his name sang, a little tentatively first time round but after getting a wave from Shay and Terry Mac for their efforts the fans had another more strident song for the manager. He waved, we clapped and some common ground seems to have been arrived at, this wasn't "holding onto 1-0" or "a game of chess". Manager and crowd seem to understand each other a little better and it only took eight wins in a row to get there. Easily pleased aren't we?

Now if we could just chalk up another 100 games in Europe, that would be lovely thank you. Madrid or Paris would be nice.

Chapter 34

24th March 2005

The Strong Walk Away

We used to mock those who walked away. People who gave up going to the match were weak-willed and lacking in commitment. We didn't care if you had just been made redundant or that you had to care for your cancerous budgie or you had actually died two seasons ago. Not renewing your season ticket was giving up on life, on hope, on your friends and on your team and it was not on.

Now it becomes clear that those who walk away are the ones embracing life, those of us that stay are growing greyer, more twisted, angrier, short tempered and snappy. We cling to our season tickets in the hope of something shiny coming along to make us young and eager again. Football becomes less of a lifestyle and more of an affliction, a noxious disease that we dare not seek a cure for.

In half the time it would have taken to drive to Portsmouth, Easyjet have dropped me off in Rome.

The sun is warm, the beer is cold, the food is fantastic and I am pretending that Newcastle United is of no relevance to a windswept traveller like me. The fact that I'm snatching my vibrating phone out of my pocket faster than a young Clint Eastwood could pull a Colt 45 on ill-shaven varmints is giving me away. And Wifey's not fooling anyone with her casual "Oh is that Guy, it must be half-time" act – like she doesn't care either. The game finishes 1-1, Guy wasn't actually there so the information that Portsmouth's equaliser was offside and at the end of ghost first half injury time that only the ref could see, is at least third-hand. This did not stop me feeling indignant and scowling in the direction I think Portsmouth might be in. Bastards!

A.S. Roma v A.C. Milan kicks off at 8.30 on a Sunday night and the stadium is miles away from the city centre. The game is live on TV and Roma have just appointed their fourth (yes that's fourth) manager of the season. They are a shambles and have little to play for but over 70,000 have turned up and very few leave before the end. The announcer races through the Milan team then reads out the first name of the home team player and the whole crowd stand and roar out the surname. Well that's the plan and on Francesco Totti (captain, highest ever scorer, Roman) the "TOTTI" is thunderous but all is not well and three Roma players are simply booed before they even get onto the pitch.

Booing your own players onto the pitch, what help is that going to be to your team? Disheartened and dispirited Roma have good players but they played really badly and lost first their shape, then what was left of their fragile confidence, then their composure, then the match 2-0 and they ended the game with nine men on the pitch.

The great joy of taking an interest in a team that is not Newcastle United is that you can walk away suppressing the urge to giggle when things go all wonky. "What a shambles, ha ha ha ha ha………….."

Days after we arrive back in Blighty; Newcastle United 0 v Aston Villa 3.

We end the game with eight players on the pitch and all is overshadowed because Dyer and Bowyer were sent off for fighting each other.

This game was supposed to be a celebration of Alan Shearer's decision to sign on for another year at Newcastle United. The sun was shining, we always beat shabby old Villa and there was so much confidence in the air that many pre-match rituals were ignored. For my own part Newcastle have never won a game when I wear sunglasses but fresh back from jaunting around Europe they were virtually glued to my head and I wore them without a care in the world.

After the game the media went instantly berserk over the fight – *The Pink* headline screamed "DISGRACE", and the phrase "Once again the good name of Newcastle United has been dragged through the mud" was brought out of the box marked 'Sanctimonious Claptrap' and given to those who like their horses as high as the moral ground they instantly gallop towards. Radio 5 Live were on the phone asking me for a blow by blow account, I couldn't oblige the nice lady from the radio because I didn't see what happened at the time, unlike the protagonists I was watching the ball. But it seemed to me after the 57th time of seeing it replayed that Bowyer said something to Dyer, which caused him to stop and turn round. Bowyer then pushed his forehead into Dyer's face and started swinging. For his part Dyer does his best to hold

Bowyer off before reaching the point where he would have been a big wet girl if he didn't throw a punch back.

It turned out that the ref's assessor said the ref was wrong to dismiss Dyer. Unfortunately this evidence was overlooked at Dyer's appeal against the subsequent three match ban (which would include the FA Cup semi-final), and the national and local press had already lazily lumped the players into the same steaming pile of guilt.

The fight was actually a distraction, 98% of the footballing country thought it was funny. Newcastle were already 0-3 down and playing with ten men when it happened, so people *(unaware of the impending ban)* were actually laughing in the pub instead of organising lynch mobs for ref Barry Knight who turned down three Toon penalties at 0-1. Nicky Butt got clean away with playing the game like he was waiting to die and it was all but forgotten that Andy O'Brien spent the whole match treating the ball like it was about to explode; poking it delicately away with his foot or running away with his hands over his ears every time it came near him. The worst crime was that yet another rubbish team had left Newcastle with points and that drags our mud-soaked 'good name' through the dirt more then any scuffle– the like of which happens in playgrounds all over the country.

I guess if Kieron Dyer had just walked away things would have turned out better but sometimes you just can't. In an interview with The Mag in 2007 Dyer put over things as he had seen them: "I was gutted because things had just started to drop right for me and I felt that under Graeme Souness I was playing some of my best ever football for Newcastle. After the match I was driving back to Ipswich with my mam and I was the innocent party and felt I hadn't done anything wrong. I turned to have an argument with my team mate which is something that happens all the time on the pitch, I had Five Live on the radio and fans were ringing up and saying Bowyer and Dyer should never play for the club again. I was gutted. All the hard work I'd put in to win people back seemed to have gone to waste. I started the next match which was Sporting Lisbon at home and the fans were great to me, which was a massive relief and I really appreciated that."

Chapter 35

7th April 2005

This Is So Not About Lee Bowyer

Wifey and I have a growing reputation for leaving catastrophe behind at places we have visited. Since we flew out of New York City on September 10th 2001 these places have partially collapsed, been flooded or suffered plagues and pestilence of some sort. So naturally within days of wandering happily around the Vatican, the Pope dropped dead and the streets of Rome were full of wailing Catholics.

Anyway, as requested by UEFA we had a "moment's silence for the Pope" before this game. At the risk of being condemned as a blaspheming heretic and consequently burnt alive (I presume they still do that) I did spend the 'moment' quietly discussing how long a moment should be. As a measurement of time it is somewhat imprecise, so why did the ref look at his watch? We would later learn that the ref was a cock-eyed, grinning halfwit but more of that later.

Of course it is a savage indictment of the modern world that I will get more abuse for stating that Lee Bowyer is (in my opinion) an idiotic, knob-head who we would do well to see the back of, than I will for the view that (in my opinion) the Catholic Church is a historically corrupt and greedy institution built on fear, torture and innocent blood. It's homophobic, oppresses women, covers up child abuse and they collaborated with the Nazis. But there you have it.

Let it not be forgotten that getting sent off for attacking Kieron Dyer on the pitch (as the club, the ref's assessor and I saw it) was actually the third time Bowyer has been sent off this season. The others were for: 1. running around kicking people in front of the ref at Liverpool before he was eventually given Christmas off and 2. the most pointless deliberate handball ever witnessed. He has been lucky not to get sent off on numerous other occasions, never more so than during a pathetic and embarrassing attempt to tussle with Sylvain Distin at Manchester City.

Before the match against Sporting Lisbon in the UEFA Cup quarter-final, Bowyer said he would die for this club and I for one would have donated a generous amount towards some sort of ceremonial sword BUT this game was not about Lee Bowyer, it was about Newcastle United: and for all that he is (in my opinion) an idiotic knobhead, Bowyer is also a half-decent footballer and as the injuries pile up those are getting pretty thin on the ground in these parts. So yes I clapped him onto the pitch when he replaced Dyer – I generally don't like bus drivers (because 90% of them are bastards) but I would sooner get on a bus driven by a bastard than walk ten miles.

The media were "astonished" and in some cases "sickened" by Bowyer's reception but they underestimated our intelligence and our desperation for a trophy. It's not about the player, it's about the club and while it might be in the media's interest for us to continually cut our noses off to teach our faces a lesson – at this point in time, it was not in the interest of Newcastle United to do so.

Spending a page explaining that this game was not about Lee Bowyer may seem a little perverse but what else is there to say – we've seen Sporting twice before this season and so we already knew that they are wet, cry-babies with a ghastly away kit.

The fact that they are cynical and have hair like girls also isn't news but the fact that Newcastle have learnt not to try and out-pass them is. We hit it long, rattled them in tackles and terrified them with Shola. Ameobi didn't have the best of games and the groan of frustration when he missed a good chance to make it 2-0 at the death was testament to that but Sporting were constantly nervous of him. He kicked the goalie in the head after five minutes going for a loose ball (an injury that took five minutes to treat) and should have been allowed to score after 84 minutes when he charged down the keeper's clearance. It happened to hit his arm but his arm was across his chest and the contact was not at all deliberate.

The foul that led to the goal was another example of fear over sense. Shola was on the side of the area with his back to goal and going nowhere when the defender barged into the back of him. By this point the ref had already disallowed a perfectly good Shearer goal, Robert crossed in a perfect free-kick but from about two inches away from where it should have been taken and the ref wasn't looking. Which in retrospect was somewhat bizarre because for the rest of the game, kicks were taken yards away from fouls, with rolling balls and before permission was given to do so. On our goal the ref also chose to ignore the fact that Shola flattened half the defence to leave Shearer unmarked to head smartly into the net.

At the end of the fourth minute of first-half injury time the last defender grappled Ameobi to the ground wide on the right and the ref, faced with a tricky decision, chose to end the half at once.

Steve Harper came on for the second half with Given injured, Dyer had to depart shortly afterwards which was a shame because he was playing well enough to get tripped up every time he tried to run with the ball. Bowyer came on, Harper made a smart save and Bowyer a reckless tackle to get booked.

Newcastle got edgy and the ref got madder – ignoring some fouls, making up others, smiling too much and at one point awarding a drop ball that we weren't invited to.

Milner got on and had a great run spoiled by a wild shot and special mention for Steven Taylor who was magnificent. Sporting had a lot of the ball but not in the last third, and shots were rare from both sides.

As UEFA Cup quarter-finals go, we did alright.

In the interests of balance I should point out that the Protestant Church can fuck off as well; they tried to ban Christmas you know, sixteen hundred and something, don't let them tell you otherwise.

Not that my printed opinion of the Catholic Church got me any complaints, it did however secure my eternal damnation, which after a lifetime following Newcastle United should be pretty straightforward.

Chapter 36

15th April 2005

Bastard!

Sunday April 10th and Newcastle United's fans and players landed at the first port of call on a five match journey away from home. The second and third games would define not only a season but an era.

Ravaged by injury and suspension, this first port was White Hart Lane, live on Sky Sports *Super Sunday*. I'm positive that the fans of every other team in the country were saying, "Why the hell is this on, what's so fucking super about these two mid-table teams? Who the hell wants to watch this shower of shite, it doesn't even matter who wins?"

And they would have been right because the game was awful. Barcelona played Real Madrid later the same day and you wouldn't believe they were participating on the same twatting planet, never mind in the same sport. Steve Harper fucked up with a poor clearance and Defoe scored. Spurs fucked up a lot and we didn't score.

But put into context, games one, four and five were little more than idle distractions for us, we barely gave a crap about our League position at this point. We were still in two Cups and one of them we were favourites to actually win outright.

When in all our lives had that happened before? If we could just stick together and believe, we would be back in Lisbon in May for the final. So obviously Laurent Robert chose to start shooting his mouth off about his problems with the manager and his tactics. He said the team was worse than last year's and that he got the blame when the team played badly but no praise when it played well. All true as it happened but what a fucking time to start. Stupid, stupid bastard!

Souness blew his top and then his chances with his team selection. He dropped Robert altogether and played Babayaro, Bramble, Jenas and Dyer all of whom had question marks over their fitness.

It looked like we had got away with it. Lisbon were edgy and nervous from the start. Newcastle looked composed. When Dyer scampered clear to put us

2-0 up on aggregate with the home side now needing three goals we surely couldn't lose. Then one by one the wheels came off.

It's all too easy to imagine Robert blasting in a free-kick at this point and killing the game dead but his own daft gob and the manager's pride means we'll never know.

Five minutes before half-time and Sporting had been no threat at all when suddenly they fluked an equaliser and gave themselves a shot of belief.

JJ went off injured at half-time, ten minutes later Bramble followed and the defensive

solidity shattered. Andy O'Brien emerged blinking into the floodlights alongside Steven Taylor. On the hour Dyer hobbled out of the action and our best chance of another goal vanished and we had no subs left to make when Babayaro started limping.

In agonisingly slow motion our world collapsed; O'Brien made a hash of a clearance and Sporting were 2-1 up, six minutes later Beto, unmarked, headed in the third and we were behind. God bless them, those remaining and able in black and white tried so hard it hurt to watch but in the last minute, when we should have been scoring the goal that saved us, Carr gave the ball away and a cruel fourth goal brought our lingering hopes crashing into the dust.

"I've been here eight seasons and I've never felt as low or as bad as that," said Shay Given.

Alan Shearer with glassy, almost tearful, eyes said, "In all the years that I've been here, that was the best opportunity we've had to pick up a piece of silverware."

If a man as magnificent as Alan Shearer is allowed a tearful eye, then mere mortals fighting for Newcastle would have been entitled to a hearty sob.

If the chairman and Bobby Robson had bought the defenders we so clearly needed instead of wasting time with that stupid Rooney bid. If Bellamy and Robert weren't so fucking self-obsessed, and so far up their own arses that they could see the damage their mouths were doing. If Souness could actually have managed them. If Andy O'Brien's nerve hadn't dissolved. Or simply if Kieron Dyer had poked in that easy chance to make it 2-0 on the night we could have faced anything. Now it was all ruined. Ruined by pride and stupidity. Now our hopes began and ended with Manchester United in Cardiff on Sunday. A full strength Manchester United who had spent two weeks resting players while we were emotionally and physically spent. It was hopeless. Utterly hopeless.

Bastard.

Chapter 37

17th April 2005

"Nec Spe Nec Meth"
("Without Hope Without Fear" – Caravaggio)

We knew we never stood a chance but that didn't make it any easier to live with. Manchester United have got better players than us and some of them were given two weeks' rest before this game. Our beaten, bruised, mentally and physically shattered squad hadn't even seen their own beds since the disaster in Lisbon.

As these last crucial weeks of our season have passed, black comedy has followed tragedy, injuries have piled up, unjust suspensions have been upheld and the slightest embers of hope have been stamped out. The relationship between manager and some players, fans and some players and press and some players has been fractious and harmful.

How many of the starting 11 weren't fit to play and whose fault was it that they had to? Imagine being a player with a genuine injury in the present climate, what do you do and how can you possibly win? Don't play and the local press paint you as a shirker, play whilst injured and don't do yourself justice and you are accused of not trying. We didn't have a chance in hell so why the bitter recriminations because we lost? If the two teams' situations had been entirely reversed we would have won – if we had gone into the match with the same build-up as Man Utd we would have had a chance but with all the shite we've been through recently, Christ, the Man Utd players were even more familiar with the Millennium Stadium's notoriously slippy pitch. And then there is the small matter of Van Nistelrooy being invisible to our defenders.

Yet, we knew all this before we went.

And we still went.

35,000, beautiful and doomed, singing on their way to a battle they couldn't win. Lesser men would weep at the very thought.

Blackburn Rovers fans, whose team stood more chance against Arsenal the day before, can look on their showing and know their support to be cheap and unworthy of the name. The worst fans in the Premiership exposed by the thousands of empty seats. Still we willed their team on just in case ours pulled off some kind of footballing miracle. But Blackburn's team is about as much use as their fans and having failed to kick Arsenal off the pitch, they crashed 3-0 and went home quietly. This left Newcastle United with the straightforward task of having to beat all the top three teams in the country to win the trophy we so desperately crave. Chelsea down with only Manchester United and Arsenal to go.

It sticks in the throat how the FA Cup is only taken seriously by Arsenal and Manchester United when the League is out of reach and the Champions League has trundled off without them again. We would really be better off meeting them in Round Three when participation for the old piss-pot is still considered an irritant to them.

There will be 35,000 different stories of how the next 24 hours were spent. The time between the final whistle of one semi and the first whistle of the next. Fitful sleep, anxiety, drinking, preparing, another couple of hours staring at the ceiling wishing for, yet wary of, sleep. "If only my heart would stop pounding, I could get some rest. What if I don't wake up when the alarm goes off? What if the alarm is wrong? Where did I put my ticket?" A million chaotic and nonsensical thoughts whizz round in a whirl of hopes and fears and the constant nagging that this is all going to be a horrible waste of time and effort looms large through all of it.

Those of us who went by coach met in town at an hour when even the straggliest of drunks were stumbling home. The Back Page had 27 buses booked and the chances of everything running smoothly were remote. Visions of gangs of drunken nutters wielding kebabs and pestering for sloppy kisses from the opposite sex didn't come to fruition, the Walker lasses must have made it home, unless they were already in Wales.

In return for stewarding a bus, Mark and Micky from The Back Page let me stuff it full of my own match crew. So sleep was unlikely, a thick skin to piss-taking essential and a luminous waistcoat and clipboard a severe temptation to abuse of power. "Keith are you chewing? Spit it out boy!"

We were in Cardiff with drink in our hands before half past ten in the morning.

The next three and a half hours were magnificent. Colliding with old friends, losing and finding people, hundred mile an hour jabbering, excited texts. Laughing, drinking, shouting, drinking, merciless abuse, drinking – all the stuff we do best and loving every single second and every single stupid drunken black and white bastard you laid eyes on.

Finally our destiny called us, through the dark, wet, hideous, brutal Welsh rain to the match and the day was (as we fully expected) ruined under a black tempestuous sky. Our team were unable or unwilling to perform. They slipped over a lot and they couldn't see Van Nistelrooy.

The 35,000 were brave and indomitable. 1-nil, 2-nil, 3-nil and still we came back with passion. Shola made it 3-1 and the team were at last giving it a go. We sang even harder. Amidst all the bitter post-match recriminations this 15 minute period was forgotten, Man U on the back foot with us deluded fuckers thinking we were going to get another one. The problem was that at some point we actually believed we could pull this off and the reality was heart-breaking. Nicky Butt rounded off a wretched performance by giving the ball away at the back and invisible Ruud gave the ball to Ronaldo (who was miles off-bloody-side by the way) and we were torpedoed for good – after that there was nothing left but pride.

"Your support is fucking shit!" we roared at the despicable red tourists and we did it with such passion and such astounding volume that your heart fair filled to bursting. A fifth goal would have been too cruel on the fans in black and white who were magnificent and credit to all the players who at least recognised the fact at the end.

Nicky Butt was reportedly talking to Alex Ferguson after this game when some nitwit local hack asked if he had a message for Newcastle's fans. For my own part I have gone way beyond the point of wanting to hear fucking anything, I want to see it from a player or they can save their fucking breath. Nicky Butt obliged me rather than the reporter and a campaign of misinformation began. In a pre-season friendly in 2006, after a year on loan at Birmingham, Nicky Butt came on as a sub and was booed by some Newcastle fans. He scored twice and a lad I know sought out the journalist and gave him a right gob-full, the journalist had the gall to look shocked. After Nicky Butt was named man of the match the reporter sat with his head in his hands for a couple of seconds while my friend (not a slim lad and wearing ill-

fitting and crumpled shorts), danced around waving his arms about. I laughed so hard I was nearly sick and probably weed a bit.

Kieron Dyer: "I did feel sorry for Nicky Butt because he wasn't fit when Graeme Souness arrived, he had a bad hamstring problem which probably put him at 80% fit. He tried to help the club out by playing and the fans didn't know he was struggling with injury, but that's just the man he is and he didn't want it publicised. So when you're 80% and playing against Manchester United in a semi-final, you're going to get found out. I told him to come out and publicly say he hadn't been fit but he's not that type of man, he says once he's out on the pitch he has to be doing the business which I respect."

Chapter 38

16th May 2005

Aftermath

Our coach driver for the journey out of Wales was a Smoggie and had already experienced the nightmare of getting out of Cardiff after a sold-out game. He said if we were fast back to the bus he would have us out sharp and we'd be the first bus back to Newcastle. So obviously we had to wait twenty minutes for two dozy twats who were either posing tearfully for the TV cameras or (more likely) grabbing a sneaky, selfish pint somewhere.

So it was that we became jammed in the knee-deep treacle of progress that can only add to the festering hatred that stout-hearted English folk feel towards Wales.

The stupid fucking made-up language on the road signs that you crawl past at half a mile an hour is enough to make you want to chew your own fucking legs off on its own. On top of that I'm dehydrated and my bag is full of nothing but stimulants; Red Bull, Pro Plus, Coke, Blue Charge. What I need is about four valium.

Three hours and six episodes of *Blackadder* later, Guy is still muttering "stupid made-up fucking language" at the road signs and you want to scream or cry. The only thing that raises a smile other than eight consecutive episodes of *Little Britain* is that none of us on my 'special bus' are going to Norwich on Wednesday. The very idea is horrific – six hours there and six hours back.

The coach stops for a second time, still miles from home and fans file off and wander around for fresh air or to suck greedily on tabs. Laughers, jokers and daft bastards are grim and fed up. The season is over and there is no upside.

If we could, we would have spat out the last dregs of the season on the forecourt of a South Midlands Shell garage but we couldn't. We had to live through it and it was awful. It was also frustrating, beset by niggling misfortune and very often boring.

There is no need to re-live it in any detail.

The fans who went to Lisbon and Cardiff and Norwich are the bravest, daftest and most wonderful of people and your heart had to go out to them after a Norwich goal in the fourth minute of injury time meant we lost 2-1 (Kluivert for us). The fact that they didn't think twice about going to Old Trafford four days later, for what was obviously going to be a thrashing, simply elevates them higher.

How bizarre then that we could have won. A sweet Ambrose goal put us one up and with 30 minutes remaining Man Utd had run out of ideas and inspiration. Rooney was about to be taken off and was barking in the face of the referee who was running to keep up with play. Rooney was only running in the same direction to continue his tirade when he suddenly looked up and saw the ball, which led to "The best goal I've ever scored". Wes Brown got a predictable winner.

Three days later and we were playing again. Home at last, against a Middlesbrough team pushing for Europe who lacked the balls to try and beat us. The state we were in they should have been scenting blood, instead they dug in like cowards, defended in numbers and our best chance (N'Zogbia) skimmed the bar in the last seconds. The numpties from Teesside celebrated this tedious stalemate with scenes of great jubilation. Strange folk.

Three days later we drew 0-0 with Crystal Palace and two things happened. Patrick Kluivert on as a sub, finished brilliantly but had his goal erroneously chalked off and Pepperami put promotional flyers on the backs of all our seats. Once it became clear that these could be folded into paper darts and that Agincourt could be re-enacted the crowd virtually ignored the football.

A cheer rose from the Leazes End as one expertly constructed device rode the thermals deep into the 18 yard box. The maker, rose arms outstretched, to receive generous applause while the ball bobbled around near the Gallowgate End. The pitch was soon littered with green paper planes, some stuck into the grass like javelins while the crowd whooped, clapped and encouraged the next. As a criticism of football it was probably the most hilarious and savage action this side of choosing a player, smearing him in gravy and releasing the hounds (which by this point many of us were in firm favour of). For the record, my own painstakingly folded effort spiralled violently into the back of some old lady's head five rows down.

Four days later and we finally found a team worse than us and the heroic away support finally got something back in a 3-1 win at Fulham. Ambrose, Kluivert and the sort of header Shola should score from every game (given his strength and stature) before Radzinski set hearts a-flutter with a goal for them in the 86th minute.

Three days later and we found another team worse than us. Bloody Everton. Hanging onto fourth spot and on course for the Champions League. Fucking rubbish team and hard evidence of the shoddy fucking state of English football when this bunch of huffers and puffers can finish fourth. Newcastle had been the better side for most of the first half when the ref felt sorry for the home team and awarded a free-kick for nothing. Presumably appalled by the decision our defence refused to mark as a point of principle and Weir scored.

In the second half Cahill overreacted to a Shola shove that saw Ameobi sent off and Cahill rubbed salt in by popping in a second for the Scouse mackems.

The final game of the season felt like a friendly. Our team clad in the latest kit (gold lettering and numbers – very nice) formed orderly lines and clapped Premier League Champions onto the pitch. The game ended 1-1. Well done Chelsea and congratulations on ruining football.

The sun shone and the relief that the season was actually over was too much for some. Frank Lampard was clapped by Newcastle fans when he took corners, Kluivert was cheered as he waved goodbye when substituted and unused sub Laurent Robert stole the show when he stripped down to a pair of saggy grey under-crackers and threw everything else into the crowd; boots, shorts, the lot.

Chapter 39

17th June 2005

Freedom Of Speech

In the hilarious, idiotic ballyhoo surrounding Lee Bowyer's attack on Kieron Dyer during the Aston Villa game, two people should have sat down in front of *Match Of The Day* that night and considered themselves very lucky indeed: Nicky Butt had a wretched game during which he never apologised to Steven Taylor for the terrible pass that directly led to our young defender's sending off. Also referee Barry Knight got clean away with a performance that was either bent or utterly inept. That's A: bent or B: utterly inept, there is no option C. 1-0 down and Newcastle had three solid penalties pompously waved away, whereas Villa were given a penalty for a challenge by Stephen Carr that, not only wasn't a foul but was also outside the area.

At least Knight *thought* he'd got away with it. Graeme Souness wasn't going to let it lie and brought the subject up after another display of boss-eyed buffoonery from the same official during our game at Goodison Park.

It must be said at this point that managers like Curbishley and Allardyce moaning on about the ref after every single defeat is getting very, very boring but Souness did little more than point out that the same ref had been in charge of both games and that he had been poor. For this our manager was fined £20,000 yesterday. That's twenty thousand pounds for expressing his opinion that was, as it happened, factually correct, given the chance Souness could prove Knight was in the wrong. Imagine, if after being filmed getting beaten up by the Los Angeles Police Department, Rodney King had pointed at the video and said, "Look, the police can be seen here whacking me with sticks," and was subsequently fined a five figure sum for bringing law enforcement into disrepute.

In Scotland last season Hearts asked politely for an independent enquiry into the impartiality of Scottish match officials after yet another sending off and last minute goal in favour of the Old Firm. They, like Souness, were charged with bringing the game into disrepute. It seems that you can't even ask a question, let alone attempt to come up with an answer when referees appear to be acting in a mad or irrational manner.

Are refs daft, cross-eyed, power-crazed Nazis intent on bringing ruin on the game? Is there some secret agenda afoot with Newcastle United's ruin part of some dark plot? Probably not but we'll never really know because no one is allowed to ask.

Meanwhile in Germany a third top flight match official has recently been investigated over match fixing. Presumably there they are allowed to ask awkward questions.

There is also a more fundamental point going unnoticed here, a point of great importance, which could have a massive impact on the game and what is said about it. Because yesterday the jury in the Harry Kewell v Gary Lineker trial was dismissed having 'failed to reach a verdict.' Lineker wrote a piece in *The Telegraph* about the fact that when Kewell signed for Liverpool his agent received £2 million. This upset Harry, presumably because Gary was suggesting he was a bit soft in the head.

Freedom of speech was under attack here, imagine if Kewell had won (and 'failed to reach a verdict' sounds like it was close) no one would be legally entitled to a written opinion. Film makers would be able to sue unfavourable critics for loss of earnings, bands on the cover of the *NME* would be able to sue me for telling you that they are an over-hyped bag of bollocks, with shit hair and not an original thought in their silly twattish heads. (*)

The next step from there is players, self-important little egomaniacs that they are, suing crowds for harassment when they get a hard time for being lazy, disloyal, greedy or shite.

Ashley Cole anybody?

(*)It is very important that you don't think I include Arctic Monkeys in this who are great. It's very encouraging to be assured that all you need in this country to make it in music is to write brilliant songs, be effortlessly cool and perform magnificently. No choreographed dance steps, Simon Cowell or gyrating dead- eyed sluts needed.

Chapter 40

12th July 2005

Excited Yet?

For Newcastle United the new season starts in four days' time and the giddy childish excitement that traditionally crackles around the place is notably absent. The city is baking under an unfamiliar, stifling sun and our football club is showing a vampiric avoidance of it. At St James' Park the box office is closed, you can stuff your Dubnica ticket application through the letterbox if you fancy going to an Intertoto Cup match this month but all is quiet. I pressed my ear to the door, expecting to hear some fiendish malevolent whispering from those within - but nothing. David Craig, a reporter from Sky Sports News, is perched on a wall with a cameraman in the shade presumably hoping for a burst of excitement unless they have finally taken root in that spot. A lucky, work-free few bask on the path with cold drinks outside Shearer's Bar but otherwise nothing. Scrawny young men go bare-chested rather than showing off the latest home shirt. Last week the first team squad were photographed cavorting in the sea during filthy, cold weather, presumably today they are indoors. Despite unloading six first team players many of the unloved and the unwanted remain among us, away from curious eyes.

Most fans who can be bothered to talk about football at all will have been troubled by the fact that last season Mr Souness complained about the small size of his squad and as things stand we have four players less than on May 14th. Does that mean we need at least six players in before we can consider ourselves ready for the season to start? The sale of Aaron Hughes doesn't make any sense otherwise.

This Intertoto lark has obviously knocked things a bit wonky because the first League game is four weeks away but shouldn't we be a bit more excited than this? As fans we need signings that will knock our socks off and (metaphorically at least) our socks remain firmly in place. Our chairman assured us that "everybody" wants to play here but none of us believe that. Perhaps Newcastle, like many other teams, are waiting to see who is left after Chelsea have had their pick of the world's talent. Maybe a host of quality players are waiting in the wings to avoid the embarrassment of turning out in the Intertoto fiasco. And indeed many have scoffed at what appears to be the unseemly grasping desperation of a club wanting to take part in a competition that means its players have to play more games than everybody else for a prize which is..... to play loads of games on Thursdays between now and March thus ruining any chance of domestic success.

But let us instead look on the bright side. At least this year our club can't now go swanning off on an inexplicable tour of the Far East, where everybody always seems to come back exhausted and confused.

But oh look, here's sunderland back from the lower Leagues again: standing on the doorstep like some halfwit embarrassment of a country cousin. Soppy toothless grin, cross-eyed, stains on his dungarees, frothing at the mouth and oh god, he's brought his suitcase. He thinks he can stay with us.

Chapter 41

23rd July 2005

FK ZTS Dubnica Anybody?

There was nothing to get excited about here. No Scotty Parker or Emre to inspect, no shiny new striker and no real chance of any danger to our qualification, just a lazy Saturday afternoon trying out other folks' seats. The only hint that this was a competitive European tie was the strict absence of beer for the proles and peasantry. A clever mate paid an extra couple of quid to get into the Platinum Club where you could be trusted to buy alcohol without bringing shame on the whole of European football or whatever it is they think the rest of us would do. This prohibition that UEFA enforces does seem rather daft when so many official sponsors are peddlars of beer (or "the Devil's own piss" as the black-cowled men who run European football probably call it when they are not busy cashing cheques from breweries).

Kev and Caz were even cleverer; they saved 12 quid each on match tickets, watched the game in a packed Shearer's Bar and got very, very drunk.

My normal row of seats was entirely empty of any company so I wandered off in search of familiar faces. These faces were found in seats with an annoyingly much better view of the pitch than my own seat affords. Bront, Frankie and Kev have been treated like ginger step-children by the club, turfed out of their seats in the Milburn Stand to make way for more upmarket clientele. For a while they had terrible seats low in the East Stand/Leazes corner, but fortunately they had the good sense to behave like ginger step-children and cried and complained until they were moved again. From this vantage point, central in the Leazes End, I enjoyed plotting a route into the Gallowgate. I was distracted from my plans with sporadic and rare outbreaks of football, a Jenas free-kick, the same player heading against the bar but mostly the mind was free to wander.

At last half-time came and I could set off on my adventure. My friend Guy had moved to the Gallowgate End and I intended to visit and inspect his new view. The one he had in the East Stand was clearly faulty and his opinions of games were often insanely wayward and wrong. I zig-zagged down from behind the goal, across the cinder into the East Stand, convinced I would be spotted and ordered back to my proper seat. But no, and out and along by the pitch I skulked, past a disinterested steward and free into the Gallowgate and a choice of views amidst the banks of empty plastic. It's dark and cold in this end and I don't like it. In the distance I could see the exact spot I had left, marked by the lurid green of Kev's lucky poker shirt (which once again would let him down) and a slumped mass of black that suggested Frankie had nodded off again. At this point I got a text from Guy demanding to know where I was because he had changed ends as well, this of course meant he got a view of the backs of Newcastle defenders heads for 90 minutes and I saw close up Shearer's two neat headers that won us the game. Apart from the goals the only thing that kept me plotting a third, more sensible, journey from seat to bar was the on-ball trickery of James Milner but I stuck it out and courtesy of a half-full ground, beat Guy back to The Three Bulls by a good ten minutes. Which was more exciting than the rubbish football match.

Chapter 42

10th August 2005

A Football Fan's Prerogative?

Football fans, it is always assumed, are a fickle breed of person. As a football fan I don't like this view and rage against it because it makes us sound stupid or shallow. It gives the impression of feeble minded sheep-like folk and pot-walloppers, easily hoodwinked by our betters, little more than a mindless mob who can be distracted or won over.

We have principles, dammit, and we will cling to them ferociously and proudly.

So how do I explain the following: 1) I wrote a happy little chapter celebrating our a hundred games in Europe but I now claim to be glad not to be in the UEFA Cup this year; 2) I have been spitting poison at Emre for years but now consider him a delight; 3) I spent three decades belittling, mocking and scoffing at cricket yet last Saturday showed more interest in it than in a home fixture at St James' Park; 4) I have always loathed Chelsea and consider them to be in the process of ruining football in this country, yet I clapped Frank Lampard at a corner in the last game of last season; and 5) as to my "favourite Newcastle player ever" I am now all, "Laurent who?"

The evidence looks damning – I appear to be more flighty than a daft girl in a Jane Austen novel, likely to giggle, faint or burst into tears because I got mud on my new dress.

Well, as Ms Austen wrote in Mansfield Park, "Let other pens dwell on guilt and misery. I quit such odious subjects as soon as I can" and as I write now, "Bollocks!"

It is the circumstances that have changed, not my morals, so…

The UEFA Cup has become a long drawn-out bore of a competition, packed to the doors with dull peasants, fearsome tramps and Middlesbrough. You are unlikely to play anybody interesting before the semi-final (which takes two thousand games to get to) and unless you actually win it, it is an utter waste of time and effort. Of course I like drinking and watching football on a Thursday night but that costs us football on a Saturday and unlike the Champions League, which is played on a Tuesday or Wednesday, our players seem unable to cope with the extra strain. This is in itself a savage indictment of the present state of Newcastle United, in that we simply haven't got enough top quality players to cope with two games a week and presumably most of the money the club earned last season from Europe was negated by our appalling League position (half a million pound a place). Obviously I write this before a smiling Freddie Shepherd drives a charabanc full of international signings through the gates of St James' the day before the Arsenal game but there is the outside chance that this won't actually happen. You could argue that as fans we will miss travelling to new and exotic places but I say, "What about Wigan?" So we should thank Robbie Elliott for the dreadful backpass against Deportivo that saw us dumped out nice and early.

Emre was the enemy and now he plays for us. Damn fine he looks too on the evidence of the Deportivo game, obviously it is going to take a little while for our club to iron out some of the bad habits he has picked up along the way. He, like Scotty Parker, must understand that this is a special club with different standards to those they are used to. So this wanting the ball, passing it to players on the same team and showing obvious enthusiasm and intelligence is going to have to come to a stop but we should enjoy it while it lasts.

Cricket used to be dull, boring, pointless and frustrating. Now Geoff Boycott drones on at length about "this is not proper test cricket" as balls are clobbered out the ground and wickets are violently uprooted every two minutes. Sport has to be exciting and cricket wasn't – now it is and compared to watching a glorified training session against a cockney pub team (Yeading) there is no competition. Only six thousand people on the planet disagreed with me by paying into the Church Of St James, which is great because what the people running this club have to understand very fucking quickly is that we are not going to turn up and empty our money into their pockets for pointless bloody games unless they put a team on the pitch that's worth paying to see.

I mention this because *The Mag* and *True Faith* were stuffed to bursting with bitter sniping about the reception afforded to Lampard but my point is this; the lad played a hundred games last year and ran his bollocks off in all of them, making the moaning of some managers about players being tired a pile of crap. Lampard has also gone from being a half-decent player to being a very good player by sheer force of will and never appears to moan about 'living in a goldfish bowl' like Mr Jenas and doesn't drift through games wasting his life like some snivelling, peanut-headed little fucking baby. Will I clap him against us in a game that actually means anything and will I stop hoping that Abramovich gets locked up for something awful and Chelsea end up £200 million in debt? No.

Robert has gone and I will try not to mention him again this season, even when we are struggling to score and there is a great big gap on our left hand side.

So as I said, it's the circumstances that have changed, not my loyalty and with the aid of strong drink I can sleep sound in my bed, thank you very much. Now can we please get on with the football?

Chapter 43

20th August 2005

There's A Coffin In My Soul

In the deepest pit of my living soul there is a coffin. I can't remember exactly when I became aware of it but it is one of those crude wooden affairs you find leaning against a wall in an old Spaghetti Western. Within it lies the twitching, barely alive and yet decaying stinking remains of My Love For Football.

My Love would shake me awake eagerly on the morning of any match but on the first home game of the season the excitement would make sleep impossible from first light, regardless of what time my head had hit the pillow the night before. The urge to run to the pub hand in hand had to constantly be restrained, the giddy joy of stepping into the Church Of St James together would almost make me cry. The sights, the smells, the noise. We used to dance drunkenly through the night streets of this beautiful city together without a care in the world. Either fat of wallet, pure of heart and gleeful in victory or skint, wet, filthy and defeated, we stood together, always at the start of something exciting.

Now the nails, long and cruel, are hammered home THUMP THUMP!

At first I felt quite pleased with the performance at Highbury but the more I thought about it the more it boiled my piss. Arsenal cheated and no one thought to accuse them in public. Arsene Wenger likes to play the role of cool ambassador with the game's higher principles, and his duties to them, close to his heart and the daft media are utterly hoodwinked. The ref had no view of the Jenas tackle on Silva and was conned, after all why would a six foot four inch hard-tackling man squeal like a tortured piglet if he hadn't been violently assaulted? And why would Ljungberg crash to the ground so, if he hadn't been tripped or shoved? Yes, yes, teams have always cheated and players have always dived but they were abused for it and questioned but no, not anymore. It is accepted, it is fair enough. THUMP THUMP!

International friendlies, one game into the new season? THUMP THUMP!
I got the new home shirt for my birthday and I would be lying if I said I didn't feel a tingle of excitement when I hauled it on for the first time. I did want to run to the pub and I would be insulting you if I even dared to suggest that hooking up with my crew of degenerates wasn't life affirming. In the ground it was a pleasure to see so many familiar faces who really should know better by now and the players coming out on a sunny summer afternoon on Tyneside... well where else would you rather be?

The banging from within the coffin was approval for Taylor and Da Boum at centre half and the firmest of nails were loosened by the performance of Scotty Parker who is quick, aggressive and assured. But...

No urgency, no width, no belief. The old fella struggling vainly around on his old knees up front by himself was tragic, the quality of his support frustrating and the performance of Jenas irritating beyond measure. The pouting little fucking baby.

He ponces about offering nothing and we are asked to love him, to encourage the poor lamb when we should be kicking him out or better yet, throwing him in the fucking river. THUMP THUMP THUMP!

West Ham were poor but we didn't have the brains to muster the intensity needed to break them down. Everybody could see that Konchesky made a brilliant saving tackle when foiling Jenas, who had a clear run at goal, but his sending off gave us a brief lift. Harewood (already booked) deliberately handling the ball should have given us another but you wonder how many men West Ham would have to lose before we scored a goal, seven or eight maybe?

Many have questioned the wisdom of playing Lee Clark but what a delight to see him home and on present form he is better than Jenas. He also had our best chance, darting into the box only to be thwarted by Carroll at full stretch.

The final whistle brought the expected jeers, a fine way to start a new season.

In this state of mind I am expected to hand over £36 to get into scabby bloody Bolton? To see us play with the same pitiful lack of imagination that went into the designing of our drab green/grey away kit, to see us lose 2-0 to Allardyce's odious fucking rabble? I don't bloody think so. THUMP THUMP THUMP THUMP!!

Chapter 44

7th September 2005

A Moment's Clarity

It was a Sunday morning some weeks back, I don't know what time it was because I couldn't muster the enthusiasm or energy to move my head to look at the clock. This being the case there was little point my bladder trying to get me out of bed, no matter how full it reckoned it was. A more pressing urgency was Newcastle's need for a new striker. Who was available? "Michael Owen isn't getting as many games as he hoped at Real Madrid. Yeah right, now if I can get to the toilet and back without opening my eyes all the way, I'm technically still asleep."

But I'm not asleep, the idea has wormed its way into my head, I'm convinced Newcastle are going to sign Michael Owen. I rushed to the TV and sure enough a panel of journos on *Jimmy Hill's Sunday Supplement* on Sky Sports were discussing Mr Owen's future. No mention was made of it concerning our club, I was unconcerned and merely imagined a smiling Freddie Shepherd steepling his fingers and saying "Excellent" like Monty Burns from *The Simpsons*. I instantly struck a deal with my (dark) self: as long as I didn't mention my belief it would happen.

Before you gasp at my powers as an oracle and politely enquire as to the winner of the 4.15 at Kempton or (more likely) demand to see my pants for evidence of lie-induced fire damage I should point out that Owen was only half the deal I had in mind, with David Beckham also, obviously, on his way. Sometimes, despite my best efforts, enthusiasm sweeps me away onto a steed of wild-eyed optimism.

Owen to Newcastle was a deal that made perfect sense providing our management and board had the balls to go for it. Michael Owen has always seemed more interested in England than any club side he may or may not be playing for, Liverpool fans have been grumbling about this for years. Fact:

there is a World Cup next summer, the lad needs games and goals and he wasn't going to see either at Real. Fact: Chelsea don't need him and nobody else can afford him. Arsenal and Man Utd said they didn't want him when in reality one has a new ground to pay for and the other blew this season's budget and more when we forced them to pay over the odds for Rooney last year.

It made sense that Owen would have to come here but that is not to say I was ever complacent because football often doesn't make sense and the words "Newcastle United" and "sense" only usually appear in a sentence also containing the words "no", "bloody" and "whatsofucking ever".

However, with the facts laid out and broken down, Michael Owen was bound for Newcastle like a Tall Ship last July.

Liverpool?

Bollocks, they were never going to pay £16 million for a player that they sold for £8 million a year ago and that is where our chairman deserves his pint bought. Whatever you think of Mr Shepherd (and I like to take a perverse view of liking him – mostly to annoy people) he played a blinder. Striding down Barrack Road with £16 million and his enormous balls in an enormous wheelbarrow, wearing nothing but a confident smile. *(I don't have to say "not literally" here do I? Obviously this is a metaphor, a heroic and enduring image, but a metaphor).*

"Real Madrid would only talk about £16 million," said Rafa Benitez *(not adding "and where did Freddie Shepherd get a wheelbarrow big enough for those enormous testiculos")* after the Liverpool talks crumbled. No shit Sherlock? The only thing that was odd was that Owen spoke to Liverpool at all. Owen may well have wanted to go there but I wanted to go to Chicago to see the Alkaline Trio play live this summer instead of going to work – life stinks, make the best of it and in Owen's case being paid a fortune to score goals for Newcastle is hardly working on the Burma bloody railway.

So you will forgive me for being more than a little pissed off at the attitude of the media when young Michael turned up at SJP with his shiny new contract, having to justify himself and explain the situation to people whose bastard job it is to think and write about football. A senior journo (Brian Woolnough) eventually asked why Michael was spending so much time talking about Liverpool when he was wearing a black and white shirt, Souness jumped in with a polite answer when the correct one was; "He's only answering the questions you dumb-ass, dimwitted drunks are asking, for Christ's sake."

Worse was to follow when Sky News somehow got control of Owen being introduced to the crowd, with newsreader Jim White in the role of ringmaster. White is a crocodile of a man, gleamy of eye and smiling all the time he is trying to eat you alive. His first question in front of 20,000 excitable children, their more excitable parents and a mass of people who were supposed to be at work was why didn't our new boy sign for Liverpool?

If they wanted to be unfair and unreasonable to the lad why didn't we go the whole hog and get Jeremy Paxman to ask Michael why he hadn't stopped New Orleans getting flooded?

An accidental window into the view of the media occurred later when White, introducing a piece from the Wales training camp, said, "Roy Evans was surprised none of the big clubs came in for Owen". Firstly Evans said nothing of the sort (he said he was surprised *more* big clubs didn't come in for Owen) and secondly, how big do you want us to be, bitch? Second in crowd only to Man Utd and second in money spent this summer only to Chelsea. Michael Owen signed for Newcastle United not fucking sunderland.

As to Beckham? Who needs the fucka when you've got Nobby back? So credit also to the fans who turned up at Owen's unveiling for singing Solano's name and by all accounts nudging the deal on. Souness could be seen encouraging the singing at this point, Nobby saw it and later said, "They have to understand that I love them too" as he dived through the closing transfer window from Aston Villa with James Milner going on loan the other way.

In the madness the fact that we had spent £10 million on Albert Luque and that Jermaine Jenas had been shipped out to Spurs was all but overlooked.

Chapter 45

10th September 2005

My Name Is Michael, Who The Hell Are You Lot?

Circumstances dictated that Newcastle had to give the rest of the Premiership a month headstart. The season was already up to September when we completed our squad building, which some were saying showed how truly crap our club is at planning for the future but the more charitable were saying, that's how long it took to get the players we wanted *(as the poet Bernard Wrigley said in 2007, "The early bird may catch the worm, but it's the second mouse that gets the cheese")*. We could have had a striker six weeks ago but that striker could not then have been Michael Owen and there would have been no Solano. So with that in mind, as well as the fact that half the first team squad has been away on international duty for the last ten days and with the terrible hamstring plague still afflicting all who enter the Old Indian Burial Ground at Longbenton (where the players are supposed to train), it was a bit much to expect this gang of strangers to hit the ground running.

But expect we did because we have seen it before, when our magnificent collective enthusiasm has defied all logic and produced a performance that renders circumstance irrelevant. There was even an element of old-school Keegan in the air: happy smiling drunk people in the sunshine, almost bouncing up to the ground, all thinking, "just chuck out the best 11 we've got and we'll roar the buggers home".

But it could never really be like that today. If Michael Owen had learnt the names of his comrades in the one day of training he had with them in the ten since he signed, he would have done well and he barely got a kick in the shambolic bloody bollocks-up that was the England defeat in Belfast.

Does circus music sometimes start playing in everybody's head at the match when Newcastle are defending? Well it does in mine, it did in Andy O'Brien's (all last season) and now it does in Steven Taylor's too. Oh good. One stupid back pass, easily intercepted and away we go; prat-falls, people falling over their own feet and crashing down on their stupid arses, big comedy double-takes and finally the ball dollied nicely into the Gallowgate End net. 1-nil to Fulham. Well done everybody, well fucking done.

It is well documented that Alan Shearer played a big part in getting Michael Owen to Newcastle United. You could forgive the latter for saying to the former at the restart, "Who are these fucking clowns and what the twatting hell have you done to my bloody career?"

It got worse, by half-time Luque had ruptured his hamstring and Taylor had wrapped himself heroically round the post clearing off the line. Both were replaced, by N'Zogbia and Bowyer respectively, by which point the heady atmosphere of the first five minutes had long since fizzled out.

It took our army of coaches over 70 minutes to realise what most people knew before the kick-off and Lee Clark eventually came on for Faye. Six minutes later Newcastle had scored their first Premiership goal of the season.

Owen was trampled on the edge of the box and from the free-kick N'Zogbia curled the ball into the keeper's top right corner with a velocity that momentarily stunned the crowd. Perhaps we had all forgotten what to do on seeing a goal but on *Match Of The Day* you could see Charles arms aloft and the East Stand utterly still.

We would have won from there. The crowd were up, the belief was flooding back, we had movement and enthusiasm but five minutes later Claus Jensen got through and Parker in pursuit put a hand on his shoulder. Jensen said later that Parker didn't pull him back but his first instinct was to go to ground and our best player was off and Newcastle were back to being a shabby mess.

We should improve as the players get to know each other, especially if we can find and kill the Hamstring Fairy.

Chapter 46

23rd September 2005

A Duty To Entertain

Football crowds are down. The banks of empty seats in this country are widening, the press, somewhat belatedly, have caught on and the hot topic is why?

Overpriced? Too many games on TV? Chelsea?

Maybe they are factors but the truth is most games in this country are now boring and a waste of time. Except for Newcastle United games where every kick is of vital importance to us – how many other teams in the country do you want to watch 90 minutes of?

Winning teams have always been strong at the back but now we have Greece as European Champions, Liverpool as European Club Champions and Bolton perceived to be a strong domestic team (who are also in Europe) on the back of tactics which involve organisation and safety above all else. And it's bloody awful to watch.

The game is riddled with cowards pretending to be football managers.

Blackburn Rovers manager Mark Hughes, at home, faced with a team who have won no League games this season and who had scored one goal, started with a lone striker. Arguably his best creative midfielder, Tugay, remained on the bench until his side went behind and afterwards he said, "I felt sure that if we had scored first we would have seen the game out." Do you think he wonders why all those people aren't in his ground on a match day? Yes, yes Blackburn have the worst fans in the League but at least some of them used to turn up.

Perhaps it was the sight of Craig Bellamy flinching when faced with the prospect of shaking hands with Alan Shearer before the kick-off but Blackburn lacked the gumption to win the game and even with Steven Taylor getting sent off, Newcastle won comfortably what should have been a tricky game. (Shearer: fucking rocket of a free-kick, Owen header and N'Zogbia performing the cutest trick to beat the keeper for the third).

Middlesbrough manager Steve McClaren: "If we had won a couple more games last season we would have been in the Champions League." And exactly whose fault was it that they didn't win a couple more games – if the evidence of the game at SJP against Boro and the grumblings of discontent from Teesside are anything to go by – that would be you Stevie old son and your yellow-bellied fucking attitude.

It gets worse because Alex Ferguson settled for a 0-0 draw at Anfield on Sunday and whatever your opinion of Manchester United you have to admit they always used to try to win games. It was frightening the way they just used to keep chucking on more strikers, yet Ryan Giggs stayed on the bench until the 89th minute and the match, like so many others already this season, drifted drearily towards its obvious, goalless conclusion.

Something has to be done now before the rot really sets in because getting crowds back is going to be harder than keeping them. Firstly the phrase, "It's not my job to entertain people" as uttered by Mourinho and Bryan Robson going into games last weekend should be considered to be bringing the game into disrepute and punished accordingly. Robson can be forgiven because his game turned out to be hilariously entertaining (last minute equaliser at sunderland) but it costs between 48 and 60 quid to pop into the Bridge for a match this season so the obvious message to Jose is, "yes it bloody well is".

The problem is that you can't make teams attack. Everton got into the Champions League with a negative goal difference last season and to not get relegated all you had to do was scramble six wins and sixteen draws out of thirty eight matches (West Brom).

The problem isn't making Newcastle games more interesting because we are always a calamity waiting to happen which is to be enjoyed as far as the rest of the country is concerned. What we need is to reward the adventurous at the expense of the cautious. So I will be proposing a fourth point for teams scoring three goals or more at all future opportunities. A 3-3 draw has to be preferred over a 0-0 and teams getting two up are bound to leave the back door open a bit whilst going for a third. Instead of games tailing away after one team has gone 2-0 up, sides will be going at it like rabbits in spring until the 94th minute. No one will dare leave early and Steve McClaren will never get to be

England manager – so we all win.

I've just saved football – hooray for me!

Obviously no one paid serious attention to this sound reasoning; the majority of games still remain dreary drivel and Steve McClaren did get to become England manager. Now England are boring as well as bollocks. Why won't people listen?

Chapter 47

8th October 2005

Missing Home Matches

Traditionally one feels a mixture of disgust and pity at the news that a fellow season ticket holder is due to miss a home match. Work, weddings, funerals and especially holidays are things that can be manoeuvred around and failure to do so shows a lacking of essential moral fibre. How can someone claiming to be a Newcastle fan allow themselves to be coerced into a position where something other than the match takes any kind of priority. Knowing their excuses to be as flimsy as their backbones, they smile thinly and make pathetic claims of having a radio in their pocket in the church / on the beach / as granny coughs out her last goodbyes but we all know it won't do and we all know where they would rather be.

Well, between the start of the season and Christmas I plan to have missed four home games, wilfully and with malice aforethought.

Life's too short and the world's too big to spend every waking hour waiting for our latest bunch of feckless underachievers to get their arses in gear. It's not a case of wanting to see them win trophies (we never expected that) and it has now gone beyond the point where it would be nice to see them play to their potential. The hope of them collectively arriving on any given pitch, fit and ready to play, now seems like wishing for the moon on a stick and the endless waiting for it to happen is maddening. So "fuck it", thought Wifey and I, "let's miss some games and see what happens."

We had a little warm-up by missing the Man Utd match. Choosing the Leeds Festival instead was easy because Newcastle nearly always play well but lose at home to Man U, which is always hard to witness in the face of those smug red swine. The non-appearance and subsequent disappearance of Transplants from the festival (just as they were about to break big style with their infectious rap/punk mash-up belligerence) was slightly offset by England beating Australia in the Test Match and an incendiary set from Rise Against.

A sterner test was deliberately putting ourselves in a situation where we couldn't even find out a game's score if we wanted to – so after eight months of preparation (basically lots of walking and getting Solano put on the back of my Toon top) we found ourselves on a plane to Peru as Newcastle kicked off against Manchester City.

At Lima airport we were met by our guide, Shane, and taken through the dusty ramshackle streets of Nobby Solano's home town to a hotel that was miles better than we had been given to expect. The crapping in a hole in the ground would come later.

If you read enough guide books about Peru you come to expect amoebic dysentery and a violent mugging within an hour of getting off the plane ("you may wish to line the inside of your rucksack with chicken wire to prevent it getting slashed" – were people really prepared to go to such extreme lengths to steal my spare pants?) Shane put our party's mind at ease and more importantly told me that Owen had scored for Newcastle and that he thought we had won 1-0, which wasn't the solid information we needed but it had to do until the morning.

Wifey and I, excitement and wonder getting the better of fretful and travel-frazzled, set out to explore. The impoverished traveller look is advised, no watches, wallets or jewellery on show *(and I do so like to dress as Mr T when on holiday)*, we still felt we were glowing shiny white and touristy, while leathery women of indeterminate age stared at us. A few beers took the edge off but the nagging doubt that we might not actually be able to manage this holiday was ever present. Lima is at (Pacific) sea-level but the majority of our adventure would be at altitude. Would our heads explode, would the four day walk along the Inca Trail be too hard, would the food or snakes or our new travelling companions kill us?

You have little option but to get another beer in and think "probably not".

Peru is a fascinating and fantastic country, a mass of contradictions and climates. Coasts, deserts, snowy mountains, jungles, cloud forests; the Incas understood architecture, trigonometry and astronomy and could build perfect walls without mortar (that we still can't replicate). This is even harder to get your head round when you consider that they never had any concept of the wheel or Hell until 150 Spaniards conquered a nation of millions and grafted

Catholicism to the indigenous religions.

An example of which is a reworking of 'The Last Supper' in Cusco (the ancient Inca capital) that has Christ and the apostles at a table which has the traditional Peruvian dish of guinea pig served on it.

We didn't eat guinea pig but we saw one cooked and it looks horrible. For a start they leave the head on, so you can tell you are not getting cat or rat. Then it looks like they set fire to it and wallop it with a shovel, so it's flat and black and its face is twisted into a last silent scream. It's apparently also picky and unsatisfying, unlike alpaca, which is a smaller cuter cameloid than a llama, that provides softer wool and scrumptious low-in-cholesterol steaks. Salads should be avoided because they are washed in the water, which the European constitution can't stomach unboiled. What a world, where steak, chips and beer is health food.

Our tour worked its way higher as the days went on to make the acclimatisation as gentle as possible but it's still hard, Wifey's nose bled intermittently for the first few days, we felt light-headed and breathless, walking half a mile was an ordeal but then comes the coca tea. A handful of the dried leaves with boiling water has a miraculous effect. There's no head rush, (you have to add chemicals and process the stuff to get cocaine) but you feel almost instantly better. Powered by the stuff we hiked to hot spring water pools, white water rafted on the Urubamba River, got up at the crack of dawn to see condors rising on the early morning thermals over the Colca Canyon and eventually started the Inca Trail.

The Inca Trail is brutal, even with eight months of struggling around the Cheviots, the Lake District and up Ben Lomond under our belts, we suffered. Hot and rocky, you climb for hours but then going down is no bloody picnic either with irregular steps jarring your knees and ankles. You are surrounded at different points by wild orchids, humming birds, mountains, bubbling streams and vast blue skies and all you can think about is putting one dusty foot in front of the other.

At the end of the first day Wifey and I got into a campsite game of football with the porters. On a bumpy pitch, viciously booby-trapped with tent ropes and with no suitable footwear I may well have disgraced our entire hemisphere, except for an unexpected dominance in the air (Peruvians are generally hardy, skilful but tiny) which will come as a surprise to anybody who has played with me over the last 30 years. Then, as if by magic, a boss-eyed girl appeared with a bucket full of bottles of cold beer, we drank them all, paid her and asked nicely for more. Half an hour later she was back, smiling and looking happily in different directions, her wonderful bucket (which we christened 'The Inca Arms') re-stocked. I sat talking with our guide Edwin who looked calmly at my sweaty black and white shirt, then waving at all the porters and cooks said, "We are all Newcastle United fans here. We are very proud of Solano". Over the next few days he added, "Howay the Lads" and "I hate sun' land" to his impressive English, although the phrase "rough as a badger's arse" left him blinking in the early morning Andean sunshine, when he asked how I was on the morning of the last day. He in turn introduced us to Cienciano who play in Cusco and are fiercely provincial and well supported: two years previous they won the South American equivalent of the UEFA Cup. They were a team lacking in stars but they defended heroically away from home, then at altitude at Cusco merely waited for the opposition to lose the ability to breathe before winning the game. In the two-legged final, however their Argentinean opponents refused to go to Cusco and so the home game was played in Lima. Reportedly 30,000 fans descended on the capital and Cienciano won and then went on to Miami to win the Super Cup the year after.

Second day in and a fellow traveller said, "I haven't come halfway round the world to talk about football," and Shane replied, "In that case you have come to the wrong continent."

The same day Newcastle were scratching out a point at Portsmouth, Cienciano scored to make it 2-1 with four minutes left, and the opposition players (Alliance from Lima) pursued the ref from the field who promptly abandoned the match. The porters, with enormous radios strapped to a couple of the awesome piles of luggage on their backs, shoved one another and laughed.

I think it was at this point that I got too cocky. I was shovelling some yellow gloop into my face at lunchtime and Wifey asked, "What's that?"

"Dunno", said I, "but it's nice, I'm getting some more." The afternoon was dreamy, we were now so high that the exhausting climbs were over for the day, the sun shone radiant beams through the lush green cloud forest and humming birds and butterflies danced across the flowers. Our porters had set up camp on some cliff tops that overlooked the mountains that hid the ancient, abandoned Inca city of Machu Picchu, the view was stunning and we were rewarded for our having done the hard part of the Trail with a bottle of rum.

Something happened between the yellow gloop and the rum; I will spare the obvious details but the highlight of a long fucking night was a desperate scramble to get out of my tent that ended with me sliding out on my knees like David Beckham, after his goal against Greece but with one boot on (the wrong foot) and violently projectile vomiting over the cliff edge.

The next day was hot and hard as we climbed up to the Sun Gate and there was a lot of slumping on my behalf but the dub reggae on my Walkman and a determination to not be the soft shite got me there. Out of our party of ten, everybody had been ill to some degree at some point, with one lad having to be taken back after the first night, so the pace was never explosive but the outbreak of communal relief and emotion at the Sun Gate was enthusiastic.

The Sun Gate looks down on Machu Picchu, if you've seen pictures of this world wonder, they are probably from this point and it is beautiful and magnificent. For a second or two you don't even notice the tears running down your sweaty, grimy face. A rainbow appeared below us on the climb down and it felt like a reward from the Inca Gods.

The hot shower and the cold bottle of beer we had that night in Aguas Calientes were two of the most luxurious things I've had in my whole life. Aguas Calientes looks like a wild west frontier town with a rail track running up the main street, walking boards for paths and wooden houses built into the mountainside.

The next day you feel inclined to haul your scruffy clothes back on when revisiting Machu Picchu, so as not to get confused for one of the fucking daytrippers. The train from Cusco is the only other way to the ancient city and you have to suppress a loathing for the well-scrubbed fuckers with their pristine hiking gear and their stupid fucking little foldy-up walking sticks. The fact that we were cooked for and had our heaviest gear carried for us is irrelevant. Obviously.

When Edwin had guided us up to the centre of the city a pair of condors flew low over us, casting shadows like a pterodactyl attack. In all his trips there, Ed said he had never seen such a thing and we felt lucky and special. We gave him a Newcastle shirt and he e-mailed us to say he wears it all the time on the Trail.

The train back to Cusco takes four hours and what a city; vibrant and buzzing after the silence of the mountains. It has shops, markets and bars including the highest Irish owned bar on the planet and the famous Cross Keys which is run by the British consulate, has football shirts all over the walls and has beer and chips and beer and chips and beer and chips.

In the streets a Newcastle shirt is greeted with a smile; people who are on the whole reserved, stop you or shout "Solano" at you but my favourite moment was whilst stumbling back to the hotel when a guy said "Ah, Newcastle, Nobby eh, you wanna buy some coke, ees very good?"

We returned to the UK in good time for the game at Wigan utterly guilt free, safe in the knowledge that Wayne, who had my season ticket, would have done equally as well as I ever could in the drinking beer and shouting incomprehensible garbage at the pitch duties. I was, (slightly) wiser, fitter and better travelled while my team and manager appeared to have learnt little. Newcastle United's performance in the Wigan game was a fucking disgrace and I wondered if the Cross Keys needed bar staff.

Chapter 48

23rd October 2005

Newcastle United 3 v sunderland 2

If the balance of power between Newcastle United and sunderland over the last 25 years were represented by people on either end of a see-saw the black and white end would have Brian Blessed, Geoff Capes, Audley Harrison, The Denver Broncos and the population of fucking China on it whilst trying to balance this out on the daft deckchair coloured end would be Jarvis Cocker in his silliest glasses and the girl from *Little House On The Prairie*, weeing herself. Newcastle regularly qualifying for Europe while sunderland are perpetually making fools of themselves and getting relegated.

However, sunderland insist on being treated as equals which means the perception of the relationship in the media has got twisted out of shape. So in the interest of balance when reporting an up and coming derby, the media must rehash one of two somewhat bizarre sunderland wins in 25 years. So they get to keep their finest moment alive whilst setting the clock back quicker than a dodgy second-hand car salesman within a month of us beating them, yet again, on their way to another relegation. At which point like a yappy dog they will start barking at us from the safety of another division.

The drunkest Newcastle fan should be able to humiliate up to half a dozen sober mackems if the mood takes him/her otherwise he/she should be getting along home because it's that fucking easy. The best idea, if stuck, is just to soak up all the hatred, then just laugh in their slack-jawed faces.

So, people singing "Stand Up If You Hate sun/land" are shouted down in my area of The Leazes End because it's better to give the impression that they are irrelevant and shouldn't be taken seriously. However, if you should find yourself in The Stadium Of Light (not the real one in Portugal obviously) when the inbred, rat molesters are at home, a large number of their songs are about Newcastle. This is because they are obsessed with us and hide in the metaphorical bushes of our life, wearing filthy trousers and rubbing themselves furiously when stuff goes wrong for us. We should get a restraining order on them where they have to stay at least two leagues away from us at all times. But instead we have to put up with their fucking stupidity.

If there is one thing they are consistently good at in sunderland it's being a pack of self-deluded fucking gasbags. They went into this game surprisingly full of themselves. It seems getting battered 3-1 at home by Man Utd had given them cause for unbridled optimism, ignoring the fact that Man Utd are a bit shit at the minute and the ease with which Van Nistelrooy brushed past Caldwell for one of the goals. At work I was trying to maintain a look of calm confidence, this was misinterpreted: "Youse are scared!" declared one of the enemy.

"I am scared of many things my good man, but your fucking football team is not one of them." It's my own team that scares me but I'm not letting him know that.

The odd thing was the amount of Mags who were struck down with serious fear, whose heart rates fluttered to the tune of Owen's twanging hamstrings. Shame on you, cowardice in the face of the enemy simply will not do. And anyway, standing in for Owen we had Shola.

It may seem all well and good being wise after the event but Ameobi was obviously going to win us this game. Partly because we have seen Caldwell play for us and we know he is a useless bag of arse, partly because the service from midfield would be better with Emre and Solano playing but mostly because Shola's brilliance would be a huge double-edged sword; winning us the match but condemning us to countless future games where we wonder what the hell it is that he is actually trying to do.

I explained this argument in the pub to bemused faces. Our company has been at civil war over Shola for ages, Guy leading the pro-camp in the face of, what sometimes seem like insurmountable odds, against Bront who recently took to calling the coat stand in the bar Shola due to its lack of mobility. Guy is invariably hopelessly outnumbered, I stay out of it but, like the British during the American Civil War, amuse myself by selling arms to both sides. But not today, to squash my own fear I hung my coat on Shola and shared the abuse that Guy usually has to manage alone.

I had in my heart the belief that this game was Shola's *Motown Junk* (the precise moment when Manic Street Preachers stopped being rubbish gits and started being brilliant) that he would suddenly be the player England need to stop Peter Crouch playing in the World Cup – but was I ever that optimistic? Well by ten o'clock that night, maybe, but I digress too far.

The familiar revulsion at the sight of the Legion Of The Unbathed in their clown suits in our ground is always jarring, a festering ugly sore up on Level 7. Communally this is easily suppressed because beer and hate had eventually dimmed the fear in the nervous. Also as a crowd we get heroically offended by those contrived little huddles stupid teams do to convince the world they are a bonded unit (Madonna and her dancers were doing the exact same thing 15 years ago – make of that what you will).

A booking for Whitehead's awful tackle on Emre inside 40 seconds set the tone for a decent show from ref Styles and bad tackles were fewer and further between than we would expect against sunderland and credit to Mick McCarthy for actually coming for a game of football.

And a game of football he got, with Newcastle slick in possession and Solano and Emre's extra class obvious. Rarely trapping a ball, they just passed it instantly and moved. More of this please, but from the start Shola Ameobi was awesome; his control, so often bewilderingly bad, was excellent, his power was frightening and most of all his obvious desire to impose himself on the game was thrilling. He had already had a header and a shot saved when Emre put a corner right on the crest of his leap and the ball tore into the net.

Lawrence's shot, seconds later, looked to have taken a deflection from where I was sitting but I might just be being kind to Given, who moved late. Whatever, after half an hour of utter dominance we had let the fuckers straight back into the game.

A minute later Carr crossed deep, the Zog pulled it back and Shola headed down and off Caldwell to put us back in front. Now we would win easily because there was no way this shower of shite were going to get two and anyway what would be the chances of them belting two from distance past a keeper as good as Given and ….oh bollocks. Elliott's shot was unsaveable.

The second half took about four hours. Short of games, Solano and Emre understandably ran out of steam. Parker and Boumsong were unaccountably awful. Carr was hobbling and Ramage (out of position at left-back) looked all too vulnerable.

Then on the hour Caldwell clumsily brought down Shola ten yards outside the penalty area. Emre, Solano and Shearer stood over the ball as the red and white wall twitched and shuffled away. After a brief chat, Shearer trotted goalwards and Emre Belozoglu scorched his name into the brains of all who bore witness. An evil, spinning shot fizzed round the wall, biffed off the post and delightfully billowed the Gallowgate End net. While the fat end of 50,000 fans exploded into each other's arms, Emre sprinted to Souness to do the same. A nice touch.

Two minutes later Steven Taylor had a close range header blocked that would have settled matters, he knew it too and stood for a second with his shocked head in his hands.

If you were at the game and heard a faint crash 20 minutes from time, that was my bottle and I wasn't alone. We started giving the ball away (even Emre), losing our composure and the panic spread faster than fire on dry grass. Taylor cleared off the line from Lawrence who might have had a penalty if he hadn't thrown himself down so desperately. Too many of our player's legs had gone and sunderland, happy to be relegated if they win here, pressed forward.

Ameobi was replaced by Chopra, Faye came on for Emre and Clarkie came on for Nobby. Lee Clark would surely sooth my jangled nerves, "sit in deep kidda, keep the ball, pass sensibly. No don't go up there near Shearer, retreat boy retreat!"….then from horrid defending, Stephen Elliott was clear on our left and he instantly chipped Shay and the world stopped.

Everything stopped because the ball was on its way to the net and it would be 3-3 in exactly half a second. Home crowd and home team resigned themselves to the worst.

Real time caught up with the rattle of the cross-bar and Given instantly uprooted from the spot, and with the tattered remains of our defence, he scrambled the ball clear.

Boumsong and Parker were our men of the last ten minutes. Leading by example, tackle and boot it. Chopra had the chance to win the game for sure, with sunderland pushed up he got the ball on the halfway line. He didn't even have to score as long as he didn't lose it. He lost it. Amazingly he got it back and instantly lost it again. This rendered me a gibbering wreck to the point that I couldn't scream abuse at the whistling home fans who were making the panic worse.

The relief took two pints to wash away leaving only purest joy on the faces of the delirious degenerates who call Newcastle home. The city was alive with the sloshing of innumerable drinks and endless cheering at re-ran televised goals.

Years ago sunderland hijacked the draw (home or away) as a moral victory, which was fine because it displayed an admission of inferiority but we can not have them claiming anything out of losing surely. Amazingly there was a gobshite mackem on the Metro as the emotionally drained stragglers went home; "Youse were lucky". Really? They get to play us with eight players who could have expected to be in our starting 16 injured (Owen, Dyer, Luque, Harper, Babayaro, Elliot, Moore, Bowyer) and we were lucky? Not to mention the five who were or should have been replaced in the actual game (Carr, Parker, Emre, Solano, Ameobi).

They haven't outplayed us over 90 minutes since the play-off game in 1990 yet still they whine on. Wanting to be treated as our equals but also demanding the right to be heroic underdogs, their finest hour since then did us a favour (ridding us of mad-boy Ruud) and we have now beaten them four games in a row. Taking 12 points to their none and can you imagine the noise they would have made if they had taken us on with six local lads in their squad – I give you Taylor, Ramage, Clark, Shearer, Chopra and man of the match, Mr Shola Ameobi).

I don't say any of this to Captain Gobshite, I just laugh. As ever this plugs into a nerve; "What ave youse ever won?" he demands.

"Plenty of games of football, playing better football than you could ever imagine?" Behind me someone cheers, which gives me the confidence to add a smile.

"We ate yers, we really fucking ate yers!" he rants as the doors open at our stop.

"Good," I say, but Wifey upstages me with just about the perfect answer; "We think you're funny."

mackems man – self-deluded fucking gasbags!

Chapter 49

6th December 2005

Missing Home Matches (part 2)

I flickered into life the morning of the Birmingham game in a Berlin hotel thinking I had taken this cutting my nose off to spite my face thing too far. I was desperate to see Newcastle play, St James' Park, my favourite place in all the world would be hosting another grand party and here I was in bloody Germany.

I felt another pang of homesickness when I came across a gang of fat blokes in football shirts, drinking in the rain at 10.30 in the morning. Hertha Berlin were at home and many of our party of 18 lads and lasses, over to celebrate the birthdays of The Big J.Bizzle and The Boy Rangecroft, would be going. Personally I couldn't see the point of watching another football match instead of Newcastle United and wandered up to the Brandenburg Gate in the rain instead, but they had a fine time and Hertha won 3-0.

But the harsh truth is that I had made a choice and it was the right one. Not just because Newcastle v Birmingham stank like the Devil's own privy but because I will remember Berlin and the fine people who went, longer than I would yet another non-descript Premier League fixture.

Anyway, God bless Easyjet, cos Berlin rocks. Its metro ran all night and the drinking establishments stayed open to provide its passengers. The people were helpful and friendly and aside from ending up in a club where they played Wham back to back with Rage Against The Machine, you couldn't knock the atmosphere. We all had our perception of the world rocked a bit as well; after growing up with old war films, *'Allo 'Allo* and the German stereotype perpetuated by the crappy end of the media, you couldn't shake the feeling that we Brits have got the Germans all wrong. Even drunken youths dropping bottles on the pavement at three o'clock in the morning had a polite gentleness that made you feel embarrassed in advance of the England fans who would be descending on the place for the World Cup. Mock Nazi salutes, with their hilarious T-shirts and comedy goose-stepping.

And what did I miss? The Birmingham game. By all means form a queue over here to tell me I made the wrong choice.

Nationally this season is a write-off, Chelsea are going to win the League and sunderland and two other nests of pointless knackers will drop out with them. For all they are wobbling, Man United and Arsenal will finish in the top four which means the battle for fourth place will be the only story of interest, which is a pretty shabby state of affairs. Winning a Cup or finishing fifth or sixth will only subject a team to the dreary, tramp-ridden UEFA Cup with games against A.Z. Bumzbollix and a once in a lifetime chance to travel to Shaktar Kuntbuket.

Why do you think the media went so overboard on the death of George Best, he hasn't kicked a ball in 30 years? It's because football can't generate enough interest to fill the massive media monster that it's created for itself. Hourly updates on the fading health of an old drunk haven't dominated as much headline space since the Queen Mother pegged it and most normal people didn't give a fuck about her either.

Oh and while we're on the subject, many of our papers had quotes in from loveable old George but I didn't see anyone reproduce the one published in *The Guardian* the week Newcastle sold Andy Cole to Man Utd: "It's a lot of money to spend on a nigger". And I'm expected to stand still and shut up for a minute for that feckless twat am I?

Missing a live football match this season is little more than missing the opportunity to get pissed with your mates and I'm not alone in widening my horizons on a traditional match day. It has become obvious that a lot of Newcastle fans are missing home games; our pub-crew numbers have been fluctuating wildly and within the ground even the most regular faces are becoming distinctly irregular.

But here's the killer, I can't actually stand it. It's awful, my world is disjointed, the local press seems silly but at the same time I have been struck by this insane notion that Newcastle United have got the players to finish the season strongly and that I want to see it happen. Our surprising and spectacular 3-0 away win at West Brom, where Michael Owen scored twice, only fuelled my belief. The abject second half at Everton and the awful 90 minutes against Wigan have only partially dampened my enthusiasm because

I was not there. I also missed the 1-1 Villa draw at home (because Easyjet can get a scruffy, comprehensive school-educated oik like me to Rome to look for Caravaggio paintings as well), which proves an age-old point of mine – that people who miss matches don't know what the fuck they are on about and they should be ignored.

Chapter 50

10th December 2005

I Don't Like Arsenal Either

Arsene Wenger is clearly a wizard of some sort, taking the most boring, ugly team in England and turning them into a thing of staggering beauty is some feat. However, a tatty blonde wig would make him look so much like an old transvestite that it is often difficult to take the man seriously; this allied to his wonky way of looking at the world when things aren't going well for his team make him a hard person to love. His ramblings after this game sunk him to a new low. Never shy about looking over other team's fences to pass comment on the state of their gardens (as Jose Mourinho put it recently, "he is a voyeur and it is a sickness") whilst ignoring the fact that his own patch looks like Steptoe's yard, he actually made himself look sillier than ever and that, short of wobbling about on high heels, takes some doing.

"I do not want to go overboard on Alan Shearer…" then he proceeded to do just that for Sky and then the BBC, "I would like someone watch the video with me and explain…"

Ooo oo me me me me – please me!!

If Madame Wenger has nothing better to do with his time than sit around watching controversial stuff from Newcastle/Arsenal matches and he wants some company then pleeeeese let me do it.

You see no one bears a grudge like me when it comes to Arsenal…. I remember Martin Keown kicking Alan Shearer's legs away AND throwing him to the ground in the Gallowgate penalty area before accusing Shearer of diving. I remember Sol Campbell going through the back of Laurent Robert and Arsenal attacking the ref for giving the penalty, when Campbell should actually have been sent off as well. In the same game Ray Parlour committed five bookable offences before he was dismissed when Craig Bellamy walked for waving his fingers near an Arsenal player's face, who in turn went down like he had been hit with an axe. Arsene and I can enjoy all those again and others if he likes. I am particularly keen to open the box marked 'Ashley Cole' and if anyone from Highbury would like to explain when it was that the offside rule stopped applying to them – then I am all ears. Seriously, on this last point, once you realise that about a third of their goals are tap-ins from a yard out with the ball having been passed forward beyond the last defender it gets really bastard irritating.

Perhaps Wenger wants to limit our video session to this season – Ljungberg diving for the penalty and Silva squealing like a little bitch to get Jenas sent off at Highbury. Shit, I'm even prepared to go through just this game if time is a problem. Ljungberg diving in the penalty area. Again. Van Persie demonstrating that he is hatched from an identical egg to Denis Bergkamp by aligning sublime touch and breathtaking vision to being both sneaky and cowardly in the tackle. And that chance where Henry missed a sitter at the far post in the first half? Off fucking side!! And who mentioned it, even locally? Nobody. Henry was ahead of the last defender when the ball was passed and the ball was passed forward – not a bloody flicker – from anybody. That's because Arsenal score so many offside goals that everybody thinks it's great football – it's not, it's off bloody side. But the highlight of our little meeting, and what I really want most of all is for the snotty-faced fucker to look me in the eye and say Lehmann knocking Scotty Parker's tooth out was an accident. He would be speaking 12 different languages through bits of video recorder for a fortnight.

Arsene says he wants "protection" for his players, no he doesn't, he wants privilege for his players – to do as they please. And all too often over the years he has been getting it, remember Arsenal won the corresponding fixture here last year after committing twenty three fouls to our seven.

But we must not get too carried away, this game was a glorious oasis of justice and normal service will be resumed all too soon. Most refs are simply too daft to see how sneaky the whole Arsenal institution actually is.

Arsenal are often sumptuous of course and Henry, Van Persie and Hleb spent the first half passing the ball to each other so fast that few teams could have lived with them. It's all well and good us fans screaming at our defenders to 'close them down' but a man can't outrun a well passed ball which led to the chance Henry had, a shot that Given made such an exceptional save from that the Frenchman himself led the congratulations.

But enough of the burgundy Gunners, this game was actually Attack Of The Scapegoats with all our recent victims playing an important part. Henry never scores when Boumsong is marking him. Faye put in a hell of a shift, no one with eyes could fault Ameobi's effort and those who think Bramble's solid tackling was let down by poor passing should remember whose swift ball it was out to the wing that started the move that created our goal.

I boasted earlier that no one holds a grudge against Arsenal like I do. Obviously that was a lie in the heat of the moment that ignored every Spurs fan on the planet and Mr Alan Shearer.

Arsenal obviously get right up the old fella's nose and he set out on a personal crusade to destroy them through sheer force of will. Obstructed by Lauren, he threw his marker to the floor via a firm grip on his throat and as Arsenal dallied over a throw-in, the venom and contempt with which he lashed the ball into the advertising hoarding spoke volumes. By the time he wound up Lehmann like a clockwork dog by nudging him, then pointing at his wrist when the German complained, the crowd were shaken to life by the scent of enemy blood. Along with the magnificent Scotty Parker, our captain led a brutal, physical and mental assault on The Gunners – and we, the pessimistic moaners, shook off our melancholy and were roused. Roused! Oh how we were roused!

A Shearer knockdown saw Parker flash a shot just over, Parker then slid a ball through that Shearer smashed into the side netting and we in the stands started to believe. Intensity, urgency and aggression melded to purposeful passing and regular chances are all we require to do our part. And as we jacked up the volume so Arsenal wobbled until Gilberto, booked for a cynical foul on Shola in the first half, again stuck out a leg to flatten Boumsong and was off. Arsenal could not begin to break out at this point. Lehmann caught a corner and hurled a ball forward but Elliott crunched into a tackle and Parker flashed a shot just over.

Where the ref and linesman were standing in relation to Lehmann scooping up a ball then launching himself, elbow first, into Parker's face is beyond me. But our lad lost a tooth and we lost our Man Of The Match and Wenger's mob got clean away with it.

God love Scotty for trying to carry on but Toure landing on his head a couple of minutes later was more punishment than he deserved or needed.

The goal came when another Arsenal break was dashed on the rock that was Titus Bramble, who clipped a cute ball straight out to the wing. The possession was worked across to Solano on the right, who angled a ball in that Shearer had to rescue moving across the area. Shearer, tenaciously dug in and re-fed Nobby who took a touch then hit the ball straight back across Lehmann into the bottom corner. In slow motion it is a goal of great beauty, at the time it simply fizzed into the inside netting.

Henry would have had a chance to get a goal straight back except for a solid tackle from Ramage who had a fine game and aside from the whistling of a handful of cowards we saw out the five minutes of time added on with little concern.

I haven't mentioned Michael Owen at all yet. His inclusion gave the whole ground a lift, his menace worried Arsenal all day and the chance he had at the end was only a chance by his standards. It was only missed through lack of match sharpness, nipping in behind a defender, to pull a ball down that just got away from him with only the despicable Lehmann to beat.

I scoured the media for sympathy with Wenger's belief that Alan Shearer and bully-boy tactics beat his team and was pleasantly surprised to find nothing of the sort.

Chapter 51

12th December 2005

The Media Hates Us

Alex Ferguson recently claimed that the media hate Manchester United. It was a weird moment as every football fan in the country stopped, blinked and thought, "Not as much as it hates my team". Who do the media actually like? I can't shake the impression that they will be opening champagne in the street if Abramovich ever got carted off to some gulag in the dead of night. There was open-air scoffing at Wenger's whining about Shearer, and England's management and players are always fair game for all comers. The BBC is riddled to the core with Spurs fans but my good friend Tim, a Tottenham fan of many a painful year, is more paranoid about the media than anybody I have ever met.

As Newcastle fans, as long of tooth as we are short of patience, we scoffed hardest. The national media never seem to miss the chance to kick us when we are down and as we always seem to be down in one way or another, they always seem to be kicking us. Or do they?

Martin Samuel (a big cuddly West Ham fan and a damn fine writer) wrote a piece in *The Times* over a month before anybody else, saying Michael Owen should sign for Newcastle. *The Sun*'s top hack is Shaun Custis who never passes up an opportunity to nail his Geordie colours to the mast (God bless him) and most of the other top writers I have come across recently treat us with benign indifference. This may be because we are not newsworthy at the moment.

(It's not like we hadn't provided the ammunition; you would have expected the press to gather and start whooping like hungry hyenas when Graeme Souness tried to explain Jean Alain Boumsong's propensity for calamity in October. Apparently his feet (size 13) meant he couldn't get proper boots, which is why he kept falling on his arse. Presumably he had normal feet when we paid £8.5 million for him and they only grew into cumbersome great flippers after Graeme's mate David Murray, the Rangers chairman, had cashed the cheque.)

In last month's *The Mag* when our old sparring partner Brian McNally (of the *Sunday Mirror*) said of Souness, "He's keen to point out that what he has achieved is getting Newcastle off the back pages of the papers and the front pages in some cases." Which is true but are we happy about it? As fans maybe, as newspaper buyers probably not. So where does that get us, to the point where it is not worth buying a paper in the morning? Like many I was a bit shocked to discover that *The Pink,* a former integral part of the Newcastle fan's Saturday night experience, is now extinct but I can't remember the last time I bought one.

I still have, and treasure the issue where Jack Charlton took us to the top of the League as well as the one where I was stood next to 'The Face In The Crowd'. But it has of course been rendered obsolete, the massive tellys in the pubs project all the scores and the League table before we can actually get out of the ground and do so all night.

What next? Well by the time I have sat through *Football First* on Sky and *Match Of The Day*, I can often barely be bothered to walk to the paper shop for a Sunday paper.

Another thing that McNally said was that, as well as getting rid of the "bad apples", Souness had scourged the club of "the people who were leaking stuff to the press...unfortunately". This is fascinating for two reasons: 1) Who would that be then? (and there is probably only one answer if you really think about it, who have we sold recently, cheaply and for no apparent reason?) and; 2) Do managers so dislike having their day to day business broadcast across the planet that they are prepared to flush out any bean-spillers? Well obviously – the pre-match information in the press as to who is going to play for Newcastle for any game this season has proved to be little more than irrelevant speculation. So what is the point of buying a paper before a game, for the quality of the writing, for the jokes?

This is an interesting time for the printed media because clubs don't seem to think they need it any more at exactly the point where the papers themselves have given over the most space ever to football. There were over five pages in some papers about Manchester United getting knocked out of Europe, a few years ago the club would have had to have burnt to the ground to merit that mass of print. Obviously some of that wasn't very complimentary, which is why Mr Ferguson got his knickers so very twisted. Naturally the old fox may once again be trying to foster the siege mentality that has served him so well over the years but as I drive past the newsagents without stopping for the fourth day in a row, I wonder if there is not a little more to it. It's not hate that is driving the written media, it's a desperation to justify their existence and not to become extinct.

Chapter 52

2nd January 2006

Another Christmas Ruined

It has become desperately trendy to be cynical about Christmas. It's a chore and a hassle and it's rubbish and blah blah fucking blah. Kids love Christmas obviously, partly because of the lights and the magic in the air but mostly because they are grasping little monsters imagining a hoard of new treasures that they can sleep on like contented dragons. So for this argument we will be ignoring kids, OK?

Quite frankly if you have reached 41 and Christmas isn't an amalgamation of everything you love doing most then it is you who is rubbish, not Christmas. Obviously assuming no one close to you has died, been diagnosed with cancer or (worst of all) has realised they are Eamonn Holmes, there is no excuse for your Christmas not to be great. You have had years to sort out your family, deliberately estranging the members you can't be bothered with, so they should know better than expect to see you. You can eat all your favourite food, with your favourite people whilst sloshing down cold and delicious drinks that you would normally consider too extravagant. It doesn't matter that a lot of the telly is rubbish because the Good Lord not only gave us a son to torture to death but boxed set DVDs and look… more drinks.

Basically if you can shape Christmas to your own will it should be mostly magnificent. However, the problems arrive with the stuff you can't control which is why on Tyneside Christmas is invariably ruined by the fucking football.

The week before Christmas things looked to be heading in the right direction, by New Year's Eve goalkeeper Steve Harper was saying, "This place is cursed."

At West Ham on December 17th Michael Owen was the difference between the two sides; he exchanged passes with Shearer to score after five minutes and headed in a second from a Solano free-kick to make it 2-1 after Solano had scored an unfortunate own goal.

Owen set up Shearer just after half time and that should have been that but Ameobi inexplicably handled in the area and Harewood scored the penalty with 20 minutes remaining. In the 90th minute West Ham 'keeper Roy Carroll went up for a corner and was stranded as Newcastle broke. Shearer led the charge and Faye crossed for Owen to pop the ball into the empty net. A scruffy hat-trick (the 'header' actually hit him on the back) but seven goals in eight games from Owen was papering over some pretty nasty cracks.

Anfield is no place to go with a papered-over crack, especially as Steven Gerrard seemed to take our buying Owen as a personal affront. He took command of the assault, scoring first, Crouch adding a second, then both scorers led the unnecessary and repellent overreaction to a Bowyer foul that left Newcastle with ten men and no chance of even the scantest consolation.

A lot of people were in St James', including travelling Charlton fans, when it was decided that getting to and from the match was too dangerous for the game to proceed. The pitch was fine and a cynical person might have thought that Newcastle were being cute, to have the team fitter than Tottenham's for the game at White Hart Lane on New Year's Eve.

If this was the case, it didn't work very well. Sloppy defending (especially on the second Spurs goal when we looked to have about ten chances to clear the bastard ball) ruined Christmas, Michael Owen getting injured looked to have ruined the season.

I was in a packed pub with Mick and Ian watching an illegal beamback and nobody seemed to think Owen was seriously hurt, his collision with Robinson looked like nothing. (*Later, Souness admitted that the Owen injury was the moment when he knew his time at Newcastle was over*). The ugly atmosphere in the pub was only tempered by the thought that we were closer to home than our comrades in the capital and could immediately get back to doing stuff that was actually fun.

An increasing feeling of hatred towards our manager only grew in a shambolic game at home against Middlesbrough. A Solano free kick had put us ahead but goals on the break from Yakubu and Hasselbaink looked to have won the game for Boro. "We want Souness out!" was louder on the TV than from where I was sitting but afterwards a vocal minority thought Lee Clark's equaliser in the fourth minute of stoppage time was a bad thing for the club, believing losing this game would have rid us of Souness and his battalion of coaches, who, like at Spurs, had sat immobile with their team in utter disarray.

The majority, having seen Given come up for the last-ditch corner, having seen Clarkie drive the ball through a forest of legs into the bottom corner of the net and having seen the Boro players flat out dejected on our grass, were too busy ordering drinks and being thankful for the late Christmas present than to worry about such treacherous thinking.

Chapter 53

7th January 2006

Souness Out!

Even in retrospect the fall of Souness isn't straightforward: I had an argument with a vegan friend a while back, who was getting into a right old ding dong with a vegetarian about what it's ethical to kill. You see the "nothing" line simply doesn't wash because everytime you breath in and out you kill millions of tiny sub-microscopic critters. So the only way to be a proper vegan is to kill yourself, which in twisted Veganworld would probably be OK, providing nobody ate you or wore your skin as a hat afterwards. Likewise from a flesh eating point of view you can't say "everything" because 'roast person' on a menu would probably cause something of a hoo-ha, even if it was only unwanted mackem children on the spit. So it's a question of where the individual chooses to draw the line, likewise with Souness.

At what point a Newcastle fan said, "Right that's it, I want rid of this fucker" was entirely up to the individual but it had to happen. (*Alan Shearer has been recorded as saying "Newcastle fans never really took to Graeme. They wanted to...")* But undoubtedly it wouldn't have taken much of a shove to get the 'Souness out' bandwagon rolling before he even walked in the bloody door. He won a lot of games, got us to the quarter-final of the UEFA Cup that we were very unlucky not to win and the semi-final of the FA Cup. He bought Michael Owen, Scott Parker and Emre and he had no luck with injuries, suspensions and daft refs.

On the other hand he spent £50 million on the team and weakened it in the process, which takes some doing.

At the turn of the year I would rather have been caught pooing in Brian Kilcline's wife's best handbag than to have taken either side in the Souness debate. Quite simply I didn't fancy the look of either side. Some of the people wanting him out, especially in the press, only did so because they had their own axes to grind but to see Souness surrounded by his useless little gang of coaches doing nothing while the team looked so clueless filled me with utter hatred.

Would we get better if the injuries cleared up, if we had a run of wins, who knew? But a mate said to me on New Year's Eve that if Newcastle won the next twenty games under Souness he would still want him sacked. What's the point of arguing with somebody that entrenched? But the lad was so far from being alone that Souness had to go to get us all on the same side again.

It was widely accepted that Alan Shearer kept Souness in a job by equalling Jackie Milburn's record against Mansfield in the third round of the FA Cup but despite the score only being 1-0 it was a relaxing afternoon. Granted there was booing at half-time, which was a terrible example to set to all the hyperactive children in attendance. Not least because the one behind me nearly booed out his millionth Opal Fruit.

The second half brought more enthusiastic scampering from our guests but half-chances were more likely to end up in Leazes Park lake than in our goal. The exception was the player lashing his foot violently at thin air when presented with a shooting opportunity, which is the next best thing to the ref getting hit in the face with the ball, when it comes to getting an Eric Morecambe style "Wa-hey" out of even the grumpiest of crowds.

With ten minutes left the stroppy stay-away fans got their come-uppance when Alan Shearer scored his record-equalling 200th goal for us. Luque rolled a ball back cutely with the ball of his foot and Shearer came steaming onto a stationary target with no hope or help in sight for big ol'Pressman in the Mansfield goal. Whallop! Gallowgate End. Arm up.

The 1-0 loss at Fulham the next week had Newcastle fans singing, "Where were you when we were good?" at the bemused and polite home support, to add black humour to another waste of time and money on the road with Souness. Further damage was done the next week with a small but filmed demonstration after we lost 1-0 at home to Blackburn. The fact that we were robbed because Pedersen punched the ball into the goal was all but unreported but my old mate Hendy was on Sky Sports along with a number of other supposedly irate fans demanding Souness be sacked (and knowing Hendy; disembowelled, chopped into little pieces and fed to the pigs).

A nervous win in the FA Cup, away to Cheltenham, with goals from Chopra and Parker while the media vultures circled, did nothing one way or the other but by Man City on the following Wednesday Souness didn't appear to have a friend left in the world. Newcastle lost 3-0 and were unforgivably shocking, so despite the cost of paying up his and his mates' contracts, Freddie Shepherd pulled the trigger.

A prodigal fan asked if any of us at five-a-side knew of a spare seat before the Portsmouth match and the gleeful spite with which I laughed when someone said, "There is one on the bench that Dean fucking Saunders won't be needing" betrayed
my true feelings.

I didn't like a lot of what Souness did and said but in retrospect it was some of the things he didn't say that gave him away: "Good players don't need motivating" and "Good defenders don't need coaching, they have a sixth sense that alerts them to danger" all sounds well and good on the surface, especially to a manager intent on filling his team with "proper" and "real" men. But the more you think about it the more you think: hang on, does that mean you don't expect to do any actual managing at all, ever? Complain about injuries, pin up team sheet, complain about ref – job's a good'un.

Glenn Roeder made a point in his first week as caretaker manager of saying, "Why does Tiger Woods have a coach?" which suggested that the lack of guiding hands had been a real issue for our players.

Another stock phrase was, "Looking at the fixtures this was a game that you would think we can win". Robson used to say this as well and it boils my piss because it infers that you sometimes look at the fixtures and decide that there are games you can't win.

"We have to learn to win games 1-0," Mr Souness said early on in his reign and even those of us keen to give him a chance thought, "That's not really what we do in these parts. You have to learn to win games 4-0, to grab the unfortunate bastards who have come in the misguided belief that they might hang on for 20 minutes by the fucking neck, rip their fucking throats out and dance in their fucking blood. And the only weapon you can use is this football. Understand?" Perhaps this should be explained to all future managers before they sign the overly generous pre-nuptial agreement. We will not "learn to be patient" – you sir, will learn to be as impatient as we are or you sir, can bugger the hell off!

Chapter 54

4th February 2006

A New Era (What, Another One?)

There are few things we Newcastle fans like more than a new era. There is something about a departing manager that turns us from a cynical, seething mob of crusty old grumpy-panted doom-mongers into gleeful, wide-eyed, childlike optimists.

There are dozens of good reasons why Cap'n Souey had to walk the plank but beholding St James' Park, and the black and white hordes rebonded in a single cause, was all the proof needed that the right decision had been made.

In fact, all that nonsense about the need for stability should be flushed down the Lavatory Of Silliness once and for all. If you look at our home results after installing a new manager the only sensible conclusion to arrive at is that we should change our manager every two weeks – we would win the League.

For the first time in ages those with tickets felt privileged and those without felt understandably jealous. The place was buzzing, the team was straining to be let off the leash and the distinct scent of determination hung heavy in the air.

So, as is traditional on these occasions, the home team came out swinging and Portsmouth backed onto the ropes and started ducking while their baggy-faced old pirate of a manager no doubt sat a-twitching in his seat.

Graeme Souness will not be remembered kindly in these parts but we shouldn't forget to be grateful for Emre, Scotty Parker and Solano who, along with N'Zogbia were way too clever, way too quick of foot and way too good for Portsmouth's midfield five. All played as if a great weight had been lifted from them.

More chances were made in the first half than in any three other games this season and that rare old feeling that a goal was coming was another welcome sensation.

Dean Kiely in the Pompey goal was lucky not to be sent off in the game previous to this one, so free of suspension naturally had a blinder. He beat away chances from Solano, Ameobi and Shearer with such agility that you might have thought of him as unbeatable, except he couldn't hold a thing and went for one cross like a man trying to catch a plant-pot falling from a balcony. So, assured he was not and eventually the breakthrough came when, in blocking a point-blank effort from Shearer, his luck finally ran out. The ball went straight to the inrushing N'Zogbia who thumped home the rebound.

From that point Portsmouth were so poor that it was always about how many Newcastle would get and whether Shearer would score THAT goal. The goal that would make him Newcastle United's top goal scorer, ever. For his part our captain belted in a shot from outside the area which had 'declaration of intent' written all over it.

Pompey spent all of half-time warming up their reserve keeper which suggested 'Arry had a lot to think about besides an apparently growing paranoia that people think he is on the fiddle and that shady characters are emptying vanfuls of money into the moat of his Hampshire castle. Nonsense of course, nine players in through the transfer window, that smell is definitely NOT rat Mr Redknapp, calm yourself down, I'm sure Sven Goran Eriksson didn't mean you when he said some Premiership managers like to get their hands in the till. Why so sensitive?

Newcastle started the second half much slower, a worrying hangover from the Souness era, where we looked like the least fit team in the League. Fortunately Portsmouth didn't have the personnel to cause us much worry and five minutes past the hour Shearer scored THAT goal. Winning the first high ball himself, he flicked on to Shola then got on his bike. Shola back-heeled the ball into his path and our hero was clean through. The net at the Gallowgate End billowed, again the arm went up and the place went crackers.

Shola collided with Kiely a few minutes later and their trainer had to come on, which gave the crowd the chance they needed to really say thank you. Great boisterous waves of love poured noisily and unashamedly from stands to pitch. Everywhere you looked, smiling people were on the feet, punching air that seemed to be vibrating with raw emotion, one name on their lips. The noise was colossal but, as ever, Shearer looked to be taking it all in his stride. Only afterwards did he admit being choked up with it all.

Another era is ending, that of the club's greatest ever goalscorer. It is happening in our lifetime and you can't help but feel lucky because this is a special time, and the fact that it isn't over yet and that people on and off the pitch have smiles on their faces again make this more of a celebration than a wake.

To the bar!

"To Alan Shearer."

Cheers (clink).

Chapter 55

22nd February 2006

In Times Of Trouble

January 1997 Villa Park: the first game for Newcastle United after Kevin Keegan walked out. Keegan wasn't happy, you could always tell with him, as a player, as a man and as a manager feelings were not for keeping on the inside, which was one of the things that made him so adorable. Later, when he managed at Fulham, England and Manchester City he became more guarded and so was less loveable, less effective and he could no longer hold a team up with his own sheer force of will.

A 7-1 win over Tottenham and a 3-0 at home to Leeds in the League looked the perfect medicine to Keegan's growing melancholy but in between these games was a 1-1 at Charlton in the FA Cup where he snapped and snarled at the press. All was clearly not well.

In the aftermath of the Messiah's departure there was shock and confusion, there was, however, no sobbing in the streets. Sitting in The Strawberry with Mark Jensen (an emergency editorial meeting for *The Mag* had been called) you could see photographers dragging youths along by the arms and stage managing them to sit with their heads in their hands on the Gallowgate steps and it was fucking sickening.

All the stages of grief swept over you; betrayal, guilt, anger, denial and the thirst for strong drink but it was Villa Park that was the defining memory. In times of extreme duress it is basic tribal nature to come together and in doing so gather a communal fortitude. We landed on Birmingham, thousands deep, in a mass show of defiance and solidarity because while managers and players and individual fans can walk away, we as a mass, as a living entity, couldn't and wouldn't. Fans who hadn't been away for ages felt the urge to be with their own, to stand shoulder to shoulder, look the world in the eye and say, "Fuck you! Fuck all of you people because we will not be beaten down. And if we have to go to war for this club then bring it on! C'mon!"

The circumstances in 2006 at Villa Park were entirely different but the feeling was the same, in times of trouble the first instinct of the Newcastle fan is not to slope off, hide and pretend not to have any interest, it's to be defiant and the support at Villa was again indomitable.

Afterwards David O'Leary said Newcastle were lucky but not for the first or last time Glenn Roeder was on the same page as the fans: "I think that's a bit spiteful. I thought Villa were lucky to only be 2-1 down at half-time. It could have been 3-1 and 3-1 for me at this level is a case of thank you very much. I said to our lads we let them off the hook." Newcastle won 2-1 with goals from Ameobi and N'Zogbia either side of a Luke Moore header for Villa. Babayaro was sent off for a 'foul' on Baros who appeared to be running away from goal but Given saved the penalty.

Playing Southampton was something else we did in January '97, it being Kenny Dalglish's first game in charge, but this time round seeing off the Saints in our next game put us in the quarter-finals of the FA Cup. The BBC had presumably picked us to show live because they expected more humiliation to be heaped on us, but despite Shearer's absence we went through thanks to a neat Dyer goal after good work from Emre and a great run and pass from N'Zogbia. Kieron went understandably potty, having missed so many games and Tyneside was on the brink of doing the same until Robert Lee, of all people, pulled us out of the FA Tupperware bucket – away to sodding Chelsea.

The whole club seemed so fucked off with the draw that the atmosphere at the ground two days later was dead and a drab 0-0 with Charlton ensued. But it is not in our nature to be quiet for long.

Chapter 56

25th February 2006

Everybody Hates Everton

Before we get into the nuts and bolts of this particular encounter you may be interested to know that, in the result of a recent independent survey, Everton are the club that most football fans hate second or third most. Everybody obviously saves their bitterest bile to spit in the eyes of their immediate neighbours but after that Everton are the club the majority of fans, who actually go to matches, dislike more than any other.

You will notice that I say club, the players are largely irrelevant as is the individual canniness of any Toffees fan who may be come across. It doesn't really matter whether the club is managed by a man with a head like a badly stuffed medicine ball or by a droning, bug-eyed, pasty-faced Scotsman, people don't like Everton. And let's be honest here, what is there to like? Good players never stay long at Everton, interesting players seem out of place there and Goodison Park is clearly some enormous git-magnet. At any point in their history it has been possible to go through the Everton squad and find at least six of the staff to shout "Git!" at without the slightest fear of contradiction. Perhaps we can tell Lee Bowyer that Everton is near London.

As a group of supporters they obviously have the self-righteous, thin-skinned desire to feel hard done by that any collection of Scousers will give you but they have extra bitterness and, worst of all, are unforgivably and utterly bereft of any sense of fun. They manage to be puffed up and dreary which has the same effect on people as a tramp looking down his nose at you from within a stinking skip. They have that awful song as well that Celtic sing: "And if you know your history, it's enough to make your heart go whoa whoa ar whoa" – well as it happens I do know a bit of history but more crucially on this point, I know enough about biology to suggest that anyone who has a heart that goes "whoa whoa ar whoa" is in desperate need for some sort of physician and that feeling the need to scream "handball" every time an opposition player chests the ball down should be the least of their worries. Newcastle fans of course sing about being the loyalest supporters the world has ever had but crucially everybody knows that we are too daft to be self-righteous, at least not to the standard that Everton have perfected.

Everton is like some sort of anti-Football Club, like they exist to spoil football and football matches. Non-entities working hard, making up the numbers and boring people rigid, the Premiership would be a happier place for their absence. In fact here's an idea: next season print the fixture list without Everton (and Blackburn for that matter) in it. Not anywhere, shuffle everybody else up a couple of places and pretend they never had a team. Yes, they would kick up a bit of a fuss but providing everybody kept a straight face we could get away with it. "Everton? Sorry mate, never heard of them". What a fantastic idea – I should run football, me.

(sigh)

Oh well, it took thirty seconds for Cahill ("GIT!") to throw himself to the floor for the first time. We got the full range from little Timmy today, sneaky fouls, diving, scrunchy faced complaining and protestations of innocence – whatever became of David Speedie? *Match Of The Day* made Everton look unlucky and the bug-eyed pasty-faced Scotsman droned on about feeling hard done by but one of the joys of Nobby Solano winning you a football match is the warm glow of seeing class rise before your eyes (as well as the two fingers up to the spiteful so and so who sold him against our express wishes). We won because you haven't got a player who can do *that*.

Scott Parker was magnificent, Emre, although ill, still shone and if anybody asks you about N'Zogbia, claim ignorance, he's our secret weapon. Shhhhh, no one outside Newcastle seems to have noticed just how good The Zog is and I don't think we should tell them. He burst into the box to cross for Nobby's first goal and was also intrinsic in the second that went Boumsong, Babayaro, N'Zog, Emre, N'Zog, Bowyer, before it got to Nobby.

You've seen it, I've seen it and they will have seen it in Cusco (Inca capital, recently voted second best city in the world in *Wanderlust* magazine in a survey I didn't conduct 'independently' in my own head) and we all want to see it again because it is so damn beautiful. Outside of the right boot, curling across the goalkeeper into the top corner. Scrumptious. The last 14 minutes dragged over without a chance for the Solano hat-trick that would have perfected the evening and there was little else to discuss apart from the "they don't boo bad players" statement being undermined by exhibit A: former sunderland patsy, Mr Kevin Kilbane ("GIT!")

Chapter 57

11th March 2006

Other People's Children

I try not to watch TV commercials. At the adverts I frantically flick through as many of the other available channels as is possible in a fashion that is, in no way, deeply irritating for whom so ever may be in the room at the same time. And no, I don't know what I'm looking for.

In an unguarded moment recently I saw an advert for (I think) one of those ghastly people-carrier things that had the tag line, "Because no adventure is bigger than having kids!" Really? How interesting, you mean people have climbed mountains, hacked through jungles in search of lost civilisations and been fired into space and it was all for nothing? In the spirit of true adventure, Tutankhamun would have remained undiscovered because Howard Carter should have stayed at home and lived with the ramifications of one of those drunken, unprotected Saturday night fumblings that accounts for 67 per cent of this country's population?

Funny that, because if you take a moment or two to consider the amount of people on the planet, producing more people doesn't seem to be one of our shortcomings, giant pandas we are not. Working our way down the evolutionary scale; rats, jellyfish and mackems all seem to have mastered the breeding trick.

You mustn't get me wrong here, I don't dislike children, I find them hilarious and fascinating (for short periods, then you must take them away quickly). In fact I consider children to be so special that I think you should have to pass some sort of stringent exam before being allowed to have one. In this country, if you want a new cat you may be asked to fill in a questionnaire and you may even be visited to make sure you can be trusted with the responsibility, yet any number of ill-educated, ugly people can be seen blowing smoke into babies' faces the length and breadth of the country. No, it's parents I've got a problem with, specifically parents I don't know. If I know you, hell, I can spare a minute (at a stretch two) to hear about how you're exhausted, skint and a secret Calpol addict. If I don't know you, go away, I don't care, smug, self-centred bastards that you are, chopping people up in town with your over-sized buggies and driving those great big ugly 4 by 4s around that keep your children safe at a risk to everybody else's.

An increasing number of people don't want to turn into that sort of person and are choosing a life without kids.

The 'breeders' consider themselves on the moral high ground and are resentful of the freedom and opportunity a child-free life offers, so they assume there is something wrong with your workings or worse, that you are "selfish". If by "selfish" you mean that I'll be paying for your kids' healthcare and education through my taxes, that I will do your job for you while you are on paid leave and that I'll be covering for you when you have to rush off to every sniffle and school suspension, with the only thanks being that it's your kids who will beat me up in the street the second I'm too old to look after myself, then yes, I'm proper selfish, me.

For the record: Wifey's and my lack of children is a tremendously considerate act that the rest of you owe us a pint for because with her temper and my looks we would doubtless spawn some hybrid of Bonnie Langford and Hitler. We had an imaginary child once, called Joe, (after Joe Young from *A Mag For All Seasons*) but he was taken into imaginary care because we kept leaving him on the Metro.

'Baby On Board' or (please God no) 'Princess On Board', why do I need to know that? Obviously I was going to start shooting at your car with the high calibre revolver I keep under my passenger seat before running you off the Redheugh Bridge into the river but now I'll have to pick a different car, one with a less precious cargo.

I don't need to have other people's fertility dangled in my face thank you very much and neither does anybody else so this fad of footballers boasting about their new babies has got to stop. The thumbsucking goal celebration to denote a new arrival is bad enough but last week a player produced a dummy from his shorts that he put in his mouth after scoring. Apart from the obvious unacceptability of pulling things out of your underpants and putting them in your mouth in public, surely there is a hygiene issue to consider.

You have scored a goal; that is cause for celebration in itself – we don't need any other examples of your achievements, where will it end? Players producing their 25 metres breaststroke certificates, pretending to steer a little car because they passed their driving test or waving photos: "here's a picture of me meeting Nelson Mandela".

Francesco Totti recently had a plastic baby waiting for him on the Roma bench that he pretended to feed after one goal and stuffed the ball up his shirt and had a team-mate deliver it on another. What he should have been concentrating on was not getting his leg broken which would have made sure Middlesbrough got knocked out of the UEFA Cup. It's a question of priorities.

Chapter 58

13th March 2006

He Turned Ya Down

Imagining Alan Shearer in a Manchester United shirt is about the same for a Newcastle supporter's brain as the thought of kissing your Granny goodbye and her sticking her tongue in. But now in these twilight days of the playing career of our greatest ever striker, with sentimentality heavy in the air, the "what if?" question arises.

What if Alan Shearer had chosen Old Trafford over St James' Park?

At the time it was unthinkable, without Newcastle United there was no serious challenge to Man Utd's dominance: at the end of the '95/96 season Man Utd finished four points clear of Newcastle but 11 ahead of Liverpool and 19 ahead of Arsenal. Letting the best centre forward in the world join that Man Utd team surely would mean conceding the title to Salford's finest for the foreseeable future.

Only Kevin Keegan, armed with nothing but personality, dreams and a cheque book, stood between Manchester United and utter domination, a Cantona/Shearer forward line alone was enough to make the blood run cold, never mind the players they would have behind them.

It would have been good at this point if every other team in the Premiership gave Newcastle half a million quid each towards Shearer's £15 million price tag because stopping him going to Old Trafford was doing everybody else a favour. Then we could have spent more money elsewhere because the harsh, cold truth is: at that precise moment in time scoring goals wasn't a problem for Newcastle and we didn't appear to actually need Shearer.

The opening League game of the '96/97 season, away to Everton, we were all giddy with excitement but there was always the nagging feeling of "how is this actually going to work?" Sure enough; Shearer, Les Ferdinand, Keith Gillespie and David Ginola spent a lot of the game standing on the halfway line looking at our overrun midfield and defence, apparently thinking: "somebody should probably be helping those guys out but I'm damned if it's my job." Newcastle lost 2-0.

The fact that over the years Newcastle United came to rely so heavily on Shearer is hardly his fault. It's a savage indictment of our club that too many of the fantastic amount of Shearer goals have saved us from mediocrity and embarrassment. With each passing season Man Utd's regret at missing out on Shearer subsides, such is the nature of football and the ongoing success of Manchester United. They won the League four out of the following five seasons but in their more thoughtful moments they know that with Shearer they could have had so much more, especially in the Champions League. So it didn't all work out badly, eh?

Certainly the fact that the prawn sandwich brigade still booed Alan Shearer on his last trip to Old Trafford was a sign of grudging respect, despite the fact that he barely put a foot right, or got a look in, during a hideously one-sided game. Alex Ferguson, bless him, always takes Newcastle United seriously at Old Trafford, always puts out his strongest side and we never catch them on one of their occasional off-days that see the likes of Fulham or Blackburn winning there. We have never got the sweet, sweet win with Shearer grabbing the winner there in the Premiership. Three 0-0s, in the most memorable of which ('03/04) Shearer had his legs kicked from under him in front of the Stretford End when we, unsurprisingly, didn't get a penalty.

We had a moral victory there in '98 but no one remembers: when we surrendered our famous 12 point lead to Manchester United in '95/96 we were told more than once how Man Utd would never allow that to happen. Well, on the second last game of the season an unlikely hero in Andreas Andersson stole a 1-1 draw, which helped Arsenal overhaul a 13 point gap to pip Man Utd by a solitary point. The tears we witnessed that night after the game as they shuffled off defeated by a team 200 miles away seemed a sort of revenge for our losses but somehow that game has slipped out of the collective memory. It sure seemed a long time ago when Wayne Rooney destroyed our latest misguided optimism in a game we were relieved to see finish only 2-0.

In the end, the "what if?" question is soppy and irrelevant; Shearer smiles like he's answering the burblings of an imbecile when his lack of medals comes up. It's like, "if I have to explain this to you, you will never understand." Ask any Newcastle fan if they would rather have seen their team win stuff and they would say yes, ask them if they considered supporting a different team and they will laugh because it was never going to fucking happen. As if being the greatest striker in the history of Newcastle United wasn't enough, Alan Shearer often thinks like us as well. God love him for it.

Chapter 59

19th March 2006

Relentless

Some things in life might seem like a good thing but they actually turn out to be really, really bad. For example, there is a new energy drink on the market: it comes in a big gothic can and it's called Relentless which is grand because the best work from the late Bill Hicks was an incendiary piece of stand-up comedy with the same name. I was already hooked on the idea and planning to have the magnificent logo tattooed on my back before I even opened the tin. It's maxed out with additives that will probably turn out to make people's brains explode and it tastes like Red Bull – and you get nearly a pint of it. The advert should have a Motorhead *Overkill* soundtrack and feature crazed young people in a darkened club, frothing at the mouth and trying to bite their own heads off. The tag line should read: "It'll probably fucking kill you but let's drink the bastard anyway". Cool eh?

Well no, because it's made by Coca Cola and that makes it very uncool. (*)

Likewise a lot of people thought a British team coming from three goals down in the Champions League Final was a good thing. It's not a good thing, an ugly fucking monster has been spawned and we at Newcastle are more guilty than most when the history books come to apportion blame.

(Anarcho-multicorporate bashing to slagging off Scousers in one seamless step – where else are you gonna get this shit?)

Two years ago Liverpool were virtually dead in the water, they only qualified for the Champions League because we were so sackless. Even last year most of the talk after we beat them here wasn't about Laurent Robert's missile of a free-kick that won the game but about how we had just seen the worst Liverpool team in living memory. Now look at them – both games this season they have pissed it against us. Michael Owen looked embarrassed at their place and we all looked a bit sheepish after this encounter. Or at least we would have done if Cisse hadn't got us all vengeful and angry.

Liverpool's boring approach, bully-boy tactics and ruthless gamesmanship made them Champions of Europe and not the laughing stock they should have been. Bolstered by that confidence they have muscled their way ahead of all but Chelsea and Man Utd.

And here's weird, it's Man Utd who are the force for good out of that little triad and no, I don't like admitting it. Here's the proof: Chelsea v Liverpool is a game that should have most football-loving neutrals drooling but what do you get? A series of drab, grinding encounters where both teams cheat, then accuse the other lot of cheating afterwards.

You can tell Liverpool are monstrous as soon as they walk onto the pitch – look at them, they are all at least six inches taller than us. Solano shaking hands with Crouch looked like some accident with circus mirrors. Of course only one of those two players is a proper footballer, someone you could imagine playing for Barcelona, say. You could attempt to undermine my argument by pointing out that Crouch scored one and created two but that ignores the vital side issue; that Boumsong is some kind of werefool. A man who can mark Henry out of a game to the point that Arsenal's main man has never scored against Newcastle when the Boum has been playing but who, during certain phases of the moon turns into a cross-eyed dimwit, who wanders the field with no sense of positioning or direction and thinks the ball is a big silver bullet that he must avoid any contact with.

Crouch (or Timmy from *South Park* if you want to be cruel) simply leaned over the top of our werefool and nodded Liverpool one up after ten minutes.

Gerrard's movement was brilliant for the second Liverpool goal but the man's an arch-hypocrite, I don't like him and he clearly dislikes Newcastle. Hell of a player, took his goal excellently, but all that shite about not wanting Michael Owen to play against Liverpool so soon after Gerrard himself came within an inch of signing for Chelsea was a bit hard to swallow.

Shola nodded us back into it just before half-time and Boumsong had a chance to equalise straight after but the ball slid across his forehead and wide.

We played better in the second half but were constantly undone by that chicken-necked little piss-pot of a ref, Mike Riley, who also hates us.

Boumsong did deserve to get sent off, no excuses about that. He deserved to be sent off for being a daft, anvil-footed, incompetent twat who has no business being on a football pitch if he can't actually put foot to ball, not for pulling down Crouch because he wasn't the last man and Crouch would probably have missed.

Cisse overdid the celebrations after slotting away the penalty and was booked – he should have been sent off for goading the crowd after that but, as I said, Riley hates us so that was never going to happen.

After that, as a crowd we stuck in and Shay kept the score down but this was a depressing fucking experience.

(*) Optional rant warning, no football enclosed! I once tried to explain the Coca Cola = The Devil's Semen argument to my good friend Chris Tait whose eyes glazed over in precisely one and a half seconds so I am aware most people don't like being moralised at over their choice of pop. Put anti-Coca Cola into Google on a PC and you get 6,700,000 hits; go to www.killercoke.org/ and you'll only ever want Pepsi in your Jack Daniels.

Chapter 60

25th March 2006

Barcelona Of The North

Environmentally, aeroplanes are a cancer on this planet. They gobble up natural resources and pump out an horrific amount of shite. Something is going to have to be done to cut the amount of aircraft in the air or we are all going to die. Apparently.

But for the time being, this is a golden age of cheap flights and the peasantry have enthusiastically taken to the skies. Hooray! And it's so easy, dangerously easy in fact:

quarter to seven one Saturday morning, Wifey and I decided that we couldn't possibly afford to have another holiday so we would definitely not be looking to get away any time soon. By quarter past the same seven, we had booked four days in Barcelona, courtesy of our friendly orange chums at Easyjet, and midweek as well so we wouldn't have to miss another match.

As has no doubt become obvious over these last chapters I have taken a conscious decision to take a step back from football. Pretending not to care would be a pathetic lie but I have been avoiding the (easily slipped into) routine of devouring football, and letting football devour you, 24 hours a day. A game finishes, you have a drink or ten, then you make a deliberate decision not to let it eat you up, not to worry about every player's niggling injuries and not to be calculating League tables in your head every night when you should be asleep. All well and good, very healthy but.... FA Cup quarter-finals MIDWEEK. When the hell did that happen and why wasn't I told? Or at least, why wasn't I told more often and louder?

"We can probably find a bar with it on the telly."

There is a long romantic and tragic relationship between Newcastle and Barcelona that must not be overlooked or forgotten. Hundreds of men from the North East travelled to Catalonia to fight Franco's fascists while the UK government chose a path of appeasement. Just what a confused, strange and doomed conflict they got themselves into is well documented in George Orwell's book, *Tribute To Catalonia*. The patron saint of Barcelona is Sant Jordi (Saint George), which you will know since Johan Cruyff called his son Jordi because he was so in love with the place. So people from Newcastle called George (and there would have been a lot because it was more traditional to name your children after the monarch in those days) would be called Jordi / Geordie. Simple and beautiful. Well, you would think so but try explaining it to a young Catalan couple, who speak little English, while you are drunk.

We were in L'Ovella Negra in November 1997 the night before Newcastle played at the magnificent Camp Nou for the first time. L'Ovella Negra (The Black Sheep) is one of the finest bars I have ever been in; just off the top of Las Ramblas amidst a mass of wonderful record shops (selling stuff by bands you love that you never knew existed). It is rustic, with wooden benches but it has a thrilling jukebox, pool tables, and pitchers of cold, yummy lager served with free popcorn. Best of all the bar-football teams are painted in red and blue stripes versus black and white stripes.

It was during a break from one of the savagely competitive encounters which my happy band was involved in that I found myself in the role of Self-Appointed Cultural Ambassador. I was bringing our two oppressed nations together, forging a bond if you will, suffice to say the young couple in question looked at me as if I were mad (while I looked at them as if I were not).

Barca, A People's Passion by Jimmy Burns is an exhaustively researched and often fascinating history of Barcelona. It is interesting how the club was manoeuvred by some of its chairmen away from its traditional apolitical position towards aligning the club with a population who considered themselves Catalonian first and foremost, not Spanish. Interesting as well that Sir John Hall saw Barcelona as a template for how he wanted things to be at Newcastle United, embracing the idea of being a nation within a nation. Incidentally, this was the same Sir John Hall who told us off for being "tribal" when we refused to consider the idea of sharing a stadium with sunderland.

Suffice to say any idea of fraternity between Barcelona and Newcastle United is purely a one-way street these days, Barca fans only wanted Newcastle to beat Chelsea because they keep getting in catfights with Mourinho, so they don't like Chelsea. That's if they had any interest at all.

"We can probably find a bar with it on the telly." Aside from the far too cool L'Ovella Negra, we would have been hard pressed to find a bar that wasn't showing our game, it was on everywhere and they were all mostly empty. We chose a Scottish bar because there would likely be less chance of cockneys; it was deserted. The music playing was great, alternative stuff; punk rock, ska and the Corona was icy cold. A lass leant over the bar and asked if we wanted the commentary turned up and the music off? At that very second the screen flashed up: "Commentators: John Motson and Mark Lawrenson."

"Nahh!" we said together.

And so it was, to an upbeat soundtrack, Alan Shearer was denied a Cup on his final season as a player with Newcastle United. We feared a hoofing after Terry put Chelsea 1-0 up after easily losing his marker at a corner in the fourth minute, but Newcastle passed the ball well and might have had more of a chance if not for a Kent-based ref who chose to let Chelsea's gamesmanship go unpunished. No one of sane mind could argue that Newcastle have better players than Chelsea at this point in time, so why Chelsea felt the need to cheat so much can only be put down to "that is what they do". And all that crap about it being foreign players who dive, Joe Cole anybody? And Robbie Elliott was sent off for trying to get out of the way of Shaun Wright-Phillips who shamelessly threw himself to the ground.

The next day involved a lie-in, sightseeing around the warrens of magical Barca back-streets, wine on the sun terrace, a siesta, then out for a meal. Perfection. Except for the nagging injustice. I texted Guy, in chilly Newcastle, from behind dark glasses in luxurious heat with a full glass of red wine on the table; "Has anything been said in the media about Chelsea's fucking cheating?"

"Nothing," he replied and I fumed.

It doesn't seem to matter where you hide, the disappointment will find you and hurt you.

Chapter 61

10th April 2006

Down Among The Mad People

"But I don't want to go among mad people," Alice remarked.
"Oh you can't help that," said the Cat. "We're all mad here. I'm mad, you're mad."
"How do you know I'm mad?" said Alice.
"You must be," said the Cat, "or you wouldn't have come here."
(Lewis Carroll - *Alice's Adventures In Wonderland*)

Prior to this match my travelling chum, Alan Harrison, commented that nobody ever went to matches in fancy dress anymore. At some point last century he attended a game at Boro dressed as a Droog. Clad in white shirts and trousers, black boots and bowler hats, just like the menacing fellows in *A Clockwork Orange*, was the only acceptable apparel of the day and how splendid they must have looked. My own grand plan, to get everybody going to the 1998 Cup Final to dress as Cybermen, fell on deaf ears and I must learn to live with the bitter regret. The problem with fancy dress is the nagging fear that only you will turn up dressed 'fancy'. I have witnessed such a thing and it can be deeply embarrassing, or at least that's what my dad insisted had happened when I found him in the pub with my mother's dress on.

Apart from one young man with a traffic cone on his head, none of those lucky enough to get tickets for this match put any thought into making this game special. All imaginative thoughts were crushed by the need to grumble about the jumped-up little pecker-heads at Boro who keep cutting our allocation because we won't sit down.

It has now become a matter of fucking principle that we stand at Boro and our club should back us to the point of taking those snivelling little bastards to The European Court Of Human Rights. It is not illegal to stand up – in fact you are expressly allowed to stand "during periods of excitement". We are Newcastle fans, we are always thirsty and we are always excited. Providing blind panic counts as excitement of course.

Suggesting Boro DJ me Mark Page should be murdered in front of his family would be utterly wrong because he would no doubt see it as justifying his smug self-importance but I can assure him that I have never seen an episode of *The Bill* in my life. So playing the theme tune three times to amuse the knock-kneed, drooling locals who think that we watch cop dramas while they play in Europe means nothing to me, especially - and this is gonna kill you - unlike a significant number of Boro fans, I actually bothered going to their home game against Roma.

As we proved last year, getting to the latter stages of the UEFA Cup is not that difficult (unless you are Everton) and if they think they are going to win the FA Cup they are as daft as they look. Yes I'm jealous, I don't mind admitting it, but it is a little early to be gloating don't you think?

For 66 minutes we controlled this game utterly. Given didn't have a meaningful save to make, Bramble was the dominant part of an unbreakable defensive wall and Nobby was Man Of The Match by a mile. Bowyer, despite being battered about, continued his fine recent form and The Zog was a constant threat. Positionally Emre was fine, he intercepted a lot and was full of running but his passing was shocking. Up front, Boro couldn't live with Shola at all but Shearer was dreadful, I don't want to remember him like this.

Our best chance before our first goal was a sublime ball from Solano that put Shola clean through on the right. Opting for power, he launched the ball violently over the bar, then had a little chuckle to himself. I saw the chuckle later on the telly, it was at the far end from where the away support was standing and nobody has eyesight that good, which explains the two second delay before anybody in the away corner celebrated Boateng accidentally nodding the ball into his own net. George had a busy day, scoring for both teams, diving twice to get Newcastle players booked and still finding times for a handful of those sneaky fouls that he seems to like so much.

Riggott kicked Ameobi so hard in the penalty area that he put a hole in Shola's sock. Our man ran half the length of the field to show ref Alan Wiley but the official waved away the penalty and the need for any emergency darning. Some justice was done when Shola lashed in our second just before half-time.

Boro brought on Viduka at half-time and tried to up their game. For the most part this involved a lot of fouls and while Newcastle had three soft bookings, Ehiogu remained card free, despite elbowing Shola in the head and committing deliberate handball. The free-kicks, from Solano and Emre, narrowly missed a post each at a point when a third goal looked likely to bring at least a fourth.

The crucial moment in the second half came with Roeder's sensible urge to get Dyer into the fray. Boro were pushing more men forward and we had no one to exploit the huge holes at their rear. Shearer, given a five yard head start from the halfway line, was ran down with horrible ease. Taking the old fella off would have cost us little, taking Solano off cost us all measured possession. We could not keep the ball from that exact point, Emre got worse, the harder Dyer tried the more he gave the ball away and Bowyer and The Zog looked knackered. Also feeling the need to balance up the tremendous amount of fouls Boro had chalked up, Wiley started giving Boro random free-kicks, the most annoying of which was after a rattlingly good Elliott tackle.

Boro got one back thanks to a deflection and we flapped and panicked our way through ten minutes of scrambling, penalty box tumbling from men in red shirts, desperate clearances and, of course, a brilliant save from Shay Given.

Outside was odd, fans mingled quite happily until we got to the compound where the buses and most of the cops were waiting, which is where the weekend warriors chose to do their posturing. The police then decided to justify their overtime by trying to rush us through the gates that were, for the most part, blocked by police horses. Suffice to say I am now of an age where I don't appreciate being jostled by the constabulary.

But they did whisk us straight back to the A19 and we won – a good day, however you dress it up.

Chapter 62

15th April 2006

In The Standing Section

Either side of the Boro game Newcastle played home games on Saturdays at three o'clock and won them both.

After a depressing series of results Glenn Roeder, instead of moaning, making excuses and getting the whole place hysterically pissy-knickered with fear, got on with the job of coaching the players. Consequently two teams who have had praise heaped on them all season were battered half to death by a team who could almost have been forgiven for considering their season over. Roeder was publicly not having any of it, even the news that our outfield player of the season, Scott Parker, was going to miss the rest of the campaign didn't seem to knock him out of his stride.

My long time Spurs supporting mate Tim, travelled up with his lass (Karen, a Colchester fan). I gave her my ticket and bought a single ticket for myself. I mention this because not sitting in your own seat is fucking weird, the pitch and game looks different even if you are only a few seats away from normal. On top of this there is the paranoia that the people around you think that this is your first game ever because they haven't seen you before. "Another clueless glory hunter, a tourist who doesn't know how to go on," the shame of it. Fortunately I ended up near Barry, one of *The Mag's* most insightful writers, so as well as singing more than usual I got to explain how I had been turned out of the seat I have sat in "FOR OVER TEN YEARS" in an overly loud voice to allay the suspicions of those around me.

I was low down in the East Stand/Leazes corner with my back to the lower tier wall, so there was no one behind me thus no hurry to sit. Newcastle started briskly, passing fluently, Shearer dummied, Solano to N'Zogbia to Bowyer 1-0! I hadn't sat down and doing so now was obviously going to ruin everything so I stood up at home for 90 minutes, in the sunshine with Newcastle playing brilliantly.

For 20 minutes we zipped the ball about and looked confident and impressive until Lennon got forward. He beat Carr to cross for Robbie Keane who Ramage was ignoring despite my screaming, "mark him, mark him," and pointing furiously. Obviously this seat was no better than my regular one when it comes to communicating my wisdom to the players and the unmarked Keane made it 1-1.

Shola whacked in a second after a Solano shot was saved by Robinson and within half an hour Shearer had made it 3-1, cracking home a penalty after Davids had foolishly shoved Bowyer in the back.

Even the Sky extended highlights chose to ignore a reprehensible moment in the first half when Newcastle kicked the ball out to allow a Spurs player treatment. Dawson, on returning the ball, put it out for a throw-in deep in Newcastle territory. He may have mis-kicked it, we'll give him the benefit of the doubt but Keane, the Spurs captain, feverishly waved his team-mates forward to put pressure on the throw-in. The ref shrugged because there was nothing he could do but Shearer gave Keane one almighty bollocking who feigned innocence before sheepishly kicking the ball out for a goal-kick.

Alan Shearer was awesome in this game, he utterly dominated the Spurs backline and was a constant menace. Dawson was eventually sent off for pulling him back, having already had a yellow card for going through the back of our captain in the first half. The Spurs fans took to booing Shearer and afterwards Tim was livid, claiming Shearer had elbowed Dawson first and swore at length about our captain's cheating. I should say in Tim's defence that he watches more football than anyone I know and that I generally find him insightful and knowledgeable (because he generally agrees with me). His dislike for Shearer and the reasons for this dislike are universal amongst opposing fans for reasons that we will always put down to jealousy because we don't understand it otherwise. Suffice to say there was no elbow and what was Dawson doing getting the wrong side of, and choosing to pull back, a player in his 36th year.

A real hammering for a team chasing Champions League qualification was on the cards but Newcastle eased through the second half and Jenas (the peanut-headed snivelling little fucking baby) missing an open net in front of the Gallowgate End gave us all cause for celebration worthy of a fourth goal.

Two weeks later I was back in my own seat to see Newcastle and Alan

Shearer take on Wigan and our old nemesis, referee Uriah Rennie. Everybody remembers Rennie sending off Shearer on the first day of the '99/00 season and the despicable cronyism that upheld that decision but no one outside Newcastle seems aware that a grinding war between us and this ref has gone on ever since.

I don't doubt for a second that Rennie has other enemies, the man appears to be a malicious egomaniac who upsets people for his own amusement, up and down the country. But we hate him and he hates us and both sides are not shy about showing it.

Boxing Day 2002, away at The Reebok Stadium, and dead-ball specialists Bolton are given a disproportionate amount of very iffy free-kicks around the Newcastle penalty area, they score four goals. An admittedly poor Newcastle team hang in however and the score is 4-3 going into the dying minutes. In front of us in the away end Lua Lua is flattened on the edge of the Bolton penalty area. Not only does Rennie not give the free-kick, he also books Lua Lua for diving. The Bolton defender owns up to the foul, Shearer takes said defender to Rennie who promptly books Shearer as well.

15th April 2006 and Wigan are 1-0 up after Bullard has scored a superb free-kick (given for a Wigan player slipping over) when Chopra is shoved over in the area and Rennie is trotting benignly towards the Gallowgate End, which outraged, is on its feet. Our ref is seemingly intent on doing nothing. The linesman gives the penalty, so Uriah has little choice. Shearer wallops the fucker home.

Bramble heads in from a corner and Shearer makes it 3-1 late in the second half.

It seems a straightforward win looking back, but both sides had made two substitutions within the first 20 minutes and this was the first time Newcastle had come from a goal behind to win a game in two years.

Chapter 63

17th April 2006

sunderland 1 v Newcastle United 4 (Four) (Yes, Four)

"No disrespect to sunderland but…." began yet another pundit, this time after their 0-0 draw at Man Utd. And there in itself is a problem. The lack of disrespect to sunderland shown outside the North East of England has been scandalous. This is a team cast adrift at the bottom of the League (again), resigned to relegation since August and without a home win all season. Leaving aside our own view of them for a second and looking at the argument from a 'state of the game' angle: how dare they turn up this bad, this ill-prepared, this ill-equipped, this pathetic for a serious sporting competition, how dare they do that (again)? It's like letting a chimp on a donkey take part in The Grand National. It's like allowing a group of old ladies in a tin bath to compete for The Boat Race. It's like getting the vicar from *Dad's Army* to try to win Wimbledon with a frying pan instead of a tennis racket.

All very amusing but allowing these things makes a mockery of the nobility of sporting occasion. In short; bringing the game into disrepute, so every possible disrespect to sunderland and they must be punished severely, not merely allowed to slither back into the shadows for a year or two. They must be barred forever from the Premiership on the grounds of shameful ineptitude and inappropriate behaviour.

Obviously from a Newcastle point of view things are somewhat different. Over these last few years sunderland AFC (the A is a pompous affectation by the way) has appeared only to exist at all for our amusement. Best player bitten by a jellyfish, players found to be cruising around at night shooting at their own fans with an airgun, hapless clods pouring scalding drinks onto their own testicles. It's been a hoot and that's even before the clueless fuckers stepped on a football pitch. Never in our wildest dreams could we have hoped that sunderland would get back into the Premiership and be even worse than last time, where getting dumped out of the League Cup by Crewe and the FA Cup by Brentford would not even be considered to be shocks, oh joy unbounded. And the fact that some of them still walk round with their chests puffed out, feeling hard done by, then blaming Bob Murray the second the wheels come off, is even funnier. And by God, do the wheels come spinning off a lot and on they go hilariously unaware of themselves and of how daft they look. Convincing themselves that a win against us would make it all worthwhile.

The traditional chin-strokers argument about "the increasing financial gap between the Premiership and the rest, making it harder than ever for promoted teams to succeed in the top flight," looks a bit of a tawdry excuse as well when you look at West Ham and Wigan this season. So we won't be having any of that either.

They have not been unlucky in sunderland, they have been utterly shit, quite possibly the worst top-flight team in the history of football, in the entire world. Ever. Twice. And the main point of our visit today was to point out that, while the footballing community at large may be politely ignoring them and allowing them to shuffle silently from the stage we will not be allowing such an exit. The (metaphorical) rotten tomatoes were long prepared, our throwing arms well limbered up.

Thanks to splendid work by the cops we got from slamming drinks down in The Newcastle Arms, to match and back, unmolested by drooling tramps dressed as deckchairs and having seen the whole game, despite managing to get ourselves split from the main convoy of coaches by Washington.

Alan (Mr Grumpy) Harrison, of this very parish, revels in the role of pessimistic curmudgeon but when I suggested we wouldn't see the game he laughed at me and he did so again at half-time when I was convinced of our defeat. I'd like to publicly thank him for both.

Outside the Stadium Of Empty Seats you got a taste of the whole day, Newcastle fans giggling hysterically and pointing at slack-jawed, twisty-faced, angry mackems who became increasingly twisty-faced and angry when their fury was only met with more giggling and pointing.

Apparently Newcastle were lucky. No Emre (who scored the winner at our place), no Bowyer or Ameobi (both of whom have been playing well recently, whatever you think of them), no Parker (our player of the season) and no Michael Owen and we were lucky? Also we had a day's less rest over the Easter period, all of which would have been given as "reasons, not excuses" under Souness for our losing this game before it even kicked off.

A swirling, blustery wind made their tatty banners flap while we adjusted to being in shadow, looking out onto brightness. Adrenalin and nerves competed with strong drink to unbalance perception but while sunderland fans and some loons in the press thought the home side were Real Madrid in the first half, I only saw them have one decent chance other than their goal and Titus headed that away. They hurried and scurried while we were strangely numb. Too deep across midfield, we appeared to be waiting for class to come and help, rather than imposing it on this verminous rabble.

Faye had the ball spinning past his feet in front of our open goal, our third decent chance to clear in the same move, he missed it and Hoyte (who to his credit had ran the length of the pitch and is not actually a sunderland player) scored.

The second half could not have been more perfect: my first derby was the 1-4 at St James' Park in '79 and despite the fact that we have beaten them a lot and that they haven't beaten us at their filthy homes since a scabby deflection in 1980, we have never avenged that defeat in my eyes. We have spent the vast majority of the last 25 years being miles better than them but the real fucking thrashing that they so richly deserve has escaped them. They never play us in decent weather, with all our best players available, when we are in any kind of form. We only had one of those three things today and it was enough to inflict the worst day of their dismal shitty lives.

Being so bad in the first half actually turned out to be deliciously cruel of us. They got their hopes up, assuming as they always do that it is possible to hurry and scurry for 90 minutes and that our players' superior ability wouldn't shine through.

On the hour Chopra came on for Clarkie, with Dyer dropping from his isolated forward role to, presumably, help drag the midfield forward. Young Chopra (Rocky or Chops? – how about Rockychops?) trotted up towards a long Bramble free-kick, Caldwell left it, their keeper, Davis dithered and Chopra nipped in. Suddenly he had an empty goal in front of him at sunderland, how we all dream…

He popped the ball in and with a look of delighted disbelief stood in front of us with his arms raised while the rest of our team raced from the halfway line to congratulate him.

Seconds later, with the away end still bouncing with glee, Hoyte pulled back the Zog in the area and the ref had the balls to give the penalty.

This was a hard few seconds, this was either going to be really brilliant or really bad, no half measures. My mate Spuggs went to video it with his phone, for some reason I stopped him, he seemed to understand. Knuckles were clenched, lips were bitten.

Shearer, by the way he was standing and by the look in his eye, had no intention of missing and he smashed in the penalty that exorcised another couple of ghosts. He took an extra few seconds after the celebration to soak up the moment while we gushed with gratitude

Arca (the jellyfish bait) came on when they got a free-kick on the edge of our area. He got a cracker at Boro from a similar spot but Jon Stead took it instead and it was rubbish.

A nervous last half hour was likely but for three things:1. sunderland are garbage; 2. sunderland's arse fell out; and 3. Newcastle are loads better than sunderland.

N'Zogbia picked up a short pass from Dyer, twisted and ran past four defenders before slotting the ball into the corner.

The Newcastle fans exploded with pleasure for a third time but this was all the sweeter because no one could imagine the mackems getting two (remember, they count a draw against us as a win, it's a clue to their underlying knowledge of inferiority.)

25 minutes before the end and the home fans were swarming out of the ground, unable to stand in the face of such humiliation. "Down with the Hoaxer, You're Going Down With The Hoaxer", "Worst Than The Last Time, You're Even Worse Than The Last Time", the classic songs kept coming; we did a cover of their "Shearer, Shearer, What's The Score?" (which they had been singing at half-time)

and a song (to the tune of *He's Got The Whole World In His Hands*) that had the line "You've Got Steve Cram, celebrity fan" in it which actually made me wee a little bit.

Shearer went down and stayed down. He went off, came back on and dropped to the grass. It didn't look good.

Luque came on, Shearer went off, an era ended before our eyes and we were so bloodthirsty it didn't properly register. Nothing much happened on the pitch, they were all but fucked and we kept the ball better. Dyer fizzed, Nobby was ice cool and Bramble and Moore had everything in hand. The entertainment was mostly off the pitch with the most fevered and merciless ridicule echoing round the ground.

A ball got dollied over the top, Caldwell (who always said he could do a job for Newcastle) missed it again and wiped out the last defender as well. Luque ran clear with the ball bobbling up around his groin for 20 yards before he poked it past Davis. £10 million? Worth every bloody penny.

An absent fan later asked how Luque celebrated. I had no idea, I was six rows down from my seat, upside down, hanging onto some strangers.

The noise, the looks on people's faces, the screaming, the frenzy of joy was overwhelming. Then up on your feet jumping and singing, "Geordie boyz, takin' the piss, Geordie boyz, takin' the piss!" Boumsong came on to counter the limited threat of big daft Kevin Kyle.

There has to be a strange admiration for the few mackems who didn't flee in the face of such a barrage. Utterly fucking battered they still had to let us know how much they hated us; hand gestures, glaring, faces contorted but silent to us and we drank it up like ice cold beer, laughed and sang some more.

The final whistle went somewhere amidst the wildest of parties and we were kept in for an age but this brought its own joy. With Glenn Roeder coming out long after the end to applaud us and the incident with the groundsman who threw down the corner flags and tried to storm off before being ordered to go back and pick up the flags so trudging the length of the pitch while 4,000 or so Newcastle fans mocked. Some people are gluttons for punishment, an hour after their team and support had been butchered like diseased pigs, red and white fools were still hanging around for more abuse outside the ground. There were ugly scenes reported that I didn't witness but the worst injury was sustained by a mackem being trampled on by a horse, possibly not the best day of his life but definitely one of ours.

All together now! "We'll meet again….."

(Why did the mackem cross the road? – Because he couldn't get his cock out of the chicken.)

For the record sunderland finished the 2002/03 season with 19 points, a record low they went on to beat in 2005/06 when they only managed 15.

Chapter 64

22nd April 2006

Life After Shearer

We have had two years to get used to the idea that Alan Shearer's time as Newcastle United player, captain and goalscorer was coming to a close. The news came through on this day that that time had arrived a little early. Two weeks in the grand scheme of things isn't such a big deal but it is hard not to feel robbed. Suddenly it felt like we had to pedal the bike alone with no one to catch us if we fell. In the past, even with Shearer missing from the team, part of your subconscious was comforted by the idea that at some point he would be back and every game would seem winnable.

Much as we like to paint ourselves as cynical, trench-humoured old grizzlies in these parts, when Shearer went round the Wigan keeper a week ago I felt a pang of regret. The world slowed (unless that was Alan at full tilt these days) and I had time to think: "make the most of this, 'cos there's not going to be many more of these." A no-nonsense finish, then off into the Leazes/East Stand corner with his arm up and his grin solid.

"Get in ya fucka! Shearer! Shearer! Shearer!"

It's also hard to be too down-hearted when you're busy pissing on the grave of your arch-enemy. In the pub before our next home game, we saw that Barry had captured the penalty at sunderland, and the mayhem in the crowd that followed it, on his phone. Shearer bitching the ball into the bastard mackems net, what a way to go out. Sweet.

Right, who are these monkeys? West Brom? Like the Premiership is going to miss this lot. Let's kill them too.

And by Jiminy, Albion stank. If European qualification hinges on goal difference we are going to wish we'd tried in the second half of this game because West Brom were the worst team we have played here since Hapoel Bnei Sakhnin. Sakhnin, a team of mad people and pirates who we beat 7-1 on aggregate in the UEFA Cup last season, who at least had the gumption to try to kick us off the pitch. The Baggies could barely be bothered to pull their pants on the right way round, never mind try to kick anybody.

Bryan (Captain Marvel) Robson will look back at this season and think, "Thank God for sunderland because without them I'd have been a laughing stock." Robson has been a right old grumble-puss recently because Albion have had some harsh decisions not go their way. Aye Bryan, that's why you're getting relegated, 'cos refs don't like you. Not because all your players are bollocks at all then? (Not that we couldn't have used Steve Watson this season, if only to see our Geordiest team ever.)

I was led to believe that our 21 man squad announced on Friday had Owen, Taylor, Emre and Dyer in it, which caused a flutter of excitement. None of them even made the bench and we started with the Zog in central midfield and Matti Pattison on the left. Exactly what is the point of buying a newspaper on the morning of a game anymore?

We also started cautiously as though we expected West Brom to come out swinging, spitting blood and fighting for their very lives. As it became increasingly obvious that they had no intention of doing anything of the sort, we set up camp in their half and moved the ball around neatly until we scored.

Solano, who had hit a blistering half-volley off the bar earlier, scored after some tidy approach work from Ameobi, Pattison and Rockychops had been partially interrupted by an Albion defender. Surely now West Brom would…..

Nope. A soft penalty for a shove outside the area on Chopra would normally have made Mr Robson go an amusing shade of purple but he was obviously so disgusted with his players' dismal and pitiful performance that he barely flickered. Shola took the ball off Nobby who seemed to say, "are you sure?" and the big fella (pedalling all by himself) walloped the spot kick into the bottom corner and we all breathed out with relief as we celebrated.

Ameobi has really come on in recent weeks. This may be Roeder's coaching or a realisation that he can and must be a player right now but Shola was awesome at Boro, missed at sunderland and unplayable today. He was advised not to play because of the damage done to his gums and teeth last week. The fact that he had the balls to turn out at all is one thing, his performance was something else. Breathing normally with a regular gum-shield is hard if you are not used to it, Shola had what looked like a hockey puck in his mouth and he was tireless. His second goal, our third, in stoppage time was well taken and richly deserved.

Nothing else happened in the second half apart from Roeder missing the chance to milk the win over the mackems by taking Chopra off for Luque, which would have given us a chance to thank them both, as well as letting Albert take aim at some more barrel-located fish.

Shearer's name rattled round the ground as the home crowd struggled to come to terms with the mortality of a man they have treated like a God. Which I guess means we are all going to have to grow up a bit.

Chapter 65

7th May 2006

From Out Of Nowhere

The last nine days of the season were a whirlwind of excitement and activity. Weeks ago we had mentally prepared for our campaign to fizzle out. The victories at Boro and sunderland were considered to be about little more than regional pride but five wins in a row had manoeuvred Newcastle United up the table to where the teams squabbling over UEFA and Intertoto Cup places were misfiring.

The long-awaited return of Michael Owen at Birmingham (where nufc.com reported home tickets were available on the day for £15 when the away supporters were charged £39) had little effect on a surprisingly tranquil match where a 0-0 draw was of no use to either team. Newcastle, in the recent role of Angel Of Death, were on hand to witness the demise of yet another Premiership team, Birmingham going down because Portsmouth won. Our outside chance of Europe was now firmly in the hands of others, which actually made Spurs v Bolton on Sky the next day exciting. Spurs won to keep Bolton below us and while Tottenham made strange bedfellows, they were a lot less strange than Boro, who sent a young side to the Reebok and did us an unlikely favour in holding Bolton to a 0-0 draw. An Intertoto Cup place was now ours if we could beat the Champions Chelsea on the last day, but a UEFA Cup slot was still on if Blackburn imploded. This idea was ruined because Blackburn beat Chelsea midweek in a scandalous display of refereeing where Chelsea were denied three obvious penalties. "A minimum of three minutes' stoppage time" was announced with Blackburn 1-0 up. As soon as Chelsea looked like getting forward for a last attack the ref blew for time, two minutes and 14 seconds after the 90 minute mark.

You could argue that Blackburn finishing the season five points clear of Newcastle meant this result was irrelevant, until you remember that Blackburn won at SJP with a deliberate handball. We all have to bear this fact in mind the next time some idiot says, "These things even themselves out over the course of a season". Ask yourself when was the last time Newcastle won a match by a player punching the ball into the net. Think Pedersen this season and Hasselbaink last and remember that statement isn't and never has been true.

Unfortunately sunderland finally won a home Premiership game for the first time in three and a half years, beating Fulham 2-1. You would think that would be little consolation to team and fans after being so abjectly humiliated but, as ever, they lacked the decency to be embarrassed and actually did a lap of honour. A lap of honour to celebrate beating their own pitiful record in gathering the least number of points in a domestic season, virtually anywhere, virtually ever, in the world?

So we went into the last game of the season two points clear of Bolton, but with an inferior goal difference meaning we would have to at least match Bolton's result (at home to already-relegated Birmingham City) in our match (at home to Champions Chelsea, who had never lost back to back matches all season) to qualify for the Intertoto Cup.

Strange really, being in the Intertoto Cup at the start of this season seemed unseemly and grasping, now it felt like a massive moral victory. After all the shit we had put up with, to have our season turned around to the point where we might qualify for Europe was more than we could have expected when Glenn Roeder replaced Souness and his gaggle of overpaid yes men.

Chelsea arrived on Tyneside less than full strength; no Cech, Terry, Makalele, Essien, Lampard, Drogba or Crespo but still with a team of full internationals and tens of millions of pounds' worth of players on the bench. Newcastle had no Shearer, Owen, Parker, Dyer or Bowyer. Chelsea could change things by chucking a £21 million England player on at half-time; when Solano went off injured Boumsong came on in his place. As an exercise in squad strength Chelsea were obviously on another planet, yet despite that and having already won the League they also systematically ganged up on the referee at every available opportunity.

In the last game of the previous season, Newcastle fans clapped a deserving Chelsea team onto the field after they won the League. This time, a loud chorus of "Fuck Off Mourinho!" went round the ground before half-time, by the end the entire Chelsea team was being savagely booed. As Champions they were unlikely to care; as an indication of what regular fans think about football being ruined by the endemically shitty behaviour of a team with enough quality to not have to behave so deliberately unsportingly, it was something Chelsea should listen to. Under Mourinho they won't, his cocky charm has long been replaced by sneering bad grace and in defeat he can be a small, small man.

In the second half, with the home crowd already smouldering at Chelsea's applied pressure on the feeble Mike Riley, our noise got jacked up higher than at any point in the season. Firstly an Emre corner was headed back across the goal by Faye to Bramble who smashed a flying volley into the roof of the Chelsea net, then Stephen Carr was sent off for stepping near Diarra who squirmed about on the floor before looking beseechingly at ref Riley. Carr was sent straight off but the livid masses simply would not allow Chelsea to leave the scene of the crime with any points. The news that Bolton were winning may have got around the ground as well because when 'The Blaydon Races' kicked in, it appeared that 50,000 people were on their feet willing the team to hold out. The booing when Chelsea had the ball seemed to make the air shake, the cheers when the ball was cleared, lumped away or (more often than not) was passed neatly out of trouble by ten man Newcastle must have undone the visitors' resolve. Credit to William Gallas for clapping round the crowd as Chelsea left the field beaten, obviously Mourinho had seen a phantom penalty (when Boumsong had clashed heads with Carvalho) and wanted Babayaro sent off as well so he could mumble about injustice instead of affording Roeder and his team any actual credit. *Reilly's red card for Carr (his fourth awarded to a Newcastle player in the last four games of ours he had taken charge of) was rescinded.*

Chapter 66

11th May 2006

End Of An Era

You had to fear the worst, Celtic ruined Peter Beardsley's testimonial by taking it too seriously, on and off the pitch and surely anyone allergic to cheese would die before half-time as our club ladled on the cloying sentimentality. Also, experience tells us that if something is worth doing at Newcastle United it's only worth doing half-arsed. My worst fears looked to be confirmed when they appeared to have run out of both programmes and free scarves before I arrived, which given I had no interest in either was fine by me but the Shearer mask and the two empty seats next to mine were a worry. Sure enough, just before kick-off as I inspected my mask and thought, "who the bloody hell thought this was a good idea?" in wobbled my match companion, "Yorite man?" followed by his besht mate, "Hey cannae grund so at ez w'shud plai yez in I propa game, ye ken?"

"Aye mate, whatever," long fucking night this was going to be.

And the cynicism stops right there because, apart from a squawking girl before and after the game (and who is to say Mr Shearer isn't partial to a bit of opera) the evening was marvellous, wonderful and truly memorable. Our club actually did a great job and put on a fantastic show. The large cards we were given, held aloft, swamped the stands in black and white stripes with big gold number 9s behind the goals and Shearer writ large across the East Stand. As our greatest ever goalscorer strode onto the pitch, gouts of flame scorched into the spring night sky, the noise and the raw emotion crackled and it was hard to hold your card steady with a lump in your throat and trying to cuff a manly tear away without our new Scots friends noticing. Shearer kicked the game off before being replaced by Chopra.

The team in black and white was the standard one of late but with Stevie Watson included instead of the injured, absent and missed Solano. Michael

Owen had a letter from his mum, or Sven, or forgot his kit…or something.

All the match reports, especially the overly mean one in *The Journal*, said the game was nothing to write home about. In the grand scheme of things that is probably true but it was played quicker and with more fizz than a normal testimonial. For the first time the choice of Celtic didn't look that daft, their fans kept our fans on their toes and until the last five minutes they didn't roll over which made the game was very watchable.

The inexplicably exhausted Watson was first to come off, replaced by Faye to warm applause. Next up after half an hour was lovely, lovely Gary Speed (on for Clarkie) who worried us by looking really good until he suddenly belted a simple pass into the crowd and we remembered why we sold him.

At half-time there was a fans' penalty shoot-out billed as England v Scotland with one of our skinny bairns blasting his penalty into the top corner and Paul Gascoigne taking and scoring the last English spot-kick. It was three or four-one to England.

Newcastle brought on Harper, Taylor, Elliott, Pattison, Ramage and Luque at half-time and it was our enigmatic Spaniard who opened the scoring with a terrific blasted volley. However, before and after the goal the evening started to get really special. Rob Lee came on and instantly began spraying 30 yard passes around, one of which led to the goal and Les Ferdinand could be seen warming up. It was either the sight of our other beloved number 9 of recent years or the actions of the Celtic fans that we copied but black and white scarves started to be swirled around above people's heads. The movement and the colour made you giddy. Those behind both goals, the East Stand and, shock upon shock, the entire Milburn Stand, stood to join the swirling and it was quite simply one of the most beautiful sights any of us have seen in our entire lives. The singing was louder, the smiles wider and the swirling frenzied. St James' Park was alive, thunderous and awesome. Whatever it costs, even if we have to pay a supplement on our season tickets, the club has to repeat this scarf gift at least twice a season (and if we can get Les to run up and down the touchline during crucial games all the better). Whatever it costs, it has got to be cheaper and of more use than Dean Saunders ever was. At last we had 'the singing section' we have long craved and it was the whole ground and it was stunning. For the rest of the game, at every excuse, everybody was up on their feet screaming their lungs inside out and (except me, dammit!)

swirling their scarves like their lives depended on it.

Celtic looked to be spoiling things by going 2-1 up after a clumsy Ramage foul gave them a penalty and Hartson beat Boumsong in the air to head in the other.

But Sir Les drew an own goal after a run into the box to make it 2-2 then was crudely flattened in the 93rd minute to earn a stone cold penalty (pfff).

Alan Shearer came back on and bashed the ball into the Gallowgate End net for the last time with the last kick of the game.

Ant and Dec (God bless 'em) seemed genuinely chuffed to play the role of ringmasters in the post-match stuff, laughing as the crowd demanded, "Who are ya?" and seemingly stifling giggles when the chairman was cheekily booed. Al said thanks and did a lap of honour with his family, I hate goodbyes and wandered thoughtfully away before the fireworks went off. It was an honour to have been there but compared to the honour of having watched the greatest English striker of his generation play for Newcastle United for ten years, for having been lucky enough to have been alive to see our top goalscorer ever, it was just a goodbye.

We have to move on from here, we can't compare whoever comes next to the incomparable. Shearer is a one-off, a man, a hero and we will think fondly of him for years whenever we swing our scarves above our heads. Tonight we celebrated the end of an era and it was grand but now we need to be allowed to start a new one. No wallowing, not now, not ever!

Chapter 67

20th May 2006

Newcastle United & England Get A Manager

Seemingly seconds after Glenn Roeder was officially confirmed as the next manager of Newcastle United the texts started being read out on Sky Sports News. The first one read; "Roeder is the wrong choice for the job, we should have gone for Steve Bruce because he is one of us." Well, I suppose that depends on your definition of "us", Mr Bruce isn't "one of" anybody I know, what with him being from Newcastle AND being redder than Captain Scarlett's knicker drawer.

Initially the problem with the managerial vacancies at both Newcastle and England was that the lack of an obvious choice meant more people were going to be unhappy than happy. The more you thought about any of the candidates the more unsuitable they all became, so England ended up with the man nobody actually wanted but who was least objected to. A man who inexcusably tries to hide his baldness with a quiff of ginger pubes, whose tactical genius appears to be limited to: a) everybody back; b) everybody forward; or c) surrender.

Sam Allardyce seemed to want both jobs. Sam looks like the school bully but actually turned out to be the class swot and he thought he was in charge of handing out the pencils: "Miss, Miss, Roeder hasn't done his exams and he's trying to steal the chair I wanted." Allardyce thinks football is an exercise in mathematics and he is keen to let everybody know that he has done his homework, his team are Wimbledon with a lap-top and everybody hates watching them. Sam gets cross when people say things like this about him and his team, so if you will all be good enough to forward this page to him it would make me very happy.

Of the other candidates: Stuart Pearce had his name mentioned around both jobs, which was a problem for me because I love Stuart Pearce and think he should be King. At some point the Queen is going to die. After a period of enforced grieving the people of this country will have to face up to the fact that Charles and that ghastly woman he married are going to be King and (in all but name) Queen and that we will be their subjects. At this point we must rise up and cast the inbred Germans (the Windsor family) out of all of their 23 stately homes and appoint Stuart Pearce as our rightful Head Of State. We can declare war on France and the National Anthem will have raucous guitars – I am prepared to fight in the streets for Good King Stuart, just don't let him ever be manager of Newcastle United or England because he'd be rubbish at it.

The first time Alan Curbishley appeared on the front, rather than the back, of a national newspaper, he behaved like the woman from Tom & Jerry, screaming and clutching his skirts, whilst wobbling atop an unstable chair, thus ruling himself out of any job more stressful than counting the paper clips. This, at least, made a change from him looking and sounding like he was about to take the Kurt Cobain route to inner peace.

We will find out in due course if we missed a trick or dodged a bullet by not reacting quicker than Rangers to snap up Le Guen but what we know for sure is that Martin O'Neill never wanted the job, he would have been here for three months already if he had the slightest interest in managing us. Judging by the style of football played by Leicester and Celtic when O'Neill was in charge (five across the back, scrappers in central midfield and a big lump up front) those of us who didn't want him anywhere near our players can finally breathe out properly again.

What I'm getting at here is that it is going to be no use saying who we should have got as soon as we lose two games in a row under Glenn next season because there doesn't appear to have been much of a choice. Obviously we all have our reservations, Roeder can't have much in the way of a scouting network in place and he does feel to be lacking something that nobody can quite put their finger on. Maybe he is simply not as comfortable in front of the media as he is on the training ground. You have to fear for Roeder on a personal level too, most of us over a certain age have been fond of Glenn since he signed as a player here at the arse end of 1983 and would hate for that to change. Which, given that we have little lasting affection for eight or nine out of our last ten managers, is unfortunately what is most likely to happen.

For the record I wanted him to get the job. Bringing calm to our club when we were hysterical was a hell of a feat. Making Titus Bramble look like a proper defender, out-manoeuvring McClaren at Boro, whatever he said to the players at half-time at sunderland, and the efficient way he reorganised the team after Solano limped out of the Chelsea game were all the marks of a good coach. But what mostly made me want him to be our manager was the fact that people were telling us that we couldn't have him because he didn't have the correct coaching badges. Pig-ignorant dullard that he is, John Barnwell (League Managers Association) was at least entitled to a public opinion, even if that opinion was crass and wrong and fucking stupid. But Sam Allardyce *(who in Chapter 20, remember, said Graeme Souness should comment on his own club and not other people's)*? The people who publicly disapproved from Wigan and Charlton? Who the fuck do you think you are? Scabby, worthless, shit eating, scumbag fucking nobodies telling us who can and who can't be our manager, rest assured if we want a bastard dancing bear to be our next coach we will not be seeking permission from the likes of you, fuck off!

Chapter 68

29th May 2006

Other Teams In Europe

Being over 40 you have to constantly be on your guard against being sentimental and misty-eyed about 'how things used to be'. For the most part the world is better: MP3 players mean you can ignore rude strangers, draught lager is nicer than when you could only get manky McEwans on Percy Street and there is more football on TV than any normal person could ever want to watch. Your choices of food, affordable holidays, entertainment, medicine and music today were unimaginable 20 years ago.

Also whilst gazing into the past you have to be aware that your view might have become somewhat distorted. For example everybody over 40 will tell you that they loved *The Clangers* on T.V. but if you actually see it you realise it was garbage, unlike *Bagpuss*, which remains class. So was it really true that in the olden days all English football fans wanted any English team who was playing in Europe to win?

I remember being thrilled when Liverpool, Nottingham Forest and Aston Villa won the European Cup in the late '70s/early '80s, when did that change? I was relatively young at the time and there was an element of self-interest because TV only showed European games when English teams were involved. European competition effectively ended when all the English teams were out, so for there to be football on TV you had to want the English to stay in.

Now you would have to be some sort of lunatic to want a team to succeed in Europe that isn't your own, especially if you follow another Premiership team. So you want me to cheer on a side that, on winning, will then have the money and pulling power to hoover up the best talent available during the next transfer window and take away my team's best players? Oh jolly good, where do I sign up for that?

Manchester United were probably responsible for severing the idea of the English footballing community getting behind its European representatives, with national celebrations breaking out when their arrogant arses ever got dumped out of Europe. It is of course ironic that England now have four spaces available in the Champions League as opposed to two, largely due to the success Manchester United enjoyed in Europe against the express wishes of everybody else.

Nothing, however, is straightforward. The obsessive football fan (like there is any other kind) will have the ramifications of other teams' progress in Europe mapped out weeks in advance, so yes, I am quite happy for a team to be playing away in Slovenia three days before they play Newcastle United, I just don't want them waving silverware at me while I'm on my own sofa.

It was hard not to admire the way Arsenal played in advancing to the Champions League final. Often plucky underdogs, playing with verve and passion, they seemed an entirely different entity to the hateful babies we encounter domestically. You could surprise yourself by, almost subconsciously, willing them on as they beat Real Madrid and Juventus in games of thrilling excitement and intoxicating tension.

The day of the final against Barcelona I was torn. I had swapped regular texts with Bully, an Arsenal fan (former flatmate and best man at my wedding) as their campaign unfolded and his frazzled nerves brought out a loyalty to him in me. An Arsenal win would make him so happy and a Barcelona win would give me little.

I was confused to the point that I actually put Talk Sport on the radio. They were playing *London Calling* by the Clash as an introduction to the afternoon show with some nameless hack and Rodney Marsh, who said, "I never liked that song", which tells you everything you need to know about Rodney fucking Marsh. Amidst other ill-considered outbursts from Marsh there were enough gobshite Gooners on air for my loyalties to the politics and beauty of Barcelona to triumph over the happiness of my best friend. Shame on me because with our roles reversed he would want Newcastle to win. I maintained a dignified text silence when Barcelona won.

No such internal dialogue with regards to Middlesbrough's UEFA Cup campaign which dragged on all season. Jealousy is an ugly thing and not something to be proud of but that is exactly what I was feeling and you just have to learn to soldier on and suppress it.

I tried to be big about their progress, exchanging pleasantries with my friends from Teesside whilst secretly plotting against them. At one point even travelling to Boro to offer support to their opponents.

I like Rome and I like A.S. Roma so Wifey and I were never going to pass up an opportunity to see them play when they were so near to the North East of England. Roo, a Boro fan, met us and seemed delighted and surprised by our presence in our enemy's nest. But Newcastle fans take great glee in pretending not to give a damn about Boro and we maintained the charade. "This is not about Newcastle or Boro, we are here for Roma," I said, which was true but we sat grinding our teeth as daft DJ Mark Page played *The Bill* theme "for Newcastle and sunderland", then said at half-time, "we usually read out the Newcastle score at half-time but they are not playing". Twat.

Roma were on a good run at the time, but it was a Newcastle style run where the team is coming apart like a cartoon aeroplane, with all the bits falling off until the only thing Wile E Coyote is flying is the steering wheel. He travels along at the same velocity for a second before, after a delayed realisation, he plummets, crashing to earth. No Totti, then no Montella, no De Rossi and the same fur coat and no knickers attitude to squad depth as at NUFC that means no decent cover. Boro won 1-0. Then held on to a 2-1 loss in Italy. I told Roo that if he went to Rome he should go to the Campo de' Fiori for food and beer. Fortunately he couldn't get the time off work so was not at the Campo de' Fiori when the Roma Ultras attacked Boro fans, with bottles, knives and (reportedly) an axe.

As long as Roma were in the UEFA Cup Boro couldn't win it but Roma blew it and Boro bashed brazenly through to the final, coming from 3-1 down twice to win 4-3 in subsequent games that could only be described as nauseating.

Still in the FA Cup at the time as well, Boro fans sang "shall we win a cup for you" at Newcastle fans during our 2-1 win at their place. We sang anti-sunderland songs back at them and thought about unhatched chickens. Boro were dumped out of the FA Cup by West Ham and Villarreal beat them 4-0 (a record) in the UEFA Cup Final. In Newcastle we weren't watching *The Bill*, we were watching ritual slaughter, live from Holland. I sent Roo a text wishing him a safe return that he replied to some days later saying, "People have got back from fucking space quicker than we got back from there."

And we thought getting back from Cardiff was a drag.

Chapter 69

4th July 2006

How We Won The World Cup

The World Cup descended on the planet in the kind of all-encompassing way that bird flu didn't. The World Cup slops over everything and dominates all. Other stuff can take place within the World Cup like weddings and work and birthdays and holidays but the living, breathing entity is present in the consciousness of all.

As to the few heretics and loonies who claimed not to have any interest in the competition well......; It's like being down the Quayside at New Year and saying, "I have no interest in fireworks." There is colour and noise and awe assailing your every sense – your interest or otherwise doesn't enter into it, this is the world you live in right now.

The event is so huge that a passing spaceship would assume that Germany was capital of Earth and that Franz Beckenbauer was our Emperor. Beckenbauer's ability to be at every game, even when two were on at once, did give him the appearance of having the sort of super-powers needed for the post of Emperor but in reality he would have to wrestle Brian Blessed, naked and oiled, for the title.

The best place to witness the World Cup, of course, was in your own house. Even the top correspondence from those actually in Germany; David Baddiel, Frank Skinner and the Dannys, Baker and Kelly, whilst entertaining, constantly gave the impression that they had no actual idea about what was going on.

At home the flag of St George had been hijacked by Poundstretcher and you constantly expected a scooterist to fly through your windscreen having skidded on one of those cheap little flags that had become detached from its plastic moorings.

For a couple of magnificent days more English people had been arrested for public disorder at Royal Ascot than in all of Germany. This gave the impression that all the 'known hooligans', who the authorities had gone to such painstaking lengths to ban from travelling to Germany, had simply switched sports. Would there be fisticuffs in the queue for strawberries at Wimbledon, bloodshed on Henman Hill? One could only hope so and would the domestic constabulary openly curse their colleagues for leaving them to deal with the country's foremost nutters as that heady mix of sunshine and lager set them all off.

All this was spoilt by an upsurge of drunken chair throwing in Stuttgart, presumably instigated by people from Essex, that led to 300 arrests. But this was an isolated hot spot because the World Cup was magic: Iranian women with joyful, painted defiantly uncovered faces, dancing in the same camera shot as Mexicans sporting sombreros and enormous false moustaches. Balls were fizzing into nets from great distance and at extreme velocity. There were erratic refs getting things hilariously wrong, games degenerating into anarchy (Holland v Portugal) and an air of chaos that meant games were either dreadful or wonderful against all perceived wisdom. Brazil v Croatia? Brazil were dreary and Croatia fearless and magnificent but Brazil won.

Poland v Ecuador should have been irrelevant but Wifey and I stumbled across a pub in Keswick stuffed full of screaming Poles, watching a game where the ball was zipped about and crossbars were rattled. 24 hour coverage on TV and radio meant you could dip in and out of the feast at will and a shiny new game kicked off every few hours.

Then the World Cup hit a wall, came to a juddering halt and a cold familiar wind blew through us. The packed and sweaty pub Guy had dragged us to for celebration of his new child was silent. Steven Gerrard missed his penalty and England were out. We stood, stunned.

For a couple of weeks everybody in the country got to feel like a Newcastle fan, not just because, like us, England haven't won anything for ages, loads of other people are aboard that unhappy ship. It was more about a vast body of people getting caught up in an unrealistic euphoria, despite their better judgement. Where you draw optimism from the fact that your team is playing badly because you believe in the quality of your players. "Wait 'til we get everybody fit," you tell yourself, "we may be playing shit at the minute but nobody wants to play us." And the optimism just keeps surging back until, despite having a decent team, the noisiest fans and wanting it the most, you lose and the dream that seemed so vibrant sinks into an icy ocean.

At Newcastle you have to go down with the ship, with England you can instantly pipe yourself aboard another, so for the price of one bottle of Pinot Grigio and a dozen of Peroni, Wifey and I declared ourselves Italian (pausing briefly to laugh at a tearful Ronaldo as Portugal were dumped out) and won the World Cup. Andiamo Italia (Let's Go Italy), Francia Vaffanculo! (France Fuck Off!)

Unfortunately the World Cup isn't real football, it's a fantasy footballing theme park and it can't last forever. *(Unlike the Cricket World Cup in 2007, which lasted two weeks longer than forever.)* To Newcastle fans coming out of the World Cup was like coming out of Flamingo Land, realising that you're way past skint and that there is only a pile of dog-do where your car used to be. The all-our-eggs-in-one-basket signing of Michael Owen had been carelessly dropped by people who thought a little jog up and down Birmingham's pitch was preparation enough for an international tournament. As Owen crawled from the pitch in Cologne like a mortally wounded wolf, all heroic and shocked, Newcastle's immediate future looked fucking catastrophic.

Chapter 70

15th May 2007

And They Wonder Why We Drink – season 2006/07

Three or four years ago I knocked the drink on the head. A lot of people I admire had done it and hadn't, as I feared would happen to me, turned into dreadful bores. Tom Waits, Mark Lamarr, Frank Skinner, Billy Connolly to name a few, while Henry Rollins has never had a drink in his life yet remains incredibly creative and amusing. It was a piece of piss, apart from the daily realisation that the world is cruel and pointless and that OH GOD I'M BORED, I sailed through it. I enjoyed feeling fitter and sharper in the mornings and driving at night. Until it came to the fucking football, after a month on the wagon I chose to dive off it and into a vat of lager. The whole game seems intent on driving you away from rationality and towards lots of strong drink. The 2006/07 season was more of a brain fuck than usual, despite the fact that nothing much happened, apart from that cup we won.

Fortunately the city didn't reflect its football team's tediousness: the most energetic and thrilling performance in Newcastle during the season was Rancid live at The Academy; the warmest crowd reaction was for Amy Winehouse at the University ("I'm used to people just staring at me with their arms folded") and the pithiest insight at The Theatre Of The Absurd was the DJ playing The Killers' *Somebody Told Me* with its "Heaven ain't close in a place like this" line.

The Premiership has been fucking tedious for more years than we can care to count. Obnoxious managers bickering at the top of the table, brazenly filling their teams with cheats and bastards then crying shamelessly when the slightest thing doesn't go their way. From the outside choosing who you want to win the League involves working out which team is the least despicable. Below that we usually have well organised over-achievers like Everton and Sam Allardyce's Bolton, grinding out enough 1-0s to finish in the top half, who resent any actual football breaking out between their well organised free-kick routines. Below that traditionally one finds a sludge of bores competent enough to stay out of trouble and beneath that a rotation of interchangeable nobodies briefly claiming to be 'back where they belong' before disappearing back to where they really belong.

Meanwhile at Newcastle United every kick, every breath, every decision in every game has felt like a matter of life and death......

Until this season.

The 2006/07 season in the Premiership was astonishing – so thrilling in fact that at Castle Furious we took to avoiding all the scores when not at a match because *Match Of The Day* had more thrills, spills and surprises than *Dr Who* (Dugga da-dung, da dugga-da dung, da dugga da dung da woo-ooo etc). So surprising in fact that Everton started playing football instead of trying to bore everybody into a coma. At the bottom teams kept lurching back from the death, while apparently safe teams would plummet in the direction of doom. Shots were clattering off crossbars, ripping into nets and being clawed away by acrobatic goalkeepers' fingertips. At the top of the table the game was played so quickly, passionately and skilfully that even the presence of Liverpool didn't spoil things. Tottenham were worth watching, Reading were a breath of fresh air and Newcastle United were...

Well what were we? This wondrous party, this festival of football was taking place all around us, and what were we doing? Moping around with the sludge, mid-table with dimwit losers like Middlesbrough and Manchester City, wondering why nobody was looking at us and why we never get to have any fun.

Our European campaign, which began in July, now looks like a dull little hobby that we fixated on to the interest of nobody in the world, including ourselves. Really, there were games where you looked at our opponents and thought, "who are these lot again?" and couldn't actually be bothered to find out? I love the fact as well that we won a trophy and then did the equivalent of tossing it into a box of old jockstraps in the back bedroom. To qualify we had to beat (among others) sunderland, Boro, Arsenal and on the last day of the season, Chelsea, a cup run of dreams. To win the Intertoto Cup we had to stay in the UEFA Cup longer than any other Intertoto qualifier, which seemed to involve about two hundred games, and definitely made it harder to obtain than the League Cup. And when we finally got it – they presented it to Scott Parker about an hour before kick-off against FC

Hoogivzafuk so nobody could see the damn thing. A trophy – an actual trophy, now used (if my imagination is a reliable witness) to jam open Freddie Shepherd's bog door after he's had a night on the pheasant kebabs and snakebite.

Glenn Roeder said he wouldn't complain about injuries as a way of drawing attention to our long list of wounded and that he never criticises referees as a way of pointing out that the fool with the whistle just cost him more points.

Then with our long list of injuries finally clearing up to the extent that Michael Owen had been seen at the training ground in actual football boots, we simpered out of the UEFA Cup like pathetic little wankers and Roeder looked clueless as it happened.

We spent the rest of the season thinking, "can we go yet?"

We at The Theatre Of The Absurd can put up with a lot but being bored when we should be annoyed or excited is simply not on and the attitude of too many players during this season was contemptible. Aside from flashes of brilliance from Obafemi Martins (17 goals in his first season in a new country, in a poor team without a regular strike partner and still some cunts were slagging him off) and James Milner, nothing of any lasting significance happened at all. At home Newcastle didn't lose to any of the eventual top six which proved they could cut it when bothered but lost to Man City, Fulham and Sheffield United to prove that wasn't very often. The low point was the FA Cup, losing to Birmingham, 5 sodding 1.

Away from home we were generally so far beyond redemption that Johnny Cash would have given up on us and he used to play to murderers. Amazingly the fans travelled, gang-handed and hilarious – rewards like a heroic point at Arsenal and an Oba Martins goal of the season missile that helped us win at Spurs were few and far between.

My abiding memory of this season is of rolling into Wigan, five and a half thousand deep, the most awesome away support in the world, with nothing for Newcastle to play for but pride and of our players showing none. We may as well not have been there, our team were pitiful, losing 1-0.

Sometimes when you're skint you have no choice but to stop in for a couple of weeks, to work harder, try to ignore the misery and trust that things will get better – the 06/07 season felt like Newcastle United stopped in for a year.

After a final abject surrender at home to Blackburn, Glenn Roeder resigned as manager.

The other thing of note was another lie laid bare: next time someone says, "If you give 100 per cent at Newcastle the fans will love you", remember these three words, Scott Fucking Parker. Despite regularly covering more grass and getting more tackles in than anybody since the great David McCreery, Parker suffered a grinding campaign of contempt from an element of the St James' crowd, which was fucking embarrassing.

(Parker understandably buggered off to West Ham and good luck to him.)

An entirely new direction was needed and one thing of interest that we had seen was AZ Alkmaar under ex-Barcelona manager, Louis van Gaal. Despite being short of quality players they were tactically brilliant, away from home the holding midfielder and the centre backs were the only players who didn't look to get forward. They attacked in a swarm of quick passing and the imagination (free from Freddie Shepherd's toilet) fair raced. Now....

Newcastle announced their new manager to be Sam Allardyce.

As my friend Lord Flynn of Jarrow says, "Well fuck me with the Rag-man's trumpet!"

I need a drink.

Chapter 71

23rd May 2007

The March Into Darkness

I have this constant waking nightmare that Sam Allardyce was sent by the Devil to destroy football. His head is so big because it has a false top to hide his little horns, he seems so broad across the shoulders because beneath his suit jacket there are enormous bat wings and he smells of sulphur.

We Newcastle fans may look like scruffy pirates and we may have an eye for mischief and adventure but we have the game in our hearts and have the souls of footballing angels and we can smell evil. Which is why we never took to Lee Bowyer and why we instinctively distrust Sam Allardyce.

We may mask this dislike, even to ourselves, convinced of the need for a new start, for organised defending and a firm hand on the players. But deep down we can feel it –a soul-scratching discomfort for Allardyce and everything he stands for. It is nothing that he played for sunderland, a red herring to confuse ourselves and others when this primal instinct is so overpowering. I might be utterly wrong here, I might have suddenly blown so far out of touch with my fellow fan that I may be asked to leave – but Allardyce coming fills me with an underlying dread that I haven't felt since Jack Charlton turned up. All arrogant and bullish.

It's not about an aversion to long-ball football, we all like to see a well executed long pass and few people complained when we had a forward line of Alan Shearer and Duncan Ferguson battering defenders about the place, it's about a distaste for Bolton's cynical, mechanical anti-football. That a player's height appears to be more important than his intelligence.

Sam will come with maths and statistics, percentages and lap-top technology and a fundamental lie; that lie is his belief that football is an exact science. Well, we'll see about that, he may as well turn up in Newcastle and try to control the shitty weather.

Rest assured he will arrive with a coven of lickspittles so large and expensive that the Souness crew will seem positively modest. Experts, he'll call them, dragging our club into the 21st century just like happened at Bolton, who we can now look on as some sort of template to base our future on. You wonder which expert it was who came up with Jaaskelainen, the Bolton goalkeeper, wasting time from minute one of every away game. Earpieces and open-mouthed chewing will become acceptable. (But please Mr Beelzebub not music when we score, never, never, never.)

Of all the opponents we have crossed swords with over these last four years why are Bolton Wanderers the team we would want to emulate? I say four years because that is how long it has now been since we regularly performed to an acceptable standard for the players we have got. Everything since then has involved a tremendous amount of time thinking, "what's fucking well wrong with us?" and wanting to personally kick a selection of our squad up the chuff. We have regularly been less than the sum of our parts, whereas Bolton are generally better than the sum of theirs. That they have done so by playing ugly football, by being crafty and premeditated in their gamesmanship and with Big Sam having a little hissy-fit with the referee every time they lose doesn't seem to have crossed Freddie Shepherd's mind. Our chairman is too busy oafishly throwing our money at the Devil to consider the amount of empty seats one can usually see at the Reebok or that he may find himself handing our number 9 shirt to El Hadji Diouf some time in the future.

There has been an argument put forward that looking down our noses at Bolton is a bit much at the end of a season when they qualified for Europe and we have spent most of it playing like a bunch of wankers. A fair point but I hooked up with a lad in a little village in Norfolk last week: I have known him since I was nine, as teenagers we went to see Crass together in 1981. He is called ADD (the capital Ds are important to him, can't remember why), a Norwich City fan but I respect his opinion on football anyway, I know this butters no parsnips for you but just think of him as someone as far removed as it is possible to be in this country from the day to day goings on at St James' Park.

He said, "Sam Allardyce is so not a Newcastle manager" – if it's so obvious to him why are other Newcastle fans telling me to "give the man a chance", for fucksake?

My answer has been a bad tempered, "No I fucking won't!" When in truth I haven't got any choice, I hated Jack Charlton shamelessly trying to turn us into Watford but 22 years later, I'm still here.

Football is not an exact science, it's a chaotic art form, Newcastle United Football Club has that chaos in every drop of its blood and it cannot be controlled by mere maths.

Am I really prepared to buy a new season ticket when I have spent four years and a large part of this book directly opposed to the way Sam Allardyce and his like approaches football? Am I prepared to compromise more of the last of my tatty principles and no doubt waste more of my time, money and dignity supporting Newcastle United?

Quite frankly........yes. Obviously.

I enjoy meeting my mates for a pre and post-match beer too much. I'm too nosey and stupidly optimistic not to go. I can't be in Newcastle and not go and I want to go away as well, with all the other hopeless and fearless cases, gang-handed and hilarious. But I've come to realise that it doesn't matter to anybody except me if I don't go and no longer feel any guilt. I will bugger off to experience something new at every available opportunity and as for the Toon?

Newcastle United have spent 15 years trying to be popular, trying to play football that people like to watch (often failing, but to aspire is divine), frowning on the cynical and the cheats and where has that got us?

Allardyce is going to turn us into a right bunch of bastards which even if it's not much fun, should be interesting. So where can I get some big black leathery bat-wings and eyes like molten steel?

For next season we march into darkness.

Epilogue

There's No Place Like Home

In May 2007 Freddie Shepherd was quoted across the press as saying, "I am not selling. It is an impossible club to buy. If the Halls don't sell and I don't sell, there is no way anybody can buy this club."

By Tuesday the 24th July the Hall and Shepherd families had been swept entirely from any meaningful control of Newcastle United.

John Hall sold his stake to billionaire Mike Ashley for £55 million, Hall becoming our new 'honourary life president', whatever one of them is, into the bargain. *The Guardian* (July 25th 2007) estimated with salaries, dividends and perks as well as the final settlement the Hall family made more than £90 million out of Newcastle United. Shepherd, already seriously ill, was shocked and initially threatened to put up a fight. From opinion gathered across the local news even Freddie's sympathisers seemed to be thinking, "let go you fool, you'll drown us all", as a protracted struggle for power could have been catastrophic.

As it was Freddie didn't release his flying monkeys and instead agreed to sell his shares for £38 million. Quoted in *The Mail on Sunday* (July 29th) Shepherd explained, "From where I saw it, the whole thing had been done behind my back. Neither John nor Douglas had been in touch to inform me of their intentions. I was not aware of Ashley's interest in the club. His name had never been mentioned. There had been a few people expressing an interest in the club but he was never on my radar. I felt disappointed by what had happened, especially remembering our past relationship. I was too ill to put up a fight. ("put'em-up, put'em-up") Had I not been in the state I was, if I hadn't have been in hospital, things might have been different. I believe I could have found enough backing to make a counter-bid but it was more or less a fait accompli."

At first is was announced that Shepherd would remain as chairman.

Mike Ashley, who, like The Wizard of Oz, is keen to stay out of the public eye, behind the curtain if you will, brought in Chris Mort as deputy chairman to conduct a "strategic review" of the club. He also snapped up all other available shares and delisted Newcastle United from the Stock Exchange on July 18th 2007.

BBC News 24 reported that on 16th of July 2007: City of London Police raided three clubs; Newcastle United, Rangers and Portsmouth "as part of an investigation into alleged corruption." Newcastle United were quick to release a statement: "The club itself is not the subject of the investigation." The transfers of Jean Alain (friend of Dorothy?) Boumsong from Rangers to Newcastle and of Amady (ruby slippers) Faye from Portsmouth to Newcastle were reportedly the subject of scrutiny.

There was no connection between this and Freddie Shepherd being removed as chairman on Tuesday the 24th July, in fact the club and former chairman both claimed that if anything were amiss that they were victims rather than perpetrators of any wrong-doing. Chris Mort took over as chairman.

"Ding dong the witch is dead," I sang whilst happily cutting the grass.

So Newcastle United would go into the 2007/08 campaign with a new manager, a new chairman and a new billionare owner. A brighter future seemed assured for the club's fans.

Aye, that and the new public smoking ban will mean we all live in perfect health and happiness, over the rainbow, where troubles melt like lemon drops, forever.